Advanced Real-Time Manipulation of Video Streams

Jan Herling

Advanced Real-Time Manipulation of Video Streams

Jan Herling
Erfurt, Germany

PhD Thesis, Ilmenau University of Technology, Germany, 2013

ISBN 978-3-658-05809-8   ISBN 978-3-658-05810-4 (eBook)
DOI 10.1007/978-3-658-05810-4

The Deutsche Nationalbibliothek lists this publication in the Deutsche Nationalbibliografie; detailed bibliographic data are available in the Internet at http://dnb.d-nb.de.

Library of Congress Control Number: 2014938061

Springer Vieweg
© Springer Fachmedien Wiesbaden 2014
This work is subject to copyright. All rights are reserved by the Publisher, whether the whole or part of the material is concerned, specifically the rights of translation, reprinting, reuse of illustrations, recitation, broadcasting, reproduction on microfilms or in any other physical way, and transmission or information storage and retrieval, electronic adaptation, computer software, or by similar or dissimilar methodology now known or hereafter developed. Exempted from this legal reservation are brief excerpts in connection with reviews or scholarly analysis or material supplied specifically for the purpose of being entered and executed on a computer system, for exclusive use by the purchaser of the work. Duplication of this publication or parts thereof is permitted only under the provisions of the Copyright Law of the Publisher's location, in its current version, and permission for use must always be obtained from Springer. Permissions for use may be obtained through RightsLink at the Copyright Clearance Center. Violations are liable to prosecution under the respective Copyright Law.
The use of general descriptive names, registered names, trademarks, service marks, etc. in this publication does not imply, even in the absence of a specific statement, that such names are exempt from the relevant protective laws and regulations and therefore free for general use.
While the advice and information in this book are believed to be true and accurate at the date of publication, neither the authors nor the editors nor the publisher can accept any legal responsibility for any errors or omissions that may be made. The publisher makes no warranty, express or implied, with respect to the material contained herein.

Printed on acid-free paper

Springer Vieweg is a brand of Springer DE.
Springer DE is part of Springer Science+Business Media.
www.springer-vieweg.de

Never trust a live video transmission - even if you've manipulated it yourself.

Abstract

Diminished Reality is a new fascinating technology that removes real-world content from live video streams. This sensational live video manipulation actually removes real objects and generates a coherent video stream in real-time. Viewers cannot detect modified content. Existing approaches are restricted to moving objects and static or almost static cameras and do not allow real-time manipulation of video content. This work presents a new and innovative approach for real-time object removal with arbitrary camera movements.

Two major challenges are presented. A high quality image inpainting method, applicable within a few milliseconds to each frame of the generated video stream is required in addition to a frame-to-frame coherence without any knowledge about future or previous frames. To determine areas to be removed, even from heterogeneous backgrounds, our approach uses a new and powerful real-time capable selection strategy based on fingerprints. Our image inpainting approach itself was inspired by previous layered and randomized approaches. Applying a new and unique initialization strategy as well as a new cost function to minimize coherence deviations based on a combination of spatial and appearance costs, the approach provides high quality results in real-time. Our approach for frame-to-frame coherence applies a homography to remove objects from mostly planar backgrounds, and is applicable even for rotational camera movement around the object to be removed.

Applied to well-known test images, our approach guarantees similar or even better quality compared to that of other state-of-the-art inpainting approaches. In addition, it performs approximately two magnitudes faster. An initial user test revealed that video manipulations based on the approach are barely detectable even if viewers are generally aware of the possibility of changed content. Based on these results, this work opens up a world of new opportunities for interactive and real-time video manipulation especially in the fields of TV and movie production as well as in advertising.

Kurzfassung

Diminished Reality ist eine neue faszinierende Technologie, die es ermöglicht, reale Inhalte aus Live-Kamerabildern zu entfernen. Die Live-Videomanipulation entfernt reale Objekte und erzeugt in Echtzeit einen kohärenten Video-Stream. Dabei können die Betrachter keine Manipulation feststellen. Derzeit existierende Ansätze sind auf sich bewegende Objekte und statische oder weitestgehend statische Kameras beschränkt und erlauben keine Manipulation des Videoinhalts in Echtzeit. In dieser Arbeit wird ein innovativer Ansatz vorgestellt, der das Entfernen von Objekten bei beliebigen Kamerabewegungen ermöglicht.

Dabei gilt es vorrangig, zwei Herausforderungen zu lösen. Zum einen wird eine Bild-Inpainting-Methode benötigt, die innerhalb weniger Millisekunden auf jedes Kamerabild angewandt werden kann und qualitativ hochwertige Ergebnisse liefert. Zum anderen muss ohne die Verwendung vergangener oder zukünftiger Kamerabilder eine Bild-zu-Bild-Kohärenz erzeugt werden. In dieser Arbeit wird eine neuartige und leistungsfähige Selektionsstrategie vorgestellt, die auf sogenannten Fingerabdrücken basiert, damit unerwünschte Inhalte selbst auf heterogenen Hintergründen bestimmt werden können. Der Inpainting-Ansatz wurde ausgehend von bereits bekannten randomisierten Ansätzen und Verfahren mit mehreren Bildebenen entwickelt. Qualitativ hochwertige Ergebnisse können in Echtzeit durch die Anwendung einer einzigartigen Initialisierungsstrategie und einer neuartigen Kostenfunktion, die die Kohärenzabweichung miniert, erzeugt werden. Die Kostenfunktion kombiniert räumliche und erscheinungsbasierende Kosten. Der auf Homographie basierte Ansatz erzeugt eine Bild-zu-Bild-Kohärenz beim Entfernen von Objekten, vor überwiegend ebenen Hintergründen und unterstützt Rotationsbewegungen der Kamera um das zu entfernende Objekt.

Obwohl der Ansatz etwa zwei Zehnerpotenzen schneller ist als aktuelle, vergleichbare Inpainting-Ansätze, zeigt sich, dass er für bekannte Testbilder durchgängig qualitativ gleichwertige oder bessere Ergebnisse erzeugt. Ein erster Test mit Nutzern zeigt, dass Videomanipulationen, die mit diesem Ansatz durchgeführt werden, für Testpersonen kaum zu erkennen sind, sogar wenn diese sich der Manipulationsmöglichkeiten bewusst sind. Basierend auf diesen Ergebnissen eröffnet der in der Arbeit vorgestellte Ansatz eine

Fülle neuer Möglichkeiten für interaktive und echtzeitfähige Manipulationen, die vor allem in TV- und Filmproduktionen sowie im Bereich der Werbung eingesetzt werden können.

Acknowledgements

First and foremost, I would like to thank my doctoral advisor Wolfgang Broll. Wolfgang's guidance and support have made a tremendous impact on the outcome of this work. After serving as my mentor during my training at the Fraunhofer Institute for Applied Information Technology in Sankt Augustin, Wolfgang offered me the chance to pursue my doctorate under his supervision. He continually provided critical feedback and suggestions and helped me to stay on track when it seemed that progress in my research had come to a halt. He always found the right words to motivate me, and was available for questions and support round the clock for a period of several years. The discussions we had were invaluable. I would like to express my deepest gratitude for so many years of cooperation and the many shared laughs and happy moments.

I would also like to express my appreciation to Beat Brüderlin for reviewing this thesis and providing detailed feedback and advice regarding my work. The uncomplicated and direct cooperation and communication allowed me to significantly improve my thesis. His enthusiasm for my research gave me self-confidence and inspired my work.

Further, I would like to extend my thanks to my external reviewer Mark Billinghurst. I am very thankful for his detailed feedback, which made it possible for me to intensify the quality and impact of my work. In 2009, Mark gave me the opportunity to participate in an exchange program at the HIT Lab New Zealand. During this time, I had the chance to meet engineers researching similar topics. I was able to benefit from the wide variety of their experience and research projects conducted by Mark and his employees.

Advice and constructive recommendations given by Sarah Brüntje were invaluable regarding the mathematical background of this thesis. I also would like to gratefully acknowledge the support of Sandra Pöschel and the helpful suggestions she provided regarding the analysis and evaluation of my work. A big thanks goes to Lisa Czok. Lisa is a native speaker and she helped me in the last phase of my doctoral thesis. She proofread and edited the entire thesis regarding grammar and spelling issues in an incredibly short time so that it could be released within the specified time frame.

Jan Herling

This dissertation would not have been possible without the encouragement and commitment of my parents Elke and Johannes. They allowed me to experience an optimal education and provided unconditional support. They always believed in me and my work.

Thank you so much.

Contents

1	**Introduction**	**1**
	1.1 Objective	4
	1.2 Outline	8
2	**Related Work**	**9**
	2.1 Static Image Processing	9
	2.1.1 Texture Synthesis	10
	2.1.2 Image Inpainting	15
	2.1.3 Image Composition	25
	2.1.4 Image Manipulation	27
	2.1.5 Discussion	31
	2.2 Video Inpainting	32
	2.2.1 Almost Stationary Camera Motion	32
	2.2.2 Dynamic Camera Motion	38
	2.2.3 Discussion	40
	2.3 Mediated Reality	42
	2.3.1 Mixed Reality	42
	2.3.2 Diminished Reality	42
	2.3.3 Discussion	45
3	**Concept**	**47**
	3.1 Real-Time Image Inpainting	48
	3.2 Real-Time Video Inpainting	51
4	**Image Inpainting**	**53**
	4.1 Mapping Function	53
	4.2 Cost Function	55
	4.2.1 Spatial Cost	55
	4.2.2 Appearance Cost	58
	4.3 Iterative Refinement	60
	4.4 Initialization	64
	4.4.1 Randomized Erosion Filter	65

		4.4.2 Contour Initialization 66

         4.4.2 Contour Initialization 66
         4.4.3 Patch Initialization 69
         4.4.4 Discussion 79
   4.5 Implicit Constraints 82
   4.6 Explicit Constraints 84
         4.6.1 Area Constraints 85
         4.6.2 Structural Constraints 88
   4.7 Analysis 93
         4.7.1 Convergence 93
         4.7.2 Complexity 97
   4.8 Implementation Issues 99
   4.9 Results 107
   4.10 Limitations 118
         4.10.1 Pixel-based Inpainting of Homogenous Content 118
         4.10.2 Perspective Image Inpainting 120
   4.11 Discussion 121

5 Video Inpainting   123
   5.1 Object Selection 124
   5.2 Object Tracking 130
         5.2.1 Heterogeneous Environments 131
         5.2.2 Intermediate Environments 132
         5.2.3 Homogenous Environments 132
         5.2.4 Contour Refinement 133
         5.2.5 Discussion 133
   5.3 Mapping Propagation 134
   5.4 Inpainting Pipeline 135
   5.5 Compensation of Ambient Lighting Changes 136
   5.6 Extended Appearance Cost 138
   5.7 Results 140
         5.7.1 Performance Issues 140
         5.7.2 User Study 142
         5.7.3 Visual Results 157
   5.8 Limitations 161
         5.8.1 Object Selection and Tracking 161
         5.8.2 Video Inpainting 161
   5.9 Discussion 164

6 Conclusion — 165
- 6.1 Summary — 165
- 6.2 Future Work — 170
  - 6.2.1 Image Inpainting — 170
  - 6.2.2 Video Inpainting — 172
  - 6.2.3 Fields of Application — 173

7 Spatial Cost Convergence — 175
- 7.1 Spatial Cost for Local Mappings — 175
- 7.2 Spatial Cost for Neighbors — 179
- 7.3 Spatial Cost for Non-Neighbors — 187

8 Appearance Cost Convergence — 189
- 8.1 Appearance Cost for Local Mappings — 189
- 8.2 Appearance Cost for Neighbors — 193
- 8.3 Appearance Cost for Non-Neighbors — 198

A Appendix — 201
- A.1 Patents — 201
- A.2 Additional Patch Initialization Comparisons — 201
- A.3 Additional Initialization Comparisons — 204
- A.4 Additional Image Inpainting Results — 208
- A.5 Additional Video Inpainting Results — 216
- A.6 Additional Study Results — 227
  - A.6.1 User Ratings — 227
  - A.6.2 Evaluation Video — 232
- A.7 Performance Measurements — 232

Bibliography — 235

List of Tables

2.1 Summary of the introduced image inpainting approaches . . . 26

3.1 Overview of the derived image inpainting approach 51

4.1 Performance values of patch initialization 77
4.2 Performances of individual initialization approaches 81
4.3 Performance comparison for the *Elephant* image 109
4.4 Performance comparison for the *Bungee* image 110
4.5 Performance comparison for the *Outlook* image 111
4.6 Performance comparison for the *Blobs* image 113
4.7 Performance comparison for the *Baby* image 115
4.8 Performance of our image inpainting approach 117

5.1 Performance of fingerprint selection 140
5.2 Performance of the video inpainting 141
5.3 The five values the test subjects could select as answer 144
5.4 Distribution of the test subjects 145
5.5 T-test analyzing ratings for individual backgrounds 155

A.1 Accumulated ratings of the test subjects 231

List of Figures

1.1	Pictures of the *Basilica St Mary of Health* in Venice	2
1.2	Live video manipulation	5
1.3	Inpainting result example for the *Train* image	7
2.1	Image processing overview	10
2.2	The two steps of texture synthesis by Efros and Leung	12
2.3	Texture synthesis result by Efros and Leung	12
2.4	Texture synthesis by Wei and Levoy	13
2.5	Texture synthesis result by Xu et al.	14
2.6	Texture synthesis by Efros and Freeman	14
2.7	Image Inpainting vs. Image Completion	16
2.8	Image restoration by Bertalmio et al.	17
2.9	Image inpainting result by Drori et al.	18
2.10	Image inpainting scheme by Criminisi et al.	19
2.11	Image inpainting results by Criminisi et al.	21
2.12	Image inpainting scheme by Sun et al.	22
2.13	Gradient-based image inpainting by Shen et al.	23
2.14	Information propagation of PatchMatch by Barnes et al.	28
2.15	Seam carving image resizing by Avidan et al.	29
2.16	Update step of the completion approach of Wexler et al.	37
2.17	Scheme of the active contour tracking approach	40
2.18	Mixed Reality continuum as defined by Milgram	42
2.19	Diminished Reality result of our previous approach	44
4.1	The two cost constraints of the mapping function f	55
4.2	Spatial cost for neighboring mappings	57
4.3	Two symmetric neighborhoods	58
4.4	Scheme of the pyramid refinement	61
4.5	Iterative layer refinement	62
4.6	Comparison of individual spatial weightings	62
4.7	Scheme of the multithreading inpainting realization	64
4.8	Comparison of the standard and randomized erosion filter	66

4.9	Contour mapping initialization scheme	68
4.10	Contour mapping initialization for a real image	68
4.11	Patch similarity determination for patch initialization	71
4.12	Inpainting priority of the patch mapping initialization	73
4.13	Determination of the direction of the inpainting border	74
4.14	Area of interest for randomized searches	75
4.15	Patch initialization of the *Pyramid* image of Xu et al.	77
4.16	Comparison of individual patch initialization modes	78
4.17	Initialization comparison for the *Elephant* image	79
4.18	Initialization comparison for the *Sign* image	80
4.19	Initialization comparison for the *Bungee* image	81
4.20	Inpainting with individual data formats	83
4.21	Inpainting with additional texture information	84
4.22	Inverse importance map of an area constraint	86
4.23	Inpainting result for the *Ruin* image	87
4.24	Constraint weighting graph	89
4.25	Line constraint costs	89
4.26	Distance determination for finite lines	90
4.27	Constraint image inpainting example	92
4.28	Appearance neighborhood for a given point $p \in T$	95
4.29	Determination of the appearance cost difference	96
4.30	Performance comparison for a mask with constant size	98
4.31	Performance for a growing mask with constant image size	99
4.32	Convergence of the number of optimized mappings	101
4.33	Convergence of the ratio of optimized mappings	102
4.34	Convergence with weak spatial weighting	102
4.35	Convergence with strong spatial weighting	103
4.36	Comparison of spatial weightings on a fine pyramid layer	104
4.37	Comparison of spatial weightings on a coarse pyramid layer	104
4.38	Cost ratio for individual pyramid layers	105
4.39	Mapping changes for individual inpainting images	106
4.40	Cost ratio for the exact inpainting approach	106
4.41	Visual comparison between exact and fast inpainting	107
4.42	Result comparison for the *Elephant* image	109
4.43	Result comparison for the *Bungee* image	110
4.44	Result comparison for the *Outlook* image	111
4.45	Result comparison for the *Blobs* image	112
4.46	Result comparison for the *Blobs* image of Kwok et al.	113
4.47	Result comparison for the *Sign* image	114
4.48	Result comparison for the *Baby* image	115

List of Figures XXIII

4.49	Inpainting result for the *Wall* image	116
4.50	Image inpainting with a soft gradient background	119
4.51	Image inpainting with perspective distortion	120
4.52	Inpainting of an individually transformed artificial image . . .	121
5.1	Real-time selection results using fingerprint segmentation . .	126
5.2	Object selection and tracking scheme	128
5.3	Contour tracking scheme	131
5.4	Mapping forwarding by application of a homography	134
5.5	Lighting compensation of the reference model	137
5.6	Comparison of a default and a corrected reference model . . .	139
5.7	Age distribution of the test subjects	145
5.8	Test subject rates for evaluation background B_0 and B_1 . . .	146
5.9	Averaged ratings for all backgrounds	147
5.10	Test subject ratings for twelve manipulated video sequences .	147
5.11	Comparison of subjects for manipulated videos	149
5.12	Comparison of subjects with and without knowledge	150
5.13	Test subject ratings for all twelve original video sequences . .	150
5.14	Comparison of subjects for original videos	151
5.15	Subjects with and without knowledge for original videos . . .	152
5.16	Average rating $\bar{x}$ of the test subjects for individual groups . .	153
5.17	Comparison of averaged ratings for individual groups	153
5.18	Averaged ratings for nonbriefed subject without knowledge .	154
5.19	Averaged ratings for briefed subject with knowledge	154
5.20	Comparison of the amount of undecidable ratings	156
5.21	Video inpainting with a heterogeneous background	159
5.22	Video inpainting of a coat of arms	160
5.23	Real-time selection results of the fingerprint segmentation . .	162
5.24	Video inpainting of a volumetric object	163
7.1	Visualization of the neighborhood $N_s(p)$	176
7.2	Visualization of the subsets T_x and $\overline{T_x}$	178
7.3	Visualization of the rearrangement of the distance measure .	183
7.4	Scheme of the direct and indirect spatial cost	186
8.1	Visualization of the neighborhood $N_a(p, f)$	190
A.1	Patch initialization for the *Elephant* image.	202
A.2	Patch initialization for the *Window* image	202
A.3	Patch initialization for the *Bungee* image.	203

A.4	Patch initialization for the *Wood* image	203
A.5	Initialization comparison for the *Wall* image	204
A.6	Initialization comparison for the *Biker* image	205
A.7	Initialization comparison for the *Blobs* image	206
A.8	Initialization comparison for the *Window* image	207
A.9	Initialization comparison for the *Wood* image	207
A.10	Inpainting result for the *Bungee* image by Pritch et la.	208
A.11	Inpainting result for the *Window* image	209
A.12	Inpainting result for the *Wood* image	210
A.13	Inpainting result for the *Universal Studios* image	211
A.14	Inpainting result for the *Still Life with Apples* image	212
A.15	Inpainting result for the *Microphone* image	213
A.16	Inpainting result for the *Dog* image	213
A.17	Inpainting result for the *Train* image	214
A.18	Inpainting result for the *Chair* image	214
A.19	Inpainting result example with leaves in the background	215
A.20	Constraint image inpainting example	215
A.21	Video inpainting removing a window in a house facade	217
A.22	Video inpainting with ivy plants in the background	219
A.23	Video inpainting with a homogenous background	220
A.24	Video inpainting with a grass background	221
A.25	Video inpainting removing a drain	222
A.26	Video inpainting recovering a straight line	223
A.27	Video inpainting recovering an circular object	224
A.28	Video inpainting with a homogenous background	225
A.29	Video inpainting recovering a volumetric object	226
A.30	Test subject rates for evaluation background B_2 and B_3	228
A.31	Test subject rates for evaluation background B_4 and B_5	228
A.32	Test subject rates for evaluation background B_6 and B_7	229
A.33	Test subject rates for evaluation background B_8 and B_9	229
A.34	Test subject rates for evaluation background B_{10} and B_{11}	230
A.35	The manipulated evaluation video of test background B_2.	233
A.36	SPEC 2006 benchmarks	234
A.37	Visualization of the estimated performance increase	234

1 Introduction

Today, most holiday pictures do not contain undesired image content like building cranes or trash bins. Usually photographers have enough time to select the best angle for the details to be captured in the photograph and prevent that undesired objects are visible in the final picture. Further, they can move to an ideal capturing position, can zoom into the scene or can crop the final image using editing tools.

Contrarily, when holiday scenes are filmed or funny or interesting situations are recorded, the video has to be captured very quickly. There is often not enough time or not even the possibility to find a better position or camera angle to hide undesired objects in the video. Sometimes, the undesired object covers such large areas of the environment that no camera angle can prevent it from being prominent in the video.

Any time a video is captured or a camera provides a live stream, e.g., of a TV show, undesired image content may become visible in the video information produced. Independent of whether the undesired image content is only temporarily visible or can be seen in the entire video stream, the undesired content reduces the overall quality of the final video. An easy-to-use video manipulation approach, allowing the removal of undesired image content, can be used for a wide variety of novel applications.

In Figure 1.1, a series of pictures taken from an exemplary holiday video is depicted in the top row. The scene has been captured from a water taxi on the Grand Canal in Venice. The beautiful Basilica in the foreground is ruined by the building crane in the background. Although the crane obviously disturbs the impressive view of the Basilica, the photographer did not have any possibility to blind out the crane in the video. Current smartphones are equipped with powerful processing units and digital sensors allowing movies with high image resolutions to be captured. In a few short years, an application allowing the removal of undesired objects in a video sequence will become a standard tool for these smartphones. Results using such an application are shown in the lower row of scenes in Figure 1.1, demonstrating one impressive option possible with an application able to removed undesired objects in a video stream.

Figure 1.1: Series of pictures of the *Basilica St Mary of Health* in Venice. The top row shows the original image information, ©2012 Dr. Ulrich Heide, kindly authorized by the photographer. The bottom row shows the image content without the undesired building crane.

Several additional areas of application exist that will benefit from an automated video manipulation approach. The post-processing of motion pictures, especially scenes with special effects, is an expensive and time consuming step in the video production process. Undesired elements visible in a video sequence often need to be removed manually before the final video can be released. These elements may include safety ropes, undesired advertisements, or film crews mirrored in window panes. Currently, these video sequences have to be retouched manually frame by frame to achieve final image quality sufficient for cinema. An automated approach allowing the removal of arbitrary objects in video sequences would significantly speed up post-processing of motion pictures.

In addition, urban planners could benefit from video manipulation technology fast enough to be applied in real-time. In Mediated Reality [73], the environment can be modified, enhanced, diminished or augmented in arbitrary ways. A system to visually remove old furniture in a room and fill in the empty area with virtual new furniture could provide direct visual feedback without the annoying necessity to demolish the old furniture first. Further, such an application would users allow to move inside the real room and would allow to investigate the new appearance from several different viewpoints. Similar applications may be used by developers or architects of large and diverse industrial complexes. Modernization could be planned by visually removing existent machinery and replacing it with virtual new

1 Introduction

equipment. This technology would simplify and speed up development of the final machine set-up.

Unfortunately, manipulation of video information, especially the removal of undesired objects, is a non-trivial and computationally expensive task. In the previous years, several approaches have been proposed attempting to remove objects in video sequences. The majority of these approaches supports only static cameras and allows the removal of moving objects. The undesired image content is replaced by visual information from video frames where the moving object is located at a different position.

Only a minor number of approaches have been proposed for constraint camera movements and undesired static objects. In the case of static objects, the undesired image content cannot simply be copied from previous or subsequent video frames. Instead, plausible image content has to be synthesized seamlessly blending in with the surrounding video information. The majority of related approaches simply warps this synthesized image content for all remaining frames in the video sequence.

Missing image content often is synthesized by image inpainting approaches that have been mainly developed for the removal of visual information in static images. The remaining (and desired) image content is used to create a final image that does not contain the undesired image information. Depending on the visual complexity of the image content, the final picture may not be identified as a manipulated image by the majority of observers. Unfortunately, almost all approaches for static image inpainting are very slow, requiring several seconds or even minutes for image processing. The approach of Barnes et al. [8] was the first image inpainting approach that was able to inpaint images with almost interactive frame rates (on lower image resolutions). Barnes et al. balanced image quality and processing time to provide an inpainting approach that could be used in image editing software. However, the approach is still between one and two magnitudes too slow to allow real-time inpainting of entire video streams.

Presently, video manipulation remains difficult to apply real-time using current computer hardware due to the high computational effort necessary to synthesize image content. This real-time restriction is primarily problematic for live video transmissions or Mediated Reality applications. Non-time-critical video manipulation for television or motion picture post-processing is able to be applied within the time span of several days on a computer cluster. However, live video transmissions have to be processed real-time. At most, a short delay of a few seconds might be acceptable for broadcasting. Mediated Reality applications even do not allow for such delays as well. Direct feedback is required by the user of a Mediated Reality application.

The user cannot interact with the Mediated Reality if the system is not fast enough or has a noticeable latency. Nevertheless, even television or motion-picture post-processing can benefit from a video manipulation system allowing faster processing of video sequences compared to other currently used approaches. Time and money can be saved both by the significantly quicker determination of results and the reduction to computational hardware requirements.

An approach for live video inpainting needs an image synthesis approach that is several times faster than any previous approaches. It also must provide almost the same image quality as state-of-the-art approaches. Apart from the image synthesis of the visual content, live manipulation of video streams has further different challenging tasks that need to be solved. On the one hand, the object to be removed has to be identified and tracked in each video frame. On the other hand, convincing image content has to be created while matching individual video frames to each other. Imagine a tree that has to be removed in a video sequence. The tree could be removed by solely invoking image inpainting iterations for each individual video frame without considering any information contained in the remaining video content. Each individual video frame would provide a convincing image result without the undesired tree. However, if the individual frames are viewed as an entire video sequence, the missing tree would be inferred as a ghost shadow. Automated video inpainting thus has to be able to provide a coherent video stream so that concurrent frames sufficiently match each other.

In this work, a novel video manipulation approach will be presented proving to be significantly faster then all previous approaches. The approach will be fast enough to be applied real-time while creating and maintaining high image quality. Furthermore, an object selection and tracking approach will be introduced allowing a static object to be selected in a live video stream. The selected object will be tracked as long as the object is visible in the successive video frames. In real-time, the visual content of the tracked object will be removed and replaced by synthesized image content. In Figure 1.2, an application of the real-time video manipulation approach is depicted. In the following subsection, the objective of this work will be introduced in more detail.

1.1 Objective

Our goal is to develop a real-time capable video inpainting approach. The approach will allow the arbitrary removal of static objects in live video

1.1 Objective

(a) Original video stream with rough user-defined selection.

(b) Resulting real-time video manipulation without the undesired object.

Figure 1.2: Live video manipulation that can be applied for television broadcasting, Mediated Reality applications or post-processing of motion pictures. An undesired object is roughly selected by the user and removed in real-time.

sequences. The aim of video inpainting is not to reconstruct the real environment behind the object that has to be removed. Instead, video inpainting attempts to synthesize image content so that the visual result is plausible for the observer. Therefore, a video inpainting approach does not need any information about the real environment or background behind an object but tries to synthesize this information. In Figure A.21, a window in a house facade is removed providing the visual impression of a solid wall. For this window a real background does not exist. Any approach trying to reconstruct the real environment behind this window cannot succeed. Therefore, a video inpainting approach needs to be applied synthesizing the missing image information. Ideally, results are plausible and convincing even for the observer who knows that an object has been removed in the video sequence. In reality, however, an observer that knows video content has been modified at a specific position will automatically seek until finding minor video artifacts. Therefore, our main objective is to convince or to spoof observers not knowing that an (originally visible) object is missing in a video sequence. Usually, the concentration of these observers centers on other visual elements of the video sequence. Undesired objects are generally not relevant to the main focus of the video.

No a priori information is known, neither about the video stream nor about the object to be removed in the video sequence. The approach will work without delay and will provide visual results immediately whenever a new video frame is available. Approaches that have direct access to the entire video sequence can provide better visual results as these approaches have knowledge of a significantly larger amount of video data. However, an approach that does not rely on a priori information allows video manipulation to be directly applied for television broadcasting or for Mediated Reality applications. Video streams can be processed without expensive and time consuming preprocessing steps.

The approach will not be able to remove partial elements or regions of an object but instead will be able to remove the entire object in one piece. The algorithm allows for recovering the visual background of the object but fails mainly in reconstructing a missing piece of an object. An observer usually does not know the exact visual information behind an object. At most, an observer has a rough guess what might be behind an object. If a part of an object is missing, the observer has a certain idea about how the missing image content should look, as the observer usually is quite familiar with the appearance and the shape of the object. An image inpainting approach suitable for removal of partial elements of an object would need access to a large knowledge database storing images of the reference objects. However, an image database would violate the condition that no a priori information is available. Figure 1.3 shows an example of a well known image inpainting benchmark image. The inpainting result is given for two individual inpainting masks. One mask removes a partial element of a visible train in the foreground, the other mask removes the entire train. The algorithm fails (like all other related image inpainting approaches) to reconstruct the missing train fragment but succeeds to synthesize an image without the train.

In the next chapter, recent approaches to video inpainting will be introduced and discussed in detail. Unlike our work, none of the previous approaches is real-time capable and can be applied for live transmission as the entire video data has to be known in advance. Nearly all approaches investigate removal of dynamic or static objects temporarily hidden by a moving object (e.g., a person walking) with almost stationary or restricted camera movement. This work will investigate and present a video inpainting approach applicable for unconstrained camera motions to allow the removal of static objects.

The constraint for only removing static objects is based mainly on real-time detection and tracking complexity. As no a priori information is given, an approach would be necessary that is able to track an arbitrary visual element that may temporarily be occluded by other visual content in the video stream. Related approaches overcome this complex task by a manually created video inpainting masks for each video frame in advance. None of the recently proposed tracking approaches is fast enough and provides accurate

1.1 Objective

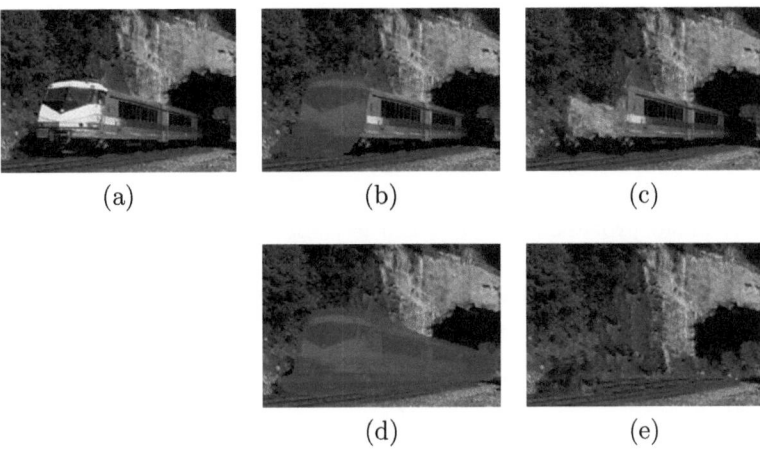

(a)   (b)   (c)

(d)   (e)

Figure 1.3: Result comparison for the *Train* image. a) Original image, b) original image with small inpainting mask, c) our inpainting result for the small mask, d) original image with large inpainting mask, e) our inpainting result for the large mask. The original image has been taken from [30], kindly authorized by the author, ©2003 ACM.

selection and tracking of almost arbitrary objects, as the video manipulation algorithm also has to be processed in the short real-time processing slot. To realize the tracking of arbitrary objects as well as to improve the coherence accuracy of the resulting video stream, the direct visual environments of the undesired objects have to be almost planar. On the one hand, the backgrounds of undesired objects are normally almost planar by default. Thus, the background constraint is not a real restriction. On the other hand, most backgrounds that are non planar such as a landscape behind an object have a large distance to the camera and thus can be supported by the approach as well.

The video inpainting approach introduced in this work has to create high image qualities. Further, the resulting video must provide a visually coherent stream not showing any artifacts or ghost shadows between successive video frames. As any a priori information about the undesired object, the environment or camera motion is not taken into account, the system needs to allow intuitive and rapid selection of an undesired object at any moment during a live video stream. The user must have the possibility to roughly select an undesired object. At the same time, the approach has to separate visual content into undesired foreground and desired background information in real-time. This undesired image content has to be tracked during the video sequence and needs be reliably removed without visual artifacts.

1.2 Outline

In Chapter 2, we will review recent approaches directly related to our work. Recent image processing approaches as well as approaches proposed to manipulate video streams will be introduced. The chapter is complemented by a discussion of approaches developed for Mediated Reality with research focusing on Diminished Reality. Following, in Chapter 3, our approach to real-time video manipulation will be derived and discussed in detail. In Chapter 4, an approach for static image inpainting will be discussed and visual results will be compared to recent state-of-the-art approaches. Generalization of the image inpainting approach leading to an approach capable of manipulating video streams will be presented in Chapter 5. The real-time approach that is able to track arbitrary objects to be removed in a live video transmission will be introduced. Accurate performance results of our entire pipeline for video manipulation will be presented in detail, and a user evaluation verifying the validity of the approach. Finally, we conclude our work in Chapter 6 and discuss future work in the field of image and video inpainting as well as fields of application applying our approach.

2 Related Work

In this section, the most important work related to our approach is presented and discussed in detail. First, an overview of previous approaches for static image processing is provided, followed by the introduction of related approaches applying manipulation of video streams. Finally, an overview of recent Mediated Reality techniques will be given.

2.1 Static Image Processing

In the last decade, a wide variety of approaches for image processing directly related to the approach presented in this work have been proposed. Basically, these approaches can be separated into three individual categories with different goals:

- **Texture Synthesis** tries to create a new image entirely using a simple regular texture from a given reference frame. The resulting image aims to provide the same visual structure as the reference frame but has a different frame dimension (see Figure 2.1a).

- **Image Inpainting** tries to seamlessly remove user defined elements in images with complex and non regular visual content. The new created image content is created in such a manner that the final result spoofs observers not knowing that the specific image content is missing in the image (see Figure 2.1b).

- **Image Manipulation** allows individual modifications of image content. For the most part, this topic encompasses image reshuffling and image resizing. However, depending on the approach, algorithms can be used to remove visual content. Image manipulation techniques are the most powerful approaches in the context of image processing. The area of application for image manipulation does not necessarily fit into unique categories (see Figure 2.1c).

Image processing approaches can also be categorized according to their modification unit. Approaches using a pixel unit modify the result pixel by

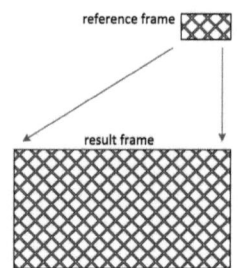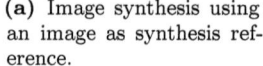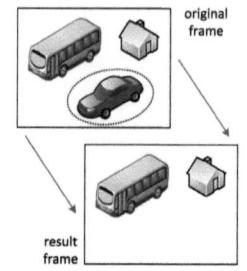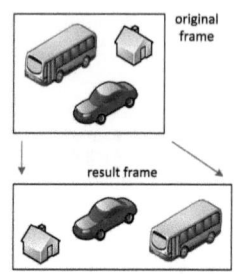

(a) Image synthesis using an image as synthesis reference.

(b) Image inpainting of a selected image region.

(c) Image manipulation resizing the original image dimension and/or reshuffling the content.

Figure 2.1: Overview of the three individual image processing categories discussed in this work.

pixel. Algorithms using image patches directly modify a set of joined pixels (mostly a squared image patch). It has to be clarified that even approaches applying single pixels as modification unit may use image patches (centered at single pixels) for similarity determination.

In the following subsections, the three main categories of image processing and their techniques are introduced in more detail. Their complexity, usability and performance is discussed.

2.1.1 Texture Synthesis

In computer graphics, textures are used intensively for creating more realistic visual results. They are often applied as simple memory storage for complex operations. The visual content of textures in computer graphics is not restricted to any specific property.

In the context of texture synthesis or image processing, textures are expected to provide simple but mostly regular structures over large image regions as depicted in Figure 2.1a. Examples for regular textures found in nature are images of regularly structured stone walls, large flowerbeds or huge sets of similar small objects. However, the synthesis of textures is not the main focus of our work as our objective focuses on natural visual content derived from arbitrary environments. Nevertheless, texture synthesis uses several basic concepts also applied in approaches suitable for images with

2.1 Static Image Processing

more complex content. An overview of the main approaches for texture synthesis is presented for a better understanding of past research. In the following, if not explicitly stated, the term texture is used in the context of texture synthesis and thus is expected to denote only the above described properties.

First, approaches applying pixel units will be introduced, followed by approaches using sets of pixels (patches):

2.1.1.1 Pixel Unit Synthesis

One of the first texture synthesis approaches was proposed by Efros and Leung [32]. They created synthesized texture from a given reference frame providing the visual structure that the new synthesized frame had to adopt. The approach created the new frame pixel by pixel starting at an arbitrary seed point in the synthesis frame. Efros created the new texture using a Markov Random Field (MRF) [59] based on the assumption that the pixel intensity value of each pixel in the texture is only dependent on a local neighborhood. The color of a new synthesized pixel p was determined by the highest probability $P(p|\omega(p))$ of the probability density function (PDF) depending on the given neighborhood $\omega(p)$ corresponding to the point p. The local neighborhood was represented by a square pixel region. Efros and Leung approximated the PDF by the application of a color intensity histogram. The histogram was composed of the center pixels from best matching patches between the reference frame and the synthesis frame. Each possible patch in the reference frame has been checked upon similarity (see Figure 2.2a) and the corresponding center pixel from the reference frame was added to the histogram if the similarity was better than a defined threshold (see Figure 2.2b). Patch similarity was determined by the sum of squared differences (SSD) of pixel color values. The approach worked well for simple and regular textures as shown in Figure 2.3. Performance and visual result directly depend on the size of the neighborhood $\omega(p)$. The size had to be chosen carefully to cover at least the lowest visible frequency (equal to the largest visible feature) in the reference frame to allow a sufficient result.

Similar to the work of Efros and Leung, Wei and Levoy [101] proposed a modified approach avoiding PDF and histogram calculation. Instead of determining a set of best matching patches between result and reference frame, they make direct use of the center pixel of the one unique best matching patch. Instead of starting at an arbitrary seed point, Wei applied a scanline algorithm in combination with an L-shaped neighborhood. This L-shape only allows for the matching of already assigned pixels between

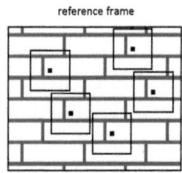 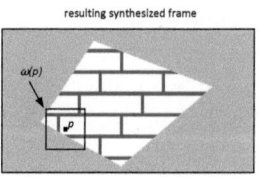 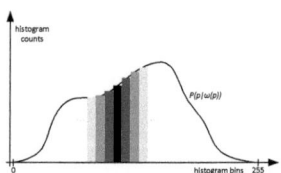

(a) Search of best matching patches for the given pixel p in the result frame; the solid blue area still has to be synthesized. The graphic has been reconstructed following [32].

(b) Resulting pixel intensity histogram of the center pixels of all patches in the reference frame best matching to $\omega(p)$.

Figure 2.2: The two steps of the texture synthesis approach of Efros and Leung.

Figure 2.3: Three results of the texture synthesis approach by Efros and Leung. Top row: reference frames, bottom row: final synthesis result with ideal neighborhood $\omega(p)$. The texture images are taken from [32], kindly authorized by the author, ©1999 IEEE.

reference and result frame. (see Figure 2.4). Wei proposed the application of a multiresolution synthesis to avoid the explicit selection of the size of the neighborhood $\omega(p)$. Several pyramid layers of the reference and result frames are created to apply the synthesis to each layer. The algorithm starts on the most coarsest pyramid layer and ends on the finest image resolution. A Tree Structured Vector Quantization (TSVQ) [37, 100] is used to avoid the brute force search of best matching pixels. However, TSVQ creation is in itself time-consuming, memory intensive and cannot guarantee ideal matchings.

2.1 Static Image Processing

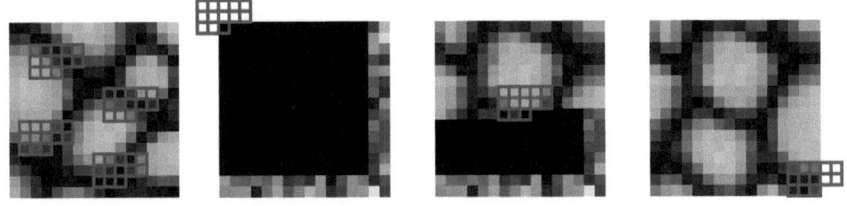

(a) Reference.   (b) Three different stages during the synthesis.

Figure 2.4: Texture synthesis by Wei and Levoy for the lowest frame resolution. The images are taken from [101], kindly authorized by the author, ©2000 ACM.

Ashikhmin [2] changed the approach of Wei by simply replacing the TSVQ application by an information propagation technique. Ashikhmin found that the usage of TSVQ is still too slow and at the same time may produce undesired visual results due to the reduced matching quality. He observed that information already found for the ideal matching of the previous pixel in the scanline order can also be used for the current pixel. The algorithm tests shifted pixels of already assigned matches in direct neighborhoods. A detailed description of a similar propagation technique is explained in Subsection 2.1.4.2. Propagation of already gathered information allows a significant performance increase compared to the performance of previous approaches. Finally, Ashikhmin introduced a possibility to create user-controlled visual results implementing the application of predefined target frames (giving a rough suggestion of the final result).

2.1.1.2 Patch Unit Synthesis

A more efficient synthesis approach was introduced by Xu et al. [105]. In contrast to a pixel-based approach explicitly synthesizing each pixel, they propose to apply an approach directly using image patches. The approach can be subdivided into three simple steps. First, Xu et al. create a tiling image by copying the reference frame as often as necessary to fill the entire new image content. Second, patches (slightly smaller than the original reference frame) are copied from one frame position to another position inside the new synthesized frame. Positioning is determined by a chaos function. Finally, the borders between copied patches are removed by cross-edge filtering within a small area around the patch borders. Figure 2.5 shows synthesis results using their approach. The approach is relatively fast due to

Figure 2.5: Synthesis results by Xu et al. From left to right: Tiling image, chaos function structure, copying of patches, final result after filtering. The images are taken from [105], kindly authorized by the author.

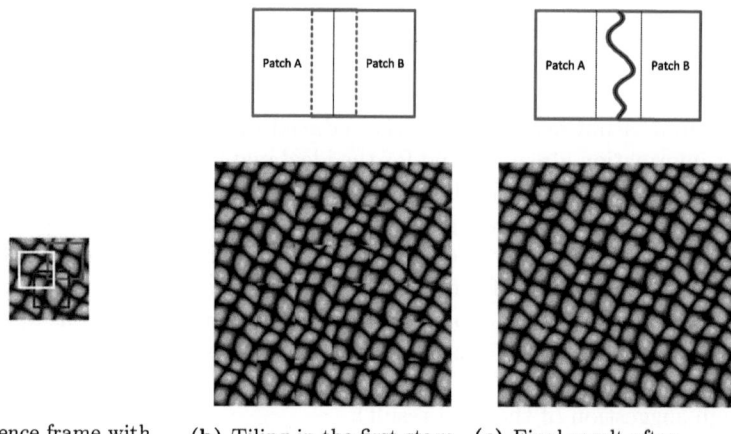

(a) Reference frame with three patches. (b) Tiling in the first stage. (c) Final result after minimal cut application.

Figure 2.6: Texture synthesis by Efros and Freeman. The texture images are taken from [31], kindly authorized by the author, ©2001 ACM. The overlapping scheme images have been reconstructed following [31].

the application of image patches, however, the border filtering needs noisy textures for visually convincing results.

A slightly different patch-based synthesis approach has been developed by Efros and Freeman [31]. In contrast to Xu, Efros does not use edge filtering at the patch boundaries but applies a minimum error boundary cut between overlapping patches. The visual result can be improved as blurring and interpolation at patch boundaries can be avoided. Figure 2.6 shows the approach of Efros and Freeman for a simple and regular texture.

2.1.1.3 Discussion

In the previous subsection, the most relevant texture synthesis approaches have been described. Some approaches apply single pixels, other apply image patches to create the final result. Approaches that do not use a multiresolution image pyramid rely on the manual adjustment of patch size with respect to texture frequency. The lower the frequency of interesting image content, the larger the patch size has to be in order to cover enough visual information for measuring similarity. The application of a multiresolution approach allows automated image synthesis without multiple adjustments by the user. Still, texture synthesis is obviously restricted to mainly non-natural images displaying regular patterns.

2.1.2 Image Inpainting

Image inpainting does not create new images by using a given reference texture, but instead seamlessly removes undesired content in images. The objective of image inpainting is to create a visual result spoofing an observer not knowing the original image. As long as observers do not notice any image manipulation although a significant portion of the original visual information is missing in the inpainted image, the objective is achieved. Several completely different visual solutions for a given inpainting image may exist, as long as the overall impression of each result allows observers to be spoofed. The manipulated image content must not disturb important visual structures such as strong borders or edges. Also, textured and blurred areas have to be sufficiently reconstructed.

In the research community, image inpainting has not yet been uniquely defined and thus also the term *image completion* is used for the same context as visual object removal. Often, the terms image inpainting and image completion are used likewise although some authors distinguish between both according to the manipulation approach used. The technique denoted image inpainting is used in combination with algorithms manipulating the image by iteratively shrinking the size of the undesired image region. In contrast, image completion is used for approaches removing (or optimizing) all undesired pixels in parallel (see Figure 2.7).

However, in the following, the notation *image inpainting* will be used for both cases, because, as a rule, the algorithms cannot be uniquely separated to denote either image inpainting or image completion. If a unique separation is necessary, the inpainting process iteratively reducing the size of the undesired image content will be denoted by *shrinking* inpainting. The

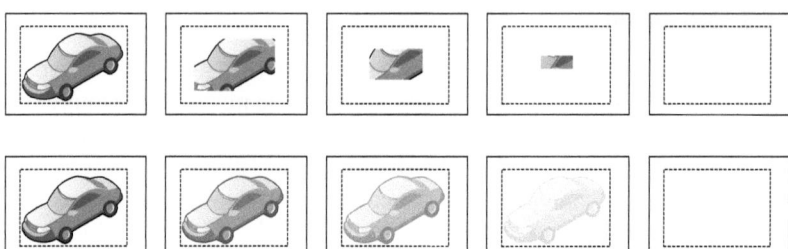

Figure 2.7: Two individual techniques to remove undesired objects in a frame. Top row: a local optimization as the manipulation starts at the boundary (sometimes mainly denoted with *Image Inpainting*, bottom row: a global optimization as the entire area is manipulated in parallel (sometimes mainly denoted with *Image Completion*). The increasing transparency stands for an abstract successive optimization of the visual result.

approach concurrently improving the entire inpainting area will be denoted by *vanishing* inpainting. Furthermore, the undesired pixel region in inpainting images will be denoted as *(inpainting) mask* or *(inpainting) hole* and the border between desired and undesired image content will be described as (inpainting) *boundary* or (inpainting) *border*.

In the next subsections, the most important inpainting approaches over the past years are introduced. Comparable to texture synthesis algorithms, two main categories of inpainting approaches exist. The first category uses pixels as the inpainting unit, approaches of the second category apply patches as the inpainting unit. However, we rather present the individual inpainting approaches in chronological order than distinguishing between those two types.

2.1.2.1 Bertalmio et al. 2000

One of the first pixel-based inpainting approaches has been proposed by Bertalmio et al. [13] to restore images with small visual errors. This approach applies a pixel-based mask filling algorithm iteratively propagating image content from the direct inpainting boundary towards the center of the hole. However, compared to a simple erosion filter [94], the approach of Bertalmio tries to explicitly propagate isophote lines (intersecting with the inpainting boundaries) into the hole to improve the visual result. Pixel values inside the undesired area are updated according to the projected 2D Laplacian [94] of the image intensities. The projection is applied onto the directions of

2.1 Static Image Processing

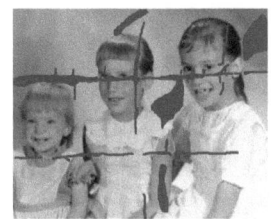

(a) Original frame.   (b) Original frame with mask covering all scratches.   (c) Restoration result.

Figure 2.8: Image restoration result for the approach of Bertalmio. This inpainting approach works well with smooth or blurred image content. The images are taken from [13], kindly authorized by the author, ©2000 ACM.

isophote lines determined by the image gradients. Several thousand iterations in combination with a pyramid layer approach are applied to produce a converged result. Figure 2.8 provides a typical restoration result using the Bertalmio approach showing that this approach works well only for images with several scattered but small pixel errors. The approach is best applied to areas with smooth image information as the algorithm basically propagates blurred image content from the inpainting boundary towards the inpainting mask. Thus, this approach is not suitable for manipulation of arbitrary natural images.

2.1.2.2 Demanet et al. 2003

A few years later, Demanet et al. [29] proposed an new pixel-based inpainting approach which iteratively shrinks the undesired pixel area by replacing pixel values at the inpainting boundary. This replacement is repeated until the hole is closed. In contrast to the approach of Bertalmio, this approach uses a correspondence map for all pixels inside the undesired pixel area. The correspondence map stores exactly one reference pixel from the remaining image content for each hole pixel. This map is defined based on the visual appearance of the eight direct surrounding neighborhoods of each pixel. Demanet et al. further introduced several optimizations such as a randomized matching search, mapping propagation for neighboring pixels (like Ashikhmin [2]) and a multiresolution approach to improve the overall performance. These optimizations are also applied in most of the approaches to be introduced. Our approach is also partially inspired by mapping pixel

(a) Original image with undesired region in red. (b) Initialization result with best matching circular patches. (c) Final inpainting result.

Figure 2.9: Image inpainting results by Drori et al. showing the individual inpainting steps of their approach. The images are taken from [30], kindly authorized by the author, ©2003 ACM.

positions and their introduced improvements. The approach presented by Demanet et al. provides neither an initialization strategy nor a possibility to preserve structural information from remaining image content. The simple hole shrinking strategy cannot produce a global optimum and thus may provide undesired results.

2.1.2.3 Drori et al. 2003

Drori et al. [30] introduced one of the first patch-based inpainting approaches. First, they applied a multiresolution approach using smoothing kernels to create an initial image. The initial image is created within several up- and downsampling iterations diffusing the content of the inpainting boundary into the mask area of the image. The initial process creates images with blurred inpainting holes visually comparable to the inpainting results of Bertalmio et al. [13] (see Figure 2.9b). A following second process then produces a high quality image. Drori et al. use best matching image patches with individual scale and orientations to successively increase the visual result of the initial process. They assign a confidence value to all image pixels. At the start, all pixels in the inpainting mask receive the lowest confidence value. Pixels from the remaining image information hold the highest confidence value. During iterative refinement, best matching (circular) patches with high confidence are merged to areas with lower confidence. This refinement is repeated until all image pixels have reached a specified confidence value. Figure 2.9 shows the visual results of Drori et al. Although the image quality is better than in previous inpainting approaches the algorithm fails in areas with strong structures. Performance is still far from real-time performance.

2.1 Static Image Processing

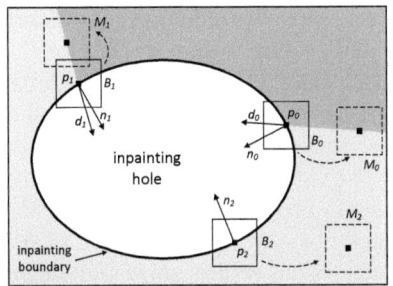 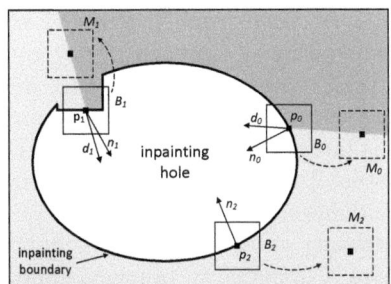

(a) Image before the first patch is copied into the inpainting hole.

(b) Result image, the inpainting priority must be re-evaluated.

Figure 2.10: Scheme of the inpainting approach by Criminisi et al. depicted for three boundary patches B_0, B_1 and B_2 with their corresponding mapping patches M_0, M_1 and M_2 respectively. The inpainting priority of B_1 is the highest as the scalar product of the normal n_1 and orthogonal image gradient d_1 at position p_1 is higher than the other products.

The overall algorithm needs between 83 and 158 minutes for an image with 384×256 pixels. Using currently available computer hardware, the approach still would require approximately 6 to 11 minutes. In Appendix A.7, the applied performance estimate approximately calculating performance using current computer hardware is described in detail.

2.1.2.4 Criminisi et al. 2003

Another patch-based approach has been introduced by Criminisi et al. [24, 25]. Their approach can be seen as an adjustment of the pixel-based approach of Demanet et al.'s [29] to a patch-based approach. Instead of shrinking the inpainting hole with single pixels during several iterations, Criminisi et al. propose to shrink the undesired frame area by the successive replacement of small image patches.

For a pixel p at the inpainting boundary, a small image patch B centered at p is defined to find the best matching patch M lying entirely in the remaining image content. The best matching patch is found by a brute force data investigation. Only the hole pixels covered by the patch B are replaced by the corresponding pixels from patch M. The replacement produces a new inpainting boundary and the process restarts (see Figure 2.10). The order of inpainting boundary pixels are selected by a priority mechanism allowing reconstruction of strong edges intersecting the inpainting boundary to be performed first. Priority is determined by the scalar product of the normal vector perpendicular to the inpainting boundary and the orthogonal of the image gradient. The stronger a line and the more perpendicular this line intersects the boundary, the earlier this area will be inpainted (see Figure 2.10). Criminisi et al. do not apply any multiresolution approaches, randomized seeking algorithms or information propagation techniques like Demanet et al. and thus the approach does not aim for interactive frame rates. Compared to previous approaches, the visual results show significant improvement as depicted in Figure 2.11.

2.1.2.5 Sun et al. 2005

Although the approach of Criminisi et al. prioritizes the inpainting of structured areas, their algorithm fails to reconstruct straight lines as depicted in Figure 2.11c. Therefore, Sun et al. [93] proposed an improved patch-based inpainting approach with two individual stages. In the first stage, the areas around user-defined lines or curves are reconstructed to fix the most important image structures first. The remaining inpainting areas are then filled as depicted in Figure 2.12. Sun et al. propose to recover the user-defined lines or curves by overlapping small image patches stringed on a chain. These patches are taken from the remaining image information, similar to Criminisi's approach. A graph optimization algorithm is used to select best matching patches. Sun et al. remove seams between overlapping patches using a gradient-based interpolation (by application of Poisson blending [79]). The structure recovering phase finally produces thin paths crossing the inpainting image dividing it into individual smaller regions as depicted in Figure 2.12b.

In the second stage, the remaining regions are recovered using the previously described approaches of Ashikhmin [2], Drori et al. [30] or Criminisi et al. [24]. Sun et al. again employ user-defined information dividing the image into individual disjoint parts to shrink the areas of influence for the inpainting algorithms. Texture information from the direct neighborhood is used. In Figure 2.12c, three individual inpainting masks A, B and C with their corresponding neighborhoods A', B' and C' are depicted showing the idea of closing the inpainting holes during the second stage.

Sun et al. claim that structure recovering (first pass) is much faster than texture recovering (second pass). Despite this claim, it is still far from real-time performance. The two-pass separation makes the entire approach inflexible especially since user-defined constraints are necessary for structure

2.1 Static Image Processing

(a) Result for the well-known *Bungee* image showing that straight lines are well preserved.

(b) The structure of the satellite image of London is preserved while some artifacts are visible in the resulting image.

(c) Inpainting of the island region, the horizon shows minor reconstruction errors.

Figure 2.11: Some of the image inpainting results by Criminisi et al. for three different images. From left to right: original image, mask image, final result. The images are taken from [24], kindly authorized by the author, ©2003 IEEE.

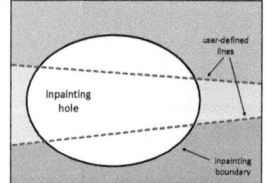 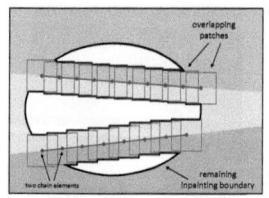 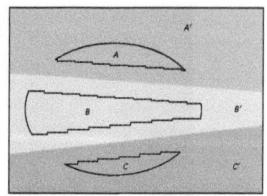

(a) Inpainting image with two user-defined lines.

(b) First phase: Structure reconstruction.

(c) Second phase: The remaining pixels are synthesized.

Figure 2.12: The two phases inpainting scheme proposed by Sun et al.

recovering. In the second pass, the usage of texture synthesis limits the application to small and textured areas. Our approach can be applied to important structures and homogenous image content concurrently while further allowing the synthesis of non-textured areas.

2.1.2.6 Shen et al. 2007

Similar to the work of Criminisi et al., Shen et al. [85] presented an approach iteratively filling the inpainting hole using patches found in the remaining image content. Instead of shrinking the hole by copying the color information from the source patches, Shen et al. copy the gradient information. This provides an intermediate inpainting result proposing the image gradients of the final image (see Figure 2.13). A color image is determined from the given gradients by solving the Poisson differential equation as proposed in [35]. The algorithm does not apply a multiresolution approach and is again not near real-time performance even though only a fraction of the entire computational time is required for Poisson solving.

2.1.2.7 Fang et al. 2009

Fang et al. [34] developed another patch-based approach mainly basing on the work of Criminisi et al. They applied a multiresolution algorithm and further reduced the search space of possible source patches. Fang et al. propose to use the eigenvalues of the Hessian matrix to determine inpainting order and direction at the inpainting border. Inpainting pixels with a strong border direction seek possible source patches only in a small image region perpendicular to the inpainting border. A brute force search is necessary only for inpainting pixels (at the inpainting boundary) with similar eigenvalues.

2.1 Static Image Processing

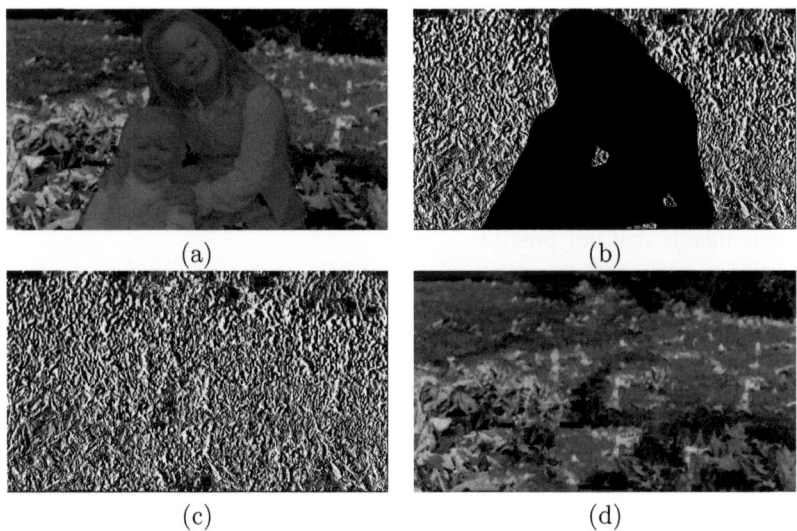

Figure 2.13: Gradient-based image inpainting by Shen et al. a) Original image with mask, b) initial (horizontal) gradient image, c) final (horizontal) gradient image, d) resulting color image after solving the Poisson equation. The images are kindly received by the author of [85].

The major difference compared to previous approaches is the application of a principal component analysis (PCA) to reduce the dimensions of the data set. Although this transformation requires a certain length of training time for each pyramid layer, the overall patch matching process can be improved due to the reduced data set. Fang et al. do not apply the PCA transformation on the most finest pyramid layer but apply a simple texture refinement step instead to avoid expensive PCA transformations for the highest image resolution. Fang et al. propose several specific optimizations and modifications of their original idea on individual pyramid resolutions. Despite this, the final approach is significantly too slow to be applied in a real-time system.

2.1.2.8 Kwok et al. 2010

A slight modification of the approach of Fang et al. has been introduced by Kwok et al. [65]. Instead of using a PCA to speed up the matching process, they propose application of the discrete cosine transformation (DCT) combined with a strong coefficient quantization to reduce the amount of information. They replace time consuming patch matching by using a comparison of a few DCT coefficients and use the parallelism capabilities of Graphic Processing Units (GPUs) to speed up the patch matching search. Unfortunately, a performance comparison between a pure CPU implementation and the GPU implementation is not provided by Kwok et al. This approach is one of the fastest approaches currently available, but real-time performance is still not possible.

2.1.2.9 Bugeau et al. 2010

Since Drori et al. in 2003, inpainting approaches mainly focused on patch-based inpainting algorithms. Bugeau et al. [21] recently investigated into pixel-based inpainting. They propose to extend the approach of Demanet et al. using a correspondence map for pixels inside and outside the inpainting boundary. The final map is determined by minimizing an energy term based on three individual appearance constraints: a self-similarity, diffusion and propagation and a coherence energy term. Within a multiresolution approach, they iteratively seek a local minimum according to their energy cost function. The approach is very slow but provides visual results comparable to other state-of-the-art approaches. For an image with 256 × 163 pixels the approach needs about 5 minutes and for an image with 750 × 563 pixels, it takes approximately 25 minutes.

2.1.2.10 Xu et al. 2010

One of the most recent inpainting approaches has been developed by Xu et al. [106]. Similar to Criminisi et al. and Fang et al., they propose a shrinking inpainting approach with explicit patch priority order. The order is determined by a patch sparsity constraint. The more unique a patch (the less similar to neighboring patches), the higher the inpainting priority of a pixel at the inpainting boundary becomes. They do not copy one best matching patch into the inpainting hole, but use a linear combination of several best matching patches. Being aware of blurring and smoothing issues whenever more than one image patch defines the final image content [103, 92, 104, 8], Xu et al. do not simply blend all patches but determine a linear combination defining the blending behavior of all patches involved. No multiresolution approach is used. The work provides convincing results compared to previous approaches, however, the algorithm is not capable for interactive or real-time applications. The C++ implementation of Xu

2.1 Static Image Processing

et al. needs 105 seconds for 5,310 pixels to be filled. The performance correlates with a fillrate of about 0.05 pixels per millisecond. The fillrate of the approach that will be presented in this work has to be higher than 1,000 pixels per millisecond to allow real-time execution for video inpainting.

2.1.2.11 Summary

The above presented inpainting approaches are a carefully selected subset of inpainting algorithms proposed in the last decade. The entire number of available inpainting algorithms is much larger. However, approaches not discussed like [16, 14, 69, 55, 108, 62, 63, 58, 75, 50, 87] mainly combine the major ideas of the approaches presented with only small variations, and are thus not introduced in more detail.

In Table 2.1, a simplified overview of the above presented approaches is given to compare the most significant differences between the individual approaches. In Subsection 4.9, a detailed performance analysis is provided for all introduced approaches.

2.1.3 Image Composition

In the following the image processing approach of Hays et al. [39] is introduced that does neither match to the category of image inpainting approaches nor to the category of image manipulation algorithms.

Hays et al. proposed a different way to handle the task of content removal. Instead of using the visual content of the remaining image, they use millions of photographs distributed over a computer cluster to fill the undesired image regions. Millions of photographs are described by a semantic scene descriptor and the gathered information is stored in a database. The direct area around an undesired image region in an inpainting image is used to find a matching photograph from the database. A Poisson blending [79] is applied to merge the original image with the photograph of the database. The visual results are promising, but the approach needs a database with a sufficient number of images. The final results are simple blendings of two images. The approach needs about one hour to process one frame (not including the time necessary to build the database).

Table 2.1: Summary of the introduced image inpainting approaches. A simplified overview is given to compare the most significant differences between the individual approaches.

Year	Author	Inpainting unit	Inpainting technique	Multi-resolution	Propagation
2000	Bertalmio et al. [13]	pixel	shrinking	no	no
2003	Demanet et al. [29]	pixel	shrinking	yes	yes
2003	Drori et al. [30]	patch	shrinking & vanishing	yes	no
2003	Criminisi et al. [24]	patch	shrinking	no	no
2005	Sun et al. [93]	pixel & patch	shrinking	no	no
2007	Shen et al. [85]	patch (gradient)	shrinking & vanishing	no	no
2009	Fang et al. [34]	patch (PCA)	shrinking	yes	no
2010	Kwok et al. [65]	patch (DCT)	shrinking	no	no
2010	Bugeau et al. [21]	pixel	vanishing	yes	no
2010	Xu et al. [106]	patch	shrinking	no	no

2.1.4 Image Manipulation

In the following subsection, recent image synthesis approaches are introduced to manipulate image content not only by image inpainting but also by image reshuffling or image resizing.

2.1.4.1 Patch-based Similarity by Simakov et al. 2009

Simakov et al. proposed a patch-based approach to manipulate images by iteratively updating the image content. They define a bidirectional dissimilarity function $d(S,T)$ giving a global measurement value to the visual dissimilarity of two images S(ource) and T(arget) with arbitrary dimensions. The function consists of two terms. The first term covers visual completeness and the second term measures visual coherence between S and T. The image T is said to be visually complete with regard to S if all information of S appears in T. T is called visually coherent if T does not have any artifacts non-existent in S. The bidirectional measurement function is defined as follows:

$$d(S,T) = \frac{1}{N_S} \sum_{P \subset S} \min_{Q \subset T} D(P,Q) + \frac{1}{N_T} \sum_{Q \subset T} \min_{P \subset S} D(Q,P) \qquad (2.1)$$

where P and Q are image patches in S and T respectively, N_S and N_T are the numbers of possible patches in S and T respectively, and $D(\cdot)$ represents the distance function between two image patches.

The higher the value of the dissimilarity function $d(S,T)$, the bigger the visual difference between the two images S and T. This function gives a simple measurement of the similarity of arbitrary image pairs. Simakov et al. analyze the error proportion of each pixel in T contributing to the entire dissimilarity value. They end up with an algorithm iteratively optimizing each pixel color with respect to the dissimilarity function. Simakov et al. additionally introduced the application of so called importance weightings. This extension solves image summarization, reshuffling and inpainting tasks using the same function. Although the patch-based similarity approach is very powerful, the brute force search of best matching patches is by far too time intensive to use for interactive framerates.

2.1.4.2 PatchMatch by Barnes et al. 2009

The previously introduced approach of Simakov et al. has been improved by Barnes et al. [8, 9] essentially combining the bidirectional similarity measure

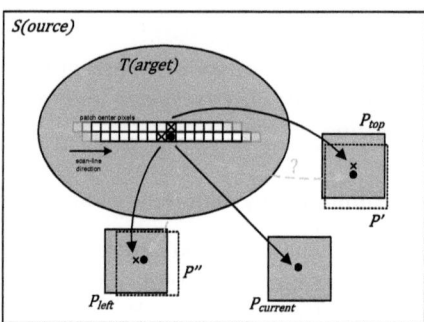

Figure 2.14: Information propagation of PatchMatch by Barnes et al. Left to right and top to bottom information propagation step for one patch, possible candidates are P' and P'' and will be compared with $P_{current}$, P' lies one pixel below P_{top} and P'' lies one pixel to the right of P_{left}.

of Simakov with the proposed randomized search and the multiresolution approach of Demanet and the information propagation as proposed by Ashikhmin. The combination of the three individual approaches allows image inpainting, resizing and retargeting of images with performance at least one magnitude faster than all previous approaches. Instead of determining exact patch matches, Barnes et al. combine a random search with already gathered information for neighboring patch matches. They argue that the amount of wrongly assigned correspondences becomes very small with the increasing number of random search iterations and therefore is negligible. The approach is separated into three individual steps:

1. **Initialization**
   The algorithm starts with an initial set of patch correspondences. This set can be defined randomly or by any a priori information providing a good initial guess.

2. **Propagation**
   Each patch match in the target region is checked for improvements by its direct two neighbors (in scan-line-order). This propagation step covers the fact that often neighboring patches in the target will correspond to neighboring patches in the source region. The scan-line-order is flipped with each new iteration step to propagate correspondences in all directions (see Figure 2.14).

2.1 Static Image Processing

(a)   (b)

Figure 2.15: Seam carving image resizing by Avidan et al. a) Original input image with one horizontal and one vertical seam (red), b) resized image after several iterations (top row), scaled original image (bottom row). The images are taken from [4], kindly authorized by the author, ©2007 ACM.

3. **Random search**
   Each patch propagation is followed by a few random search iterations trying to find a better patch in the source image. The search area starts encompassing the whole source image and decreases exponentially to determine the exact position. The propagation step alternates with the random search step until all patches in the target region have been improved. Several of those passes are necessary to receive approximated patch correspondences of sufficient quality.

2.1.4.3 Seam Carving by Avidan et al. 2007

Avidan et al. [4] developed a method to shrink, stretch or crop images while the important image content remains visible without warping. The approach is based on removing or adding horizontal and vertical seams. A seam starts at one image border and ends at the opposite border. A horizontal seam has exactly one pixel in each column and has a vertical offset of at most one pixel. Correspondingly, a vertical seam has one pixel in each row. For each seam an energy cost is determined, e.g., by summing the gradients of successive seam pixels. Removing seams with lowest energy cost allows preservation of image content (see Figure 2.15). The approach of Avidan is faster than other image resizing approach. However, the approach still does not accommodate interactive framerates for moderately sized images.

2.1.4.4 Shift-Map by Pritch et al. 2009

An approach allowing retargeting, resizing, rearranging, and image inpainting has been presented by Pritch et al. [81]. They apply a global optimization problem for single pixel mappings between a target and a source frame. Each single pixel mapping provides an appearance and a user defined cost. The appearance cost requires the image content of neighboring mappings to be similar in the target and in the source frame. An explicit user defined data term adds user guided cost to optimize the visual result. A graph labeling approach is used to seek an optimal solution over several pyramid layers. Due to the graph optimization, the overall performance does not reach interactive frame rates and thus is not real-time capable. The approach of Pritch can be seen as an extension of the approach of Demanet et al.

2.1.4.5 Darabi et al. 2012

Darabi et al. [28] combined the ideas of two previous approaches. They used the idea of Drori et al. [30] integrating orientation and scale issues into the search for best matching patches. Darabi et al. also proposed a scale and orientation invariant version of the dissimilarity approach of Wexler et al. [103]. Further, they integrated reflectance and luminance correction of image patches into the image processing pipeline. The search for best matching patches is performed randomly analog to the approach of Barnes et al. [8].

Compared to the original approach of Barnes et al., Darabi et al. receive improved results for inpainting images with regular structured image content that can be reconstructed by scaled, oriented or mirrored image patches. The approach also allows cloning and stitching of images as well as morphing between two pictures.

However, due to the significantly larger search space for the transformed image patches, the approach of Darabi et al. is several times slower than the original approach of Barnes et al. For image inpainting, they claimed to reach a fillrate of about 4.3 pixels per millisecond for an image of 1340×2048 pixels. In Subsection 4.9, the performance values of our approach are given in detail. Our approach is more than 500 times faster for an image with comparable frame dimensions while our CPU is slightly slower than the evaluation CPU of Darabi et al.

2.1.5 Discussion

The above presented approaches are briefly discussed in this subsection. Recent state-of-the-art approaches for texture synthesis, image inpainting and image manipulation share the problem that none of them allows real-time computation. A minor number of approaches can be applied with interactive framerates, achieving at most one frame per second (depending on frame and mask dimensions). The majority of approaches introduced need several minutes or even hours to process one single image.

The presented approaches may be classified according to several of their individual properties. The most important classification property appears to be the manipulation unit and the optimization process. Most approaches use patch-based image manipulation. Some of the introduced works apply individual pixels as the manipulation unit.

All introduced approaches in Subsection 2.1.1, 2.1.2 and 2.1.4 apply one of three individual optimization techniques to create the final image. Some approaches define image manipulation as a graph labeling problem and create a final image by determining a graph with minimal overall cost. Other approaches apply a brute-force search of best matching image content. Only a few approaches apply a heuristic (mainly randomized) search of matching image content.

To date, the fastest algorithm has been introduced by Barnes et al. [8, 9]. Their method reaches a fillrate of up to 60 pixels per millisecond [28] for an image resolution of 1340 × 2048 (our approach reaches a fillrate of more than 2,000 pixels per millisecond for an comparable image). The algorithm of Barnes et al. uses the content of best matching image patches that have been found in a heuristic manner and superimposes this information to iteratively create a final image result. Within several iterations, the image inpainting result is obtained by a vanishing process successively improving the visual result but not shrinking the inpainting mask. If no user specified constraints are applied, this algorithm is not able to reliably preserve structural information of the remaining image as homogenous and heterogeneous image content is handled with the same priority. The creation of a homogenous image region and the creation e.g., of a straight line, compete with each other and thus none of these two visual elements may be reliably reconstructed.

In contrast to the work of Barnes et al., approaches iteratively shrinking the inpainting mask such as that of Criminisi et al. [25], Sun et al. [93] or Kwok et al. [65] are able to preserve structure information. Significantly more time is needed for computation. Preservation of image structure is primarily governed by the inpainting order. Segments on the inpainting boundary surrounded by heterogeneous image content are inpainted first, segments with neighborhoods of homogenous image content are handled afterwards. However, approaches iteratively shrinking the inpainting mask still fail to reconstruct structure information more complex than straight lines or regular curves.

Thus, complex structure information requires explicit user-defined constraints to additionally guide the algorithm. The approach of Barnes et al. [8] allows defining of straight lines that have to be preserved during image inpainting. Even more complex structure constraints like curves are supported by the approach of Sun et al. [93]. While Barnes et al. integrate constraint handling into their inpainting pipeline, Sun et al. decided to separate the inpainting process. First, the user-defined structure is reconstructed and finalized. Then, homogenous image parts are inpainted.

None of the above presented approaches is suitable for real-time video inpainting. The most obvious problem is that no algorithm is fast enough to be applied in real-time. The few algorithms able to process an inpainting image within a few seconds require explicit user-defined constraints to make a reliable reconstruction of structural information possible. For real-time applications, user-defined constraint are not practical and should be avoided.

For high quality manipulation of live video streams, the task is to find a static image processing approach significantly faster than all state-of-the-art approaches producing comparable image quality.

2.2 Video Inpainting

In this section, the most important video inpainting approaches are introduced. First, approaches for almost stationary cameras are introduced followed by approaches proposed for dynamic camera movements.

2.2.1 Almost Stationary Camera Motion

Video inpainting approaches introduced in the following subsections all require the entire video sequence to be known in advance. None of the video inpainting algorithms could be applied for live video streams even if the approach proves fast enough to process video frames. All approaches are designed to remove a static background object in a video sequence while a moving foreground object (mostly a person walking) crosses in front of this object.

2.2 Video Inpainting

The approaches can handle video sequences captured with a static camera. Some of them allow camera movements with specific restrictions. Pure and smooth rotations or smooth camera panning (translations of the camera parallel to the image plane) can be handled by some approaches presented below.

Several user-driven preprocessing steps are necessary to provide information required for those algorithms. A large damage-free portion of the video sequence is needed so that the approaches have enough visual source information for the inpainting of the remaining video stream.

Typically, benchmark video sequences have a video resolution not larger than 320 × 240 pixels and are comprised of less then 100 frames. The image regions of objects to be removed are significantly smaller than the regions in comparable benchmark images for static image inpainting. None of the algorithms allows real-time application, as all of them are more than three magnitudes too slow (even if preprocessing steps are not taken into consideration).

2.2.1.1 Jia et al. 2004

Jia et al. [53, 54] proposed one of the first video inpainting approaches to repair damaged video sequences. They proposed to manually separate the video sequence into foreground and background content. Visual elements from the background content have to be static, foreground elements are moving objects. The approach allows removal of static background objects while repairing the video sequence for moving foreground elements. Thus, the approach is designed e.g., to remove a static tree, while in the video sequence a person crosses in front of the tree. Jia et al. propose a two-stage technique. The first stage repairs missing static background content while the second stage repairs missing visual content of the moving foreground object.

The user has to manually split the background content into individual segment layers. Several manually selected key frames equally distributed in the video sequence are segmented. This segmentation then is distributed to intermediate frames using a mean shift tracking approach [23]. For each background segment, visual motion is determined and individual homographies [94] between successive video frames are calculated. The missing content covered by static background layers is repaired by inpainting [55] the area in the very first video frame. The result of the first frame's inpainting then is warped throughout the video sequence by application of individual homographies and interpolated at the segment boundaries. A coherent video sequence without the undesired static background object is obtained. However, the video is still damaged as the moving foreground object is missing if it crosses the inpainted background region.

In the second stage of the approach, the moving foreground object has to be extracted. Jia et al. propose to capture the video sequence twice in a preprocessing step, first without the moving object and second with the moving object. Difference determination between the two video sequences allows the moving object to be extracted. The entire visual 3D content of the extracted moving foreground object is then sampled to find periodic sequences. The approach needs one damage-free periodic sequence of the foreground object to allow repair of the damaged foreground pixels. Within an iterative non-linear refinement algorithm [67], the found periodic foreground movement is optimized and seamlessly integrated into the damaged video sequence. Both results are then blended to achieve the synthesized video sequence. Jia et al. do not provide any comparable performance information for their approach.

2.2.1.2 Zhang et al. 2005

Zhang et al. [109] proposed an approach for video inpainting similar to that of Jia et al. They also segment image content into individual layers. However, Zhang et al. use an automatic segmentation approach based on the optical flow. Once accurate and joint segments have been extracted, these layers are sorted according to the overlapping order. An undesired object is erased by removing the layer of the object itself and by inpainting the region in all layers sorted behind the removed layer. Like Jia, Zhang applies a patch-based inpainting algorithm in the first frame of the video sequence and warps this reference frame to all successive video frames. The warping is defined not by a homography but by the detected motion within each individual segmentation. They apply this approach for short video sequences with an almost static camera. Neither statistical information about the frame or object dimension nor any performance values are provided.

2.2.1.3 Patwardhan et al. 2005

The video inpainting approach presented by Patwardhan et al. [77, 78] is only able to process video streams captured with an absolute static camera. In principal, they apply a 3D version of the static patch-based image inpainting approach of Criminisi et al. [25]. The 3D extension allows the inpainting of

2.2 Video Inpainting

moving objects in front of a static background or the inpainting of a static background preserving a moving object.

For the case that a moving object has to be removed, the approach has two steps. In the first trivial step, missing information is simply copied from different video frames in which the moving object is at a different position and the original background information is visible. The second step then fills in the remaining unknown video information. As the camera is static, the unknown information is missing at the identical position in each frame. Once a best matching patch is found for the missing region, this unique patch then is used for all successive frames.

For the case that a moving object intersects a static object to be removed, Patwardhan et al. apply a slight modification to the inpainting approach of Criminisi et al. First, moving image content is inpainted. Then, static image elements are investigated as the moving content is more important for visual quality than the static background. E.g., the trajectory and the visual impression of a walking person can be seamlessly preserved while the person crosses the inpainting region. As already mentioned, this approach basically is a straightforward extension of the 2D approach of Criminisi et al.

Although the presented benchmark videos are very short (less than 5 seconds) and the frame dimension is small (320×240 pixels) the approach needs between 5 and 20 minutes to provide the final video result. Respecting the increased computational power of computer hardware in recent years (see Appendix A.7) the algorithm would still need between 1 and 5 minutes on current hardware to process a video of less than 5 seconds.

2.2.1.4 Shen et al. 2006

Shen et al. [86] proposed a video inpainting approach for sequences of videos with the same conditions as with the videos handled by Jia, Zhang or Patwardhan. The main contribution of the approach of Shen et al. is warping of the video stream as opposed to warping of the inpainting result. Shen et al. propose to determine the global homographies between successive video frames to handle camera movements with pure rotation or pure zooming.

The homography is used to create a warped video stream that acts like a video stream captured by a static camera. Visual content of moving foreground objects (with periodic movements) is normalized by a transformation to accommodate a motion object with constant size and speed.

The visual content of the moving foreground object is inpainting by a 3D extension of the structure propagation approach of Sun et al. [93]. The propagation path is defined by the best fitting curve matching all foreground object pixels. The energy error function of Sun et al. is extended by a spatial temporal coherence term integrating the first and second derivative of the image content. If inpainting of the warped video stream has been finished, the final video stream is produced by back-warping of the entire video content. No performance values are provided by Shen et al.

2.2.1.5 Shiratori et al. 2006

Shiratori et al. [90] proposed a video completion approach comparable to the gradient image inpainting approach of Shen et al. [85]. Like the approach of Shen, Shiratori et al. first fill the undesired content using structure information instead of pixel color information. This structure information is then used to determine the final colored inpainting result. Instead of using 2D image patches and image gradients like Shen, 3D image patches and a local motion field are used. Shiratori et al. argue that the two-staged algorithm may perform better instead of the sole application of color patches, as the best matching color patch could produce visual artifacts in a worst case situation.

Once the inpainting hole has been filled by copying motion field patches, the final color information is determined by solving a linear equation system. The system is designed to propagate the color information of the 3D mask boundary into the inpainting mask. The direction of the propagation is specified by the synthesized motion field.

Segmentation of static background as necessary in the approach of e.g., Jia et al. [53] or Zhang et al. [109], can be avoided. Thus, the approach of Shiratori is less sensitive to segmentation errors or invalid homography determinations. However, the overall approach is only applied for almost static cameras and very short video sequences (less than 5 seconds). The approach would need about 10 minutes to proceed a video sequence of 60 frames with a resolution of 352×240 on current computer hardware (see Appendix A.7 describing the estimated translation factor).

2.2.1.6 Wexler et al. 2007

The image manipulation approach of Simakov et al. as introduced in Subsection 2.1.4.1 is a generalization of the approach of Wexler et al. [103] For the task of image or video inpainting, the coherence term of the bidirectional similarity measure of Simakov et al. is sufficient. By discarding the completeness impact, a unidirectional function is obtained, measuring in which

2.2 Video Inpainting

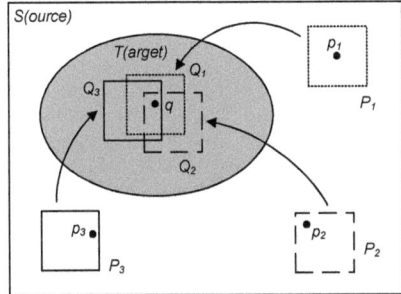 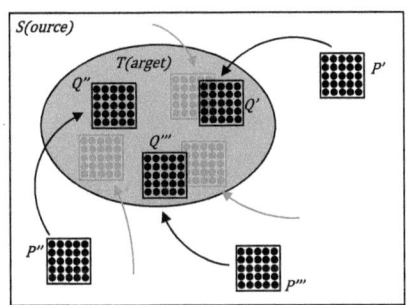

(a) Scheme of one update step for pixel q with (exemplary) three image patches; the color of q is defined by the colors of $p1$, $p2$ and $p3$.

(b) One update iteration: for each patch Q of T: accumulating all color values of the patch correspondences with following normalization at the end.

Figure 2.16: Update step of the image completion approach of Wexler et al. [103]

degree a masked image region is composed of the remaining image data. The sole application of the coherence term has originally been proposed by Wexler et al. [102]. The approach of Simakov et al. can be seen as a generalization of this approach.

Figure 2.16 shows the scheme of Wexler's update step for a pixel $q \in T$. The color value of q is defined by the color values p_i of the corresponding patches $P_i \in S$. Rather than updating each target pixel individually by seeking all patches Q_i (and their corresponding patches P_i) containing the target pixel q, the algorithm updates all corresponding pixels covered by one patch concurrently. The approach takes each patch Q_i from T and accumulates all pixel values by the colors of the corresponding patch P_i. After all patches in T have been processed, the algorithm normalizes the target pixels.

For video inpainting, Wexler et al. add the spatial and temporal motions to their similarity measure to receive a visually coherent video stream. Wexler et al. apply neither image segmentation to foreground and background objects nor explicitly determine the optical motion to apply the video inpainting algorithm. The Wexler et al. approach needs a user-defined inpainting mask for each video frame expensively created by the user in a preprocessing step. Although the approach works well for almost static cameras and small inpainting holes, the approach is very time consuming due to the large search space of matching patches. This approach only provides visual coherence between successive video frames for an almost stationary camera.

2.2.1.7 Liu et al. 2009

The video completion approach of Liu et al. [71] adopts the idea of the two-phase algorithm of Shiratori et al. First, they reconstruct video motion inside the 3D inpainting mask using the same approach as Shiratori. In the second step, color information is reconstructed. Liu et al. do not find color information by a linear equation system but by the application of an approximated graph labeling solution. A significant difference compared to other inpainting approaches also applying graph labeling optimizations (e.g. Pritch et al. [81]) is that Liu et al. do not convert each video pixel into a graph node but only a small subset of equally distributed pixels. This under-sampling allows faster calculation during the optimization process. Each video pixel corresponding to a graph node is surrounded by an image patch (larger than sampling distance) mapped to an image patch outside the inpainting mask. The similarities of overlapping pixels of patches corresponding to neighboring graph nodes define a cost measure. This measure is used in the graph labeling algorithm to find best matching patches for the inpainting mask.

Reconstructed video motion is used to guide patch optimization to improve video coherence between successive frames. Liu et al. apply a multiresolution approach to accelerate graph optimization. Unfortunately, no performance results have been presented.

2.2.2 Dynamic Camera Motion

In this subsection, approaches without constraints regarding camera movements will be presented. Video inpainting approaches allowing dynamic camera motions are more complex than approaches developed for almost stationary cameras. The number of proposed video inpainting approaches reflects the algorithmic complexity.

2.2.2.1 Shih et al. 2009

A video inpainting algorithm mainly extending the image inpainting approach of Criminisi et al. [25] has been introduced by Shih et al. [89], [88]. Comparable to Jia et al. or Zhang et al., Shih et al. automatically subdivide image data into individual layer segments with individual motion. The

2.2 Video Inpainting

averaged motion vectors of individual image segments are then used to guide the inpainting algorithm and to improve visual coherence between successive frames. Shih et al. do not restrict camera motion and allow more complex video sequences as compared to previous approaches.

Final video results are not convincing as visual artifacts can be seen even in video sequences with low image resolutions. For video sequences with constrained camera movements, the visual results are comparable to previously proposed approaches designed for almost stationary cameras. Shih et al. propose that their algorithm can be used for inpainting between 1 to 5 pixels per millisecond (not including the time necessary for preprocessing steps). In Subsection 5.7.1, the performance results of our video inpainting approach is presented showing that our approach is about three magnitudes faster than the approach of Shih et al.

2.2.2.2 Takeda et al. 2010

The approach of Takeda et al. [95] allows for removing a near object occluding a distant landscape. The approach is not real-time capable and needs the entire video stream in advance. As the object to be removed is near and the landscape distant, the relative position of the undesired object moves during the video sequence. Takeda determines the homography of the landscape for successive video frames. The near foreground object is removed by copying visual information from previous or prospective images capturing the original background. This approach is the sole video inpainting approach dependent on camera movement as this approach does not work using a static camera.

2.2.2.3 Herling and Broll 2010

The approaches presented above do not aim to achieve video frame manipulation in real-time performance. Our previous approach [40] has been developed to overcome the real-time restriction. The approach was inspired by the image inpainting approach of Wexler et al. [102] and Barnes et al. [8]. A contour tracking approach for detection of objects in almost homogenous environments has been applied to remove static objects in the live video stream of a hand-held camera. In the first video frame, an undesired object is roughly selected by the user. Active contour detection begins using this rough user-defined selection. The contour is iteratively refined. The resulting contour precisely encloses the undesired object. The precise contour is enlarged for the next video frame and the active contour approach restarted

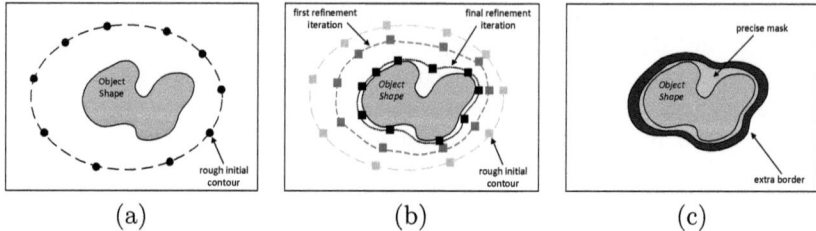

Figure 2.17: Scheme of the active contour tracking approach. a) Undesired object with rough user-defined contour, b) several iterative refinement steps finding the final precise contour, c) resulting inpainting mask.

to find the precise contour for the next frame. In Figure 2.17, the simple active contour tracking approach is depicted.

A basic frame to frame coherence has been achieved by propagation of patch matches between successive video frames followed by several optimization iterations. Information propagation provided frame coherence for panning and zooming camera motions. During sequences with high rotational camera motions or shaking movements, frame coherence sometimes failed. Significant optimization and modifications were applied to our previous approach to end up with a real-time approach. Depending on image content, the resulting inpainting image quality sometimes could not match the overall quality possible with the static image inpainting approach, e.g., of Barnes et al. In Chapter 4, an image inpainting approach will be described that is faster than our previous approach while providing significantly higher image quality. A detailed comparison of benchmark images between the previous and the current approach is given showing the differences between both approaches.

2.2.3 Discussion

In the previous subsections, the most important state-of-the-art approaches developed for video inpainting have been introduced. The presented video inpainting approaches are a subset of the large set of published approaches for video manipulation. Approaches not discussed in more detail like [12, 22, 107, 98] do not provide any significant modification to the above introduced algorithms.

Apart from our previous approach [40], none of the approaches, even if they were fast enough, could process live video streams. All approaches need

2.2 Video Inpainting

access to the entire video stream in advance. All images of the video stream have to be available in the hardware memory to process video inpainting. Several of the presented approaches like that of Jia et al. [53] or that of Wexler et al. [103] are based on preprocessing steps. Often, the user has to manually identify the object to be removed within several key frames and has to segment the video stream into individual blocks with regards to the visual foreground and background content.

The introduced approaches are mainly restricted to almost stationary cameras or strongly constraint camera motions. The less restricted the camera motion, the more complex the creation of coherent video inpainting result becomes. While the inpainting of an moving object captured with a static camera is an almost trivial task, the inpainting of a static object temporarily hidden by a moving object is significantly more complex. Some previous non-real-time capable approaches like that of Jia et al. [53], Zhang et al. [109] or Shen et al. [86] realize a coherent video stream by warping the image content of the very first video image. The sole application of image warping cannot compensate changing lighting conditions and thus may produce unrealistic inpainting fragments. Warping does not allow integration of more detailed visual information in the following video frames with zooming camera motion. Still other approaches such as the approaches of Wexler et al. [103], Shiratori et al. [90] or Liu et al. [71] do not warp the image content of the first video frame, but inpaint a 3D image block instead.

Although our previous approach [40] allowed a real-time execution for video inpainting, high performance was a trade-off between speed and image quality. This trade-off restricted the application of our previous approach to environments with almost homogenous textures without significant structured information. The creation of a coherent video stream was realized by a propagation of patch matches between successive frames. This propagation allowed creation of a coherent video stream, but only for homogenous backgrounds and linear camera movements. Fast, rotational camera motions could not be reliably compensated. Complex camera motions resulted in a non coherent video stream producing visual artifacts.

Therefore, a live video inpainting approach has to be based on an image inpainting algorithm faster or equally fast as that of our previous approach [40] with significantly higher image qualities. Video coherence has to be explicitly considered to allow non-restricted camera motion. The combination of real-time image inpainting and motion compensation is therefore the basis for creation of a real-time video inpainting approach providing sufficient image quality. Finally, the algorithm has to support zooming camera motion

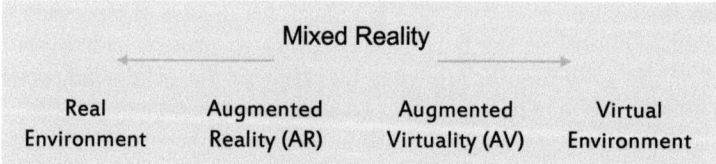

Figure 2.18: Mixed Reality continuum as defined by Milgram [74].

for the integration of more detailed visual information to avoid blurring effects whenever an object gets close to the camera.

2.3 Mediated Reality

Mann defines Mediated Reality [73] as a reality without constraints to augment, to enhance, to diminish or to modify the reality in an arbitrary way. In the following section, the specific aspects of Mediated Reality will be introduced. First, Mixed Reality will be discussed briefly, followed by a presentation of Diminished Reality.

2.3.1 Mixed Reality

Mixed Reality, as defined by Milgram et al [74], encompasses the reality-virtuality continuum. This continuum spans from the real environment to the virtual reality (VR), with Augmented Reality (AR) and Augmented Virtuality (AV) in the center of the continuum (see Figure 2.18).

AR allows for seamlessly integrating virtual content (e.g., 3D objects) into the real environment. The user has the possibility to interact with the real and virtual objects concurrently. In contrast, Augmented Virtuality integrates real objects into virtual environments.

Today, the individual subclasses of Milgram's continuum may be realized with a wide variety of visualization technologies. Simple television screens, computer displays, video and optical see-through head mounted displays, projectors, or displays of tablet computers and smartphones are all display technologies used for Mixed Reality applications [18, 5, 15, 110, 20, 19, 41].

2.3.2 Diminished Reality

As well as Mixed Reality and Augmented Reality (AR), Diminished Reality (DR) is also a subset of Mediated Reality. However, instead of adding virtual

2.3 Mediated Reality

content into a real environment as AR does, Diminished Reality aims to remove real objects from the real environment. A visual input device e.g., a digital camera of a smartphone, may be used to remove real objects in the video stream displayed by that device. Compared to the intensive research regarding to AR technologies in the previous decade, DR is presently in an early research state. Although the above introduced video inpainting approaches may be understood as indirect solutions for Diminished Reality systems, the main constraint with regards to DR is that the approach has to be applied in a real-time context.

Current research projects in the field of DR may be separated into approaches working with a single hand-held video camera as input and those approaches needing more than one video stream to diminish the reality. In the following, the most important DR approaches will be introduced.

2.3.2.1 Single-View Approaches

The simplest form of Diminished Reality applications hide tracking markers. Although the first marker tracking approaches have been developed more than one decade ago [57], these approaches are still widely used in AR applications. Normally, markers are not part of the natural environment and thus may have an undesired influence on persons using AR systems that apply marker tracking.

Siltanen [91] proposed an approach able to hide markers in real-time in an AR application. He creates one static texture at the first moment the marker becomes visible. Texture generation is based on a simple approach mirroring the visual information of the marker's neighborhood. The texture is then rendered in each frame and blended with the video background at the texture's borders.

A slight modification of the approach of Siltanen has been introduced by Korkalo et al. [64]. Their approach applies a more powerful image inpainting algorithm for static texture generation to hide tracking markers in more complex environments. They create a high resolution texture combined with a small low resolution texture created for each new camera frame and blend both textures. As a result, changing lighting conditions can be compensated and the generation of small low resolution texture can be applied in real-time.

For the sake of completeness, it should be mentioned that our previous work [40] as introduced in Subsection 2.2.2.3 also belongs to the class of single-view DR approaches. In Figure 2.19, the live result of our previous Diminished Reality system is shown for a static object lying on a table. The

44   2 Related Work

(a) Original frame with combined inpainting mask.

(b) Resulting real-time Diminished Reality result.

Figure 2.19: Diminished Reality result of our previous approach [40] allowing to remove an object in real-time from a live video sequence.

approach neither needs any a priori information about the environment nor any details about the object to be removed.

2.3.2.2 Multi-View Approaches

Multi-view based approaches to Diminished Reality use information from several additional camera locations, observing the current scene from different viewpoints in order to restore parts of the image hidden by an obstacle.

Zokai et al. [111] presented an approach using several individual images from different viewpoints. While the approach did not require dense temporal image sequences, all cameras had to be registered using marker based or markerless tracking. They applied a para-perspective projection model in order to generate the correct background. This further required the background to have a certain minimum distance from the obscuring object. Zokai et al. allowed the user to define a polygon around the objects to be removed. However, the region was fixed and could not adapt automatically to movements of the camera or the object.

Lepetit and Berger [66] applied a twofold approach: for rather small areas they applied a simple intensity or RGB texture filling, while for larger regions they used a 3D reconstruction. For the latter, they used individual triangle patches from multiple views of a video sequence, applying a homographic transformation for texturing. Their approach uses a 3D boundary to estimate the 2D outline of the occluding object for each frame. In order to obtain

2.3 Mediated Reality

the 3D boundary, the user has to first sketch the 2D boundary in a small number of key frames (similar to Jia et al [53]).

Enomoto and Saito [33] used multiple freely moving hand-held cameras capturing the same scene from different viewpoints to diminish occluding objects. They applied marker based tracking to calibrate the cameras. The approach was tested in different dynamic scenarios including moving obstacles, moving cameras, and changing scene objects. The approach was limited to planar background objects.

Jarusirisawad et al. [52] presented an approach to Diminished Reality applying a plane-sweep algorithm. The approach used projective grid space rather than the Euclidean space. While this allowed for weakly calibrated cameras, the approach used up to six cameras at once. The approach was interactive while not real-time in a GPU-based implementation.

The above presented multi-view approaches to Diminished Reality generally do not remove the undesired objects by any kind of video inpainting algorithms but by the application of visual content as seen from different views. Simple problems e.g., the removing of a static object lying on a table, cannot be processed by the presented approaches. The original visual information below an object lying on a table is not visible even if the environment is captured from several different individual viewpoints. The approaches fail if the real background of an object to be removed is physically invisible.

2.3.3 Discussion

In contrast to the introduced video inpainting approaches, Diminished Reality approaches must be applied in real-time. A DR application not able to be executed in real-time does not allow for any reasonable user interaction. Research in the field of DR is mainly based on the real-time constraint and focuses on the removal of static objects in a video stream.

Apart from our previous work [40], none of the proposed DR approaches allow for removing real objects in an unknown environment. Some approaches simply hide tracking markers with an almost static inpainting texture. Other approaches use tracking markers to calibrate frames from several individual cameras to remove an undesired object in real-time. None of the proposed approaches can be applied for Diminished Reality in an unknown environment with complex visual background information using a single hand-held camera.

3 Concept

In this chapter, the main aspects of our work and the decisions behind the individual strategies used in our approach will be described. The main differences between our work and previous research will be discussed in detail.

In Chapter 2, the most relevant approaches to our real-time video manipulation approach have been introduced. A wide variety of static image inpainting and image manipulation approaches exist that create high quality results. All related approaches so far have not been developed for real-time applications. The approaches are several magnitudes too slow and thus cannot be applied to meet our objective.

Several video inpainting approaches exist that integrate image inpainting algorithms in their pipelines to attempt creation of coherent video streams. However, a video inpainting approach using a non-real-time capable image inpainting approach cannot be applied in real-time. Even if a video inpainting approach would apply a well-known static image inpainting method in the very first video frame, and would forward this synthesized image content to the following video frames (by image warping), the creation of the first frame would still need several seconds. A delay of a few seconds is not acceptable for live video transmission or in a Mediated Reality system relying on real-time execution. Simple warping of the image content does not allow for compensation for lighting conditions and prevents the integration of more detailed visual information in following video frames.

The main objective of this work is to create a real-time video manipulation algorithm. To meet this objective, the approach can be separated into two tasks. The first task has to realize an image manipulation algorithm able to synthesize high quality images in real-time. The second task is to derive an algorithm from the image manipulation algorithm that allows selection and removal of undesired objects in live video streams. In the following sections, the main aspects of our approach will be introduced in more detail.

3.1 Real-Time Image Inpainting

Previous inpainting approaches, like those of Criminisi et al. [25], Fang et al. [34], Barnes et al. [8] or Bugeau et al. [21], create the final image by an exemplary based algorithm. Instead of creating an absolutely new image, the final image is created by copying suitable content of the remaining image information into the inpainting mask. As explained in Subsection 2.1, the modification unit may either be a single pixel or a set of joint pixels (mostly a squared image patch). Pixel-based approaches have been introduced by Demanet et al. [29] and Bugeau et al. [21]. The approach of Bugeau shows that the image quality of pixel-based algorithms is comparable to that of patch-based algorithms like those used by Criminisi et al. [25] or Xu et al. [106].

Patch-based approaches may process an image faster than pixel-based approaches as a larger amount of image content is copied into the inpainting mask within one iteration. The performance edge corresponds with the size of the image patch. The larger the image patch the faster the inpainting hole is filled (not considering the time necessary for patch matching). However, the application of patches tends to create visual blocks, as even the best matching patches may produce a noticeable border between the two image patches in a textured region. Approaches using patch-based inpainting algorithms like that of Barnes et al. [8] or Drori et al. [30] often superimpose or blend neighboring patches to overcome this block building problem. The additional blending and superimposing may create image blurring, reducing the performance benefit of patch-based approaches. Overall, the performance of pixel- and patch-based approaches is almost comparable.

Pixel-based approaches allow for direct creation of the final image by simply copying pixels between two image regions. Because no explicit normalization or blending operations are necessary, pixel-based approaches allow for a more intuitive and faster creation of the final image. Comparing the individual properties of pixel- and patch-based algorithms, pixel-based approaches seem to have a slight advantage over patch-based approaches.

In this work, an image manipulation approach will be developed based on single pixels as the manipulation unit, as already applied in the works of Demanet et al. [29] and Bugeau et al. [21]. Although the approach of Bugeau is by far too slow (needing 25 minutes for an image with 750×563 pixels), our work will show that a real-time capable approach can be realized. Bugeau et al. use three individual appearance constraints and apply a non-heuristic optimization that searches for best matching pixels. For real-

3.1 Real-Time Image Inpainting

time application, this number of expensive appearance constraints has to be reduced and an alternative optimization technique is imperative.

As discussed in Subsection 2.1.5, all the introduced image inpainting approaches apply either a graph labeling approach, or brute-force search, or a heuristic optimization for image creation. Determining a graph with minimal overall cost or finding best matching image content by a brute-force search is simply too slow. A brute-force search for an image with typically image resolution may need several minutes to process (if several iterations are applied). In Subsection 4.9 a detailed performance comparison is provided between our and previous inpainting approaches. Both techniques cannot be applied if real-time performance is required. Demanet et al. [29] proposed the application of a randomized search for best matching pixels. This idea of a heuristic optimization has been adopted by Barnes et al. [8] to significantly speed up computational time. The approach in this work will also apply a heuristic mapping optimization to find an approximated pixel matching near to the global optimum. Our previous real-time video inpainting algorithm [40] also applied a heuristic optimization approach in combination with a single appearance constraint iteratively improving the inpainting mask. Avoidance of a brute-force search for best matching image patches is the basis for real-time performance. A heuristic search provides a good but not optimal mapping, as the convergence speed of the image manipulation approach is slow, requiring more refinement iterations. Due to the real-time constraint, however, only a few refinement iterations can be applied in order to finish the manipulation in time. In our previous approach, the visual result was a compromise between speed and image quality. Almost homogenous backgrounds, less prone to blurring artifacts, were a restriction.

The convergence behavior of an enhanced inpainting approach has to be improved to produce a higher image quality with the same number of refinement iterations. The poor execution performance of the approach of Bugeau et al. (25 minutes to process a typical image) shows that more than one appearance constraint cannot be applied in a real-time system. Faster convergence behavior has to be achieved without additional appearance measurements. To overcome the convergence issue, we investigate an additional constraint not based on appearance similarities but rather on spatial matching similarities. The spatial matching constraint guides the iterative mapping refinement comparable to an elastic spring model, so that neighboring matches map to neighboring pixels. This novel cost measure is determined very efficiently and is the main contribution of this work regarding the static inpainting algorithm. The combination of the appearance constraint with the spatial mapping constraint allows for faster convergence of the heuristic optimization process. Less refinement steps are needed to provide high quality image results.

The heuristic optimization will be completed by the propagation of information from already found neighboring pixel mappings. Originally, Ashikhmin [2] proposed the idea of reusing and forwarding the information of already found mappings. Ashikhmin argued that there is a high probability that two neighboring pixels inside the inpainting mask will map to the corresponding neighboring pixels in the remaining image content. In this work, a shifted mapping derived from neighboring pixels will be considered as candidates for current pixels. It should be mentioned that the propagation of information would be wasteful in combination with a brute-force search or a non-approximated graph labeling problem. The propagation strategy has not been used intensively in previous approaches, as most do not apply a heuristic optimization strategy.

The approach developed in this work has to create the final inpainting image by either shrinking the inpainting mask or by vanishing and iteratively optimizing the undesired image content (see Subsection 2.1.2). A shrinking algorithm mainly creates the final image by finding the local optimum in a partially recovered image region. The result may not be identical to the global optimum. A shrinking approach (heuristically searching for matching image content) relies on less information that can be propagated from neighboring mappings and will often find matchings far away from the local optimum. In contrast, an inpainting algorithm iteratively vanishing the content of the inpainting mask aims to find a global optimum within several optimization iterations. A vanishing algorithm finding the global optimum or trying to approximate the global optimum will provide better image quality than that of an inpainting approach shrinking the inpainting mask. Therefore, we decided to apply a vanishing strategy allowing image quality to be iteratively improved. In Subsection 4.4.3, we will discuss the combination of both strategies, which may provide better results for structured images. Our approach will focus on the vanishing strategy and may partially use a shrinking strategy. None of the previously developed inpainting approaches combines both strategies to provide a final image.

The above described strategies of our algorithm will be combined with a multiresolution approach. The inpainting and optimization will be applied on several pyramid layers beginning with the coarsest image resolution. The application of individual frame resolutions covers a wide range of image frequencies. On coarse pyramid layers, visual content with low frequencies will be reconstructed. Higher frequencies will be recovered on finer pyramid layers. The convergence performance of the heuristic mapping approach can

3.2 Real-Time Video Inpainting

Table 3.1: Overview of the derived image inpainting approach that will be developed in this work. Bold properties represented the major strategies of our approach.

Algorithmic strategies	Techniques
Manipulation unit	Pixel-based inpainting Patch-based inpainting
Optimization strategy	Brute-force search Graph labeling optimization **Heuristic search with propagation**
Inpainting behavior	Shrinking (local optimization) **Vanishing (global optimization)**
Image resolution	Singleresolution approach **Multiresolution approach**

be significantly improved by the application of a multiresolution approach [30, 102, 92, 34, 8].

Table 3.1 summarizes the main aspects and strategies of our approach. It shows the major strategies and possible options that could be used for static image inpainting. In Chapter 4, the above derived properties of our static image inpainting approach will be introduced in detail.

3.2 Real-Time Video Inpainting

Non-real-time capable video inpainting approaches to create a coherent video stream (as presented in Subsection 2.2) are based on two different strategies. The first strategy explicitly creates a coherent video stream by inpainting the first video frame and warping this content to successive video frames. The second strategy implicitly creates a coherent video stream by successively inpainting 3D video patches with best matching image content. Both strategies have advantages and disadvantages regarding the resulting image quality, coherence accuracy and computational performance. As the first strategy applies the expansive image inpainting algorithm only once for the first video frame, the approach is faster than the second strategy. Further, image warping provides video coherence with high accuracy. If arbitrary camera motion has to be supported, an approach successively inpainting

3D video patches cannot reach the coherence accuracy that approaches with image warping can achieve. However, the determination of a correct warping transformation between successive video frames may be difficult or error-prone. An approach using the warping strategy will decrease the image quality the more frames the video sequence has. A warping strategy cannot sufficiently handle zooming camera motions, as the warping does not appropriately introduce more detailed image information. A simple warping algorithm is also not able to reconstruct the noise characteristics of the remaining video content. Briefly summarized, the first strategy typically produces video coherence with high accuracy and decreasing image quality over time. The second strategy lacks sufficient video coherence, although the image quality of individual video frames remains constant.

A combination of both strategies may provide better visual results than the application of either one by itself. None of the video inpainting approaches as introduced in Subsection 2.2 combines both strategies. In this work, a video inpainting approach combining both strategies will be described. A video stream with a high accuracy and good image quality can be achieved. Instead of directly warping the image content of an initial video frame, our approach creates a reference image for each individual frame. These reference images are created by warping a previous key frame and are only used to guide the image inpainting algorithm. Our video inpainting approach invokes an image inpainting step for all video frames, creating visual results almost similar to the reference frames. This approach will be able to create a coherent video stream with a high image quality even for video sequences with more than 700 frames (see Appendix A.5 for some examples).

Our previous approach [40] applied an active contour algorithm to determine an undesired object in a live video stream. The application of an active contour allows for tracking objects with an almost homogenous background and only needs a few milliseconds for processing. The drawback is that a simple active contour approach cannot be applied in a heterogeneous environment. State-of-the-art object segmentation and tracking methods use approaches such as minimal cut, graph labeling or mean shift approaches to determine and separate foreground and background image content. None of these approaches can be applied in real-time due to the high computational complexity involved. This work will present an object selection and tracking approach able to distinguish undesired objects with even heterogeneous backgrounds. This approach is inspired by recent image segmentation algorithms and processes several magnitudes faster to allow real-time performance.

In Chapter 5 a detailed description of our video inpainting approach as outlined above will be presented.

4 Image Inpainting

In this chapter, the implementation of the static image inpainting component as derived in Subsection 3.1 will be presented in detail. In Subsection 4.1, the pixel mapping function will be introduced. A novel cost measure is defined in 4.2 that produces a real-time inpainting result comparable to state-of-the-art approaches. In Subsections 4.3 and 4.4, the entire image inpainting pipeline is presented; composed of refinement, propagation and an optional initialization steps. Subsequently, in Subsection 4.6, extensions for the basic inpainting approach are presented which improve the visual result and quality according to individual constraints. The presented static inpainting approach will be analyzed in detail in 4.7.

4.1 Mapping Function

An image I with width w and height h is composed of $n = w \times h$ pixels. Thus $I = \{p_1, p_2, \ldots, p_n\}$ is defined by a set of n pixel positions. A pixel position $p_i = (p_{i_x}, p_{i_y})^\top$ is a 2D position storing the horizontal and vertical position in the image.

The function $i(p)$ maps a pixel position to the image pixel color value of the image I at position p:

$$i : I \to \mathbb{Q}^1, \quad \text{for monochrome images}$$
$$i : I \to \mathbb{Q}^2, \quad \text{for images with two channels}$$
$$i : I \to \mathbb{Q}^3, \quad \text{for images with three color channels}$$
$$\vdots \qquad\qquad \vdots$$

For image inpainting, a given image needs to be separated into two disjoint image domains, one which defines the desired image content and the other which defines undesired image content. The image I is subdivided into the two sets T(arget) and S(source) with $I = T \cup S$, $T \cap S = \emptyset$ and $S \neq \emptyset$. All pixels from T are replaced during the inpainting process to provide a synthesized image. Similar to the inpainting approaches presented in

Chapter 2, our method creates the content of T by directly using visual content from the source region S.

Investigation of the works of Pritch et al. [81] and Bugeau et al. [21] shows that synthesis approaches with pixels as inpainting unit are capable of providing comparable or even better results than other state-of-the-art techniques. Thus, our approach is based on using single pixels as the inpainting unit.

As we a recently showed [46, 48], image inpainting can be defined as a global minimization problem of finding a transformation function f producing minimal overall synthesis costs for an arbitrary image I according to a given cost measure. The mapping function f maps target positions $p \in T$ to source positions $q \in S$ inside an image I:

$$f : T \to S \tag{4.1}$$

For each target pixel f, one unique source pixel is defined. Once f has been determined, the final image can be created by replacing all target pixels with source information as defined by the mapping function f.

Generally, the result of a manipulated image may be considered acceptable if the replaced (synthesized) image content blends seamlessly with the surrounding image information and remains free of disturbing artifacts and implausible blurring effects. The new image information should visually fit the remaining image parts. Image content not existing in the source S cannot be used to synthesize the target T (equivalent to the coherence measure of Simakov, et al. [92]).

As derived in Chapter 3, our transformation function f is based on the following two constraints:

- Neighboring pixels defined in T should be mapped to equivalent neighboring pixels in S. This first constraint ensures the structural and spatial preservation of image information (see Figure 4.1a).

- The neighborhood appearance of pixels in T should be similar to the neighborhood appearance of their mapped equivalents in S. A visually coherent result and seamless transitions at the border of the synthesized area T are ensured (see Figure 4.1b).

The global minimization problem to solve is to find a transformation function f producing minimal overall cost for an image I and a target region $T \subset I$, with $S = I \setminus T$:

$$\min_{f} \sum_{p \in T} cost_\alpha(p, f), \tag{4.2}$$

4.2 Cost Function

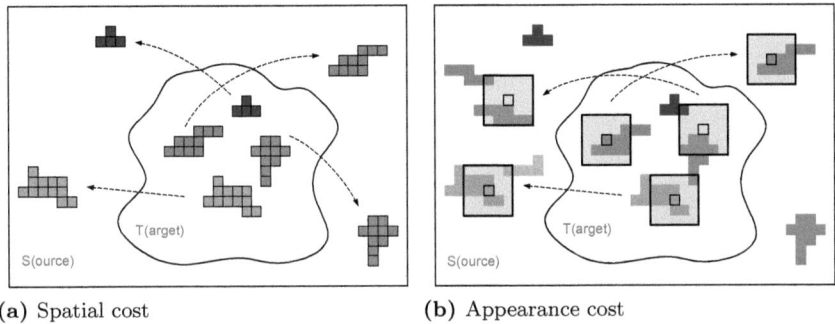

(a) Spatial cost (b) Appearance cost

Figure 4.1: The two cost constraints of the mapping function f.

while the cost function $cost_\alpha : T \times (T \to S) \to \mathbb{Q}$ is defined for all elements (pixel positions) inside the target region.

4.2 Cost Function

As described above, our approach subdivides the overall costs into a part based on the spatial impact and a part based on the appearance impact. This can be represented for any $p \in T$ by the following linear combination:

$$cost_\alpha(p, f) = \alpha \cdot cost_{spatial}(p, f) + (1 - \alpha) \cdot cost_{appear}(p, f), \quad p \in T \quad (4.3)$$

The control parameter $\alpha \in [0, 1]$ allows balancing between both types of costs. Next, the spatial cost measure $cost_{spatial}(\cdot)$ as well as the appearance cost measure $cost_{appear}(\cdot)$ will be discussed in detail.

4.2.1 Spatial Cost

Minimization of the spatial cost impact forces a mapping of neighboring target pixels to neighboring mapping pixels. This is represented for a neighborhood N_s by the spatial cost measure $cost_{spatial} : T \times (T \to S) \to \mathbb{Q}$:

$$cost_{spatial}(p, f) = \sum_{\substack{\vec{v} \in \{\vec{v} \in N_s | \\ (p+\vec{v}) \in T\}}} d_s[f(p) + \vec{v}, f(p + \vec{v})] \cdot \omega_s(\vec{v}), \quad p \in T \quad (4.4)$$

with the set N_s holding the spatial relative positions of neighboring pixels, a spatial distance function $d_s(\cdot)$ and a cost weighting $\omega_s(\cdot)$.

The set N_s of relative positions may have an arbitrary size as long as N_s is symmetric. Thus, the following must hold:

$$\vec{v} \in N_s \iff -\vec{v} \in N_s \tag{4.5}$$

The identity element must not be part of N_s:

$$\mathbf{0} \notin N_s \tag{4.6}$$

The spatial distance function $d_s : I \times I \to \mathbb{Q}$ must provide commutative properties and therefore

$$d_s(p_1, p_2) = d_s(p_2, p_1), \quad \forall p_1, p_2 \in I \tag{4.7}$$

must hold. The spatial distance function has to provide zero costs for the identity:

$$d_s(p, p) = 0, \quad \forall p \in I \tag{4.8}$$

The weighting function $\omega_s : N_s \to \mathbb{Q}$ must be symmetric and should not violate the law of conservation of energy. Therefore,

$$\omega_s(\vec{v}) = \omega_s(-\vec{v}), \quad \forall \vec{v} \in N_s \tag{4.9}$$

and

$$\sum_{\vec{v} \in N_s} \omega_s(\vec{v}) = 1 \tag{4.10}$$

needs to holds.

Ideally, any neighbor $(p + \vec{v}) \in T$ of $p \in T, \forall \vec{v} \in N_s$ is mapped to the corresponding neighbor $f(p) + \vec{v}$ of $f(p)$. The spatial cost of (4.4) sums up the spatial distances $d_s(\cdot)$ from this ideal situation for any $\vec{v} \in N_s$ and $p \in T$ (see Figure 4.1a and 4.2). Our approach fundamentally differs from previous pixel- and patch-based approaches such as [29, 25, 93, 81, 8, 21], which only apply appearance similarity costs. In contrast to these approaches, our spatial cost function allows a significantly faster convergence and reduces image blurring and geometrical artifacts. In Subsections 4.8 and 4.9 a detailed performance analysis is provided. This novel cost constraint can be seen as an elastic spring optimization automatically minimizing neighboring mapping offsets.

4.2 Cost Function

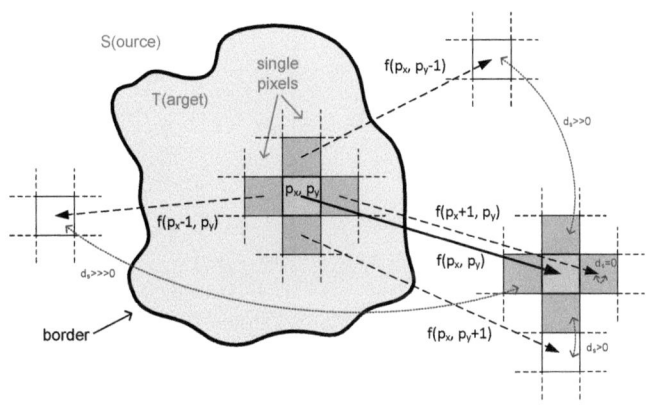

Figure 4.2: Spatial cost for neighboring mappings depicted for a four-neighborhood. Mapping $f(p_x + 1, p_y)$ is ideal and therefore the spatial cost $d_s(\cdot)$ is zero. The mapping $f(p_x, p_y + 1)$ is quite good and therefore $d_s(\cdot)$ is almost zero. Mappings for $f(p_x, p_y - 1)$ and $f(p_x - 1, p_y)$ are far away from the ideal positions, resulting in a high $d_s(\cdot)$.

While N_s allows for any size symmetric neighborhood, a common neighborhood N_s^δ is defined by:

$$N_s^\delta(\delta_s) = \{\vec{v} \in (\mathbb{Z} \times \mathbb{Z}) \mid 0 < |\vec{v}| \le \delta_s\} \quad (4.11)$$

where $\delta_s \in \mathbb{R}$ specifies the radius of the neighborhood (see Figure 4.3). We apply a symmetric neighborhood $N_s^\delta(\delta_s)$ with $\delta_s = 1$ defining a four-neighborhood or $\delta_s = \sqrt{2}$ defining an eight-neighborhood while the importance weighting for those small neighborhoods is set to a uniform weight $\omega_s(\vec{v}) = \frac{1}{|N_s|}$.

Tests showed that the spatial distance function is well represented by the squared distance clamped to τ_s:

$$d_s(p_0, p_1) = \min(|p_0 - p_1|^2, \tau_s), \quad p_0, p_1 \in I \quad (4.12)$$

The upper border τ_s crops the spatial cost to a maximal influence as the cost for mappings with an already large distance of, e.g., 200 and 2,000 pixels, should be the same. Cropping is comparable to the Tukey robust M-estimator [97, 80] where error remains constant if it exceeds a specified threshold. Tests further showed that the l^2 norm provides slightly better results but obviously requires more computation time.

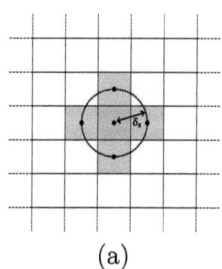 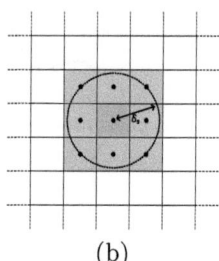

(a) (b)

Figure 4.3: Symmetric neighborhood $N_s^\delta(\delta_s)$ from (4.11) with individual distance parameter δ_s. a) four-neighborhood with $\delta_s = 1$ and b) eight-neighborhood with $\delta_s = \sqrt{2}$.

4.2.2 Appearance Cost

The impact of the appearance constraint is represented for any $p \in T$ by the cost measure $cost_{appear} : T \times (T \to S) \to \mathbb{Q}$:

$$cost_{appear}(p, f)$$
$$= \rho_{N_a}(p, f) \cdot \sum_{\substack{\vec{v} \in \{\vec{v} \in N_a \mid \\ (f(p)+\vec{v}) \in S\}}} d_a[i(p+\vec{v}), i(f(p)+\vec{v})] \cdot \omega_a^1(\vec{v}) \cdot \omega_a^2(p+\vec{v})$$
(4.13)

with the normalization term $\rho_{N_a}(\cdot)$ and with $d_a(\cdot)$ specifying a pixel intensity distance measure.

N_a defines an individual neighborhood equivalent to N_s holding the relative positions of neighboring pixels without the identity element:

$$\mathbf{0} \notin N_a \qquad (4.14)$$

The weighting function $\omega_a^1 : N_a \to \mathbb{Q}$ allows for appearance weighting according to the relative position inside the neighborhood. The absolute weighting function $\omega_a^2 : I \to \mathbb{Q}$ allows individual weighting of specific image regions.

The normalization parameter $\rho_{N_a}(p, f)$ finally normalizes the appearance cost sum according to the number of applied elements:

$$\rho_{N_a}(p, f) = \frac{1}{\sum_{\substack{\vec{v} \in \{\vec{v} \in N_a \mid \\ (f(p)+\vec{v}) \in S\}}} 1} \qquad (4.15)$$

4.2 Cost Function

It should be noted that although the cost spatial measure (4.4) and the appearance cost measure (4.13) seems to be similar, they operate on different data types. One operates on the mapping function directly, while the other operates on the image intensities according to the mapping function.

The application of an appearance cost can be found in several related approaches such as Efros [32], Demanet et al. [29], Pritch et al. [81], Simakov et al. [92] or Barnes et al. [8]. Our explicit weighting function $\omega_a^2(\cdot)$ allows for weighting appearance distances individually according to external constraints, e.g., the synthesis border between the source and target pixels. Appearance costs close to the synthesis border may have higher impact to the overall cost to avoid undesired border effects such as edges or visual discontinuities. None of the introduced related approaches applies such an individual appearance weighting to improve the visual inpainting result.

Tests with different neighborhood sets reveal that N_a provides the best results with respect to the trade-off between accuracy and performance when represented by a small image patch centered at p. Circular neighborhood sets require more processing time and produce only a negligible visual improvement. Squared patches allow the application of optimized CPU instructions to speed up the computation by at least a factor of two. Patches with a size of 5×5 pixels provide sufficient details regarding visual content while still allowing for fast computation. A square patch neighborhood $N_a^\delta(\delta_a)$ with edge length δ_a is defined by:

$$N_a^\delta(\delta_a) = \left\{ (v_x, v_y) = \vec{v} \in (\mathbb{Z} \times \mathbb{Z}) \,\bigg|\, 0 < max(|v_x|, |v_y|) \leq \left\lfloor \frac{\delta_a}{2} \right\rfloor \right\} \quad (4.16)$$

The definition of $N_a^\delta(\delta_a)$ fulfills condition (4.14).

In our approach, we use the sum of squared differences (SSD) [94] for the appearance distance $d_a(\cdot)$ as it provides a suitable trade-off between performance and quality when compared to other measures such as the sum of absolute differences (SAD) and the zero-mean SSD [60, 26].

If not mentioned differently, a uniform weighting $\omega_a^1(\cdot)$ is applied for the inpainting results in this work:

$$\omega_a^1(\vec{v}) = \frac{1}{|N_a|} \quad (4.17)$$

Compared to, e.g., a Gaussian weighting, a uniform weighting allows faster calculation of the appearance cost while still producing convincing mapping quality. We measured a performance difference between uniform and Gaussian weighting of at least a factor of 4 as uniform weighting allows the application of optimized CPU instructions. Absolute weighting $\omega_a^2(\cdot)$ provides a higher appearance impact at the inpainting border between T and S to allow seamless integration of the new image content at the inpainting border:

$$\omega_a^2(p) = \begin{cases} \tau_a, & \exists \vec{v} \in N_a : (p + \vec{v}) \in S \\ 1, & \text{else} \end{cases}, \quad \forall p \in T \qquad (4.18)$$

with the border impact $\tau_a \gg 1$.

4.3 Iterative Refinement

The cost measure for the pixel mapping function f has been introduced in the previous subsection. At this point, a mapping function f has to be determined that minimizes the overall cost for all target pixels $p \in T$ regarding condition (4.2). Finding the optimal transformation function f is done by starting with a rather rough guess of f, followed by a series of iterative refinement steps. A binary mask M separates the target and source pixels within the inpainting frame I. The mask M has the same frame dimension as I and is defined for each position $p \in I$ by:

$$M(p) = \begin{cases} 0, & p \in T \\ 1, & p \in S \end{cases}, \quad T = T \cup S \qquad (4.19)$$

In each iteration, mapping for any target pixel p with $M(p) = 0$ is sought to be improved in a scanline order. Randomly, several source positions q with $M(q) = 1$ are tested according to the cost function and accepted whenever the cost can be reduced. The random search radius is decreased with each new test for fine tuning of the mapping position. Improved matching is then propagated to neighbor positions in T. This approach is similar to that proposed by Barnes, et al. [8] and the multi-core extension of our previous approach [40]. The information propagation method of Barnes et al. has been described in detail in Subsection 2.1.4.2. Originally, propagation and randomized search methods in the context of image inpainting have been proposed by Ashikhmin [2] and Demanet et al. [29].

Our previous work and the approach of Barnes et al. applied the dissimilarity measure of Wexler, et al. [103] or Simakov, et al. [92] respectively. Each refinement needed a target information update of an entire image patch, requiring the application of the individual contribution from each

4.3 Iterative Refinement

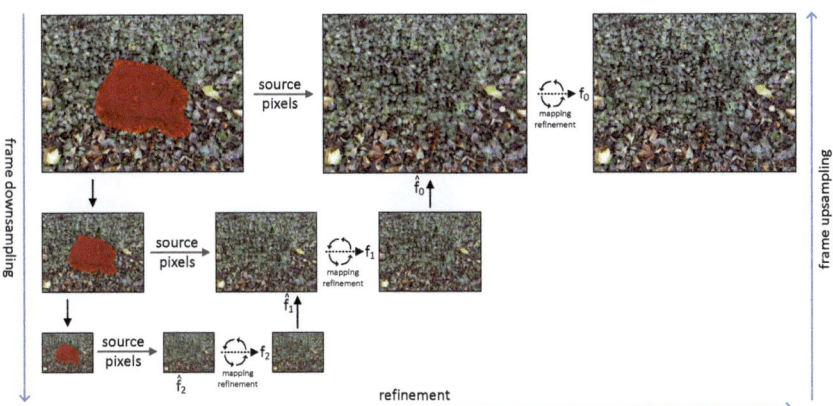

Figure 4.4: Scheme of the pyramid refinement as recently proposed in [46]: The original frame is downsampled (left) and iteratively refined and upsampled again (diagonal from bottom left to top right).

patch followed by a normalization. Our current approach directly updates only a single pixel and thus avoids expensive normalizations.

We apply a multiresolution inpainting approach. Iterative refinement is applied on an image pyramid starting with a reduced resolution layer and increasing the image size until the original resolution has been reached. Depending on the mask size and frame dimension, typically between three and eight layers are used. The coarsest pyramid layer is found by the first layer in that no mask pixel exists that has a larger distance than 3 pixels to the inpainting border. The algorithm starts with an initial mapping guess $\hat{f}_{n-1}$ in the coarsest pyramid layer L_{n-1} and stops if an improved mapping f_{n-1} with minimal overall cost has been determined. This mapping is then forwarded to the next pyramid layer L_{n-2} and is used as the new initialization $\hat{f}_{n-2}$. Again, after a series of iterations within the current layer, the optimized transformation f_{n-2} is forwarded as the initialization of the next layer until the final layer L_0 (providing the highest resolution) has been reached and processed (see Figure 4.4).

The applied image pyramid allows the covering of visual structures with individual frequency, speeds up the mapping convergence and significantly reduces the chance that the algorithm gets trapped by some local minima.

Figure 4.5: Iterative layer refinement: Original image and mask (left column), intermediate results of each layer (upper row), and corresponding neighboring blocks (bottom row).

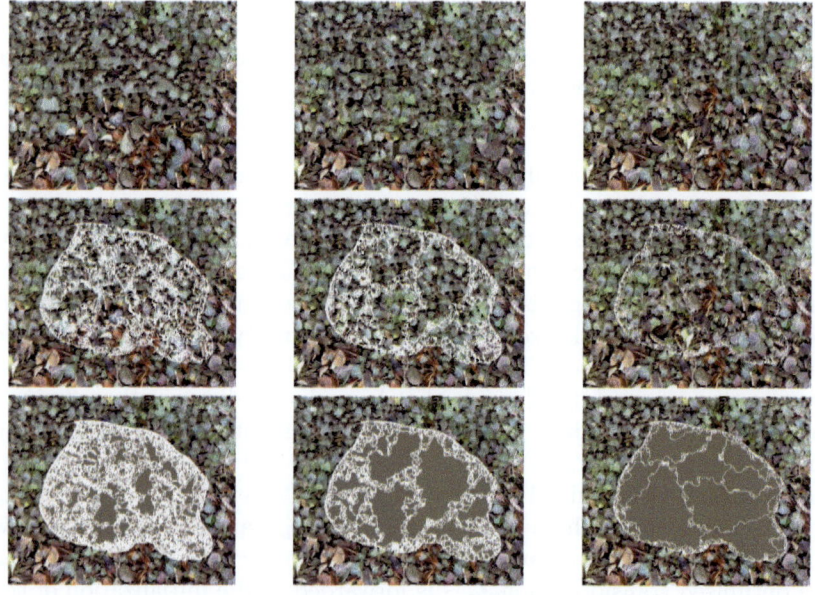

(a) Weak weighting with control parameter $\alpha = 0.05$

(b) Moderate weighting with control parameter $\alpha = 0.20$

(c) Strong weighting with control parameter $\alpha = 0.80$

Figure 4.6: Neighboring block comparison for weak, moderate, and strong spatial weighting. The top row shows the final result, the center row shows the individual pixel blocks and the bottom row shows the spatial costs. The stronger the weighting, the larger the joint blocks (zero spatial cost: gray; non-zero spatial cost: white).

4.3 Iterative Refinement

Figure 4.5 shows some intermediate results during an inpainting process visualizing the spatial cost and the corresponding intermediate inpainting result. A visualized comparison between weak, medium and strong spatial weighting is depicted in Figure 4.6 showing the characteristic joint image blocks after the final iteration. The stronger the impact of spatial weighting, the larger the joint image blocks and the thinner the gap between these blocks. Large joint image blocks prevent undesired blurring in the final image result but may produce slightly noticeable borders between the blocks due to the thin gaps between them. Contrarily, small joint image blocks may create slight blurring in inpainting images while the gap between the blocks is large enough to avoid noticeable borders. Thus, a moderate impact of spatial cost provides best inpainting results for the majority of inpainting images. A second property of spatial weighting has to be considered. Spatial weighting has a significant influence on the convergence behavior of the iterative refinement approach. The higher the spatial weighting, the faster the convergence of the number of mapping changes. A detailed analysis and comparison of individual spatial weightings is provided in Subsection 4.8.

Please note that due to the different image sizes in the individual layers, the spatial distance function d_s from (4.4) has to be normalized according to the size of the individual pyramid layer dimensions to allow consistent cost impact.

The final mapping function f_0 directly defines the image information of the target area and may thus be used to create the final synthesized image. The resulting overall cost gives a measure of the final image quality. The approach allows the application of individual image formats on each pyramid layer because the transformation function only defines pixel mappings and is therefore independent of the used color model. More detailed color information may be applied in coarser pyramid layers. The bit depth is reduced with increasing layer resolution to speed up computation of appearance costs. Significant mapping decisions on coarse layers may be computed by applying very detailed image information. Expensive fine tuning on more detailed layers may be performed with less color information. See Subsection 4.5 for a more detailed discussion of this topic.

As in our previous approach [40], the iterative refinement approach as developed in this work benefits from multi-core CPUs. Iterative cost refinement is applied on disjoint subsets $T_0, T_1, \ldots, T_{n-1}$ of $T = T_0 \cup T_1 \cup \cdots \cup T_{n-1}$ concurrently. Thus each subset T_i can be processed by an individual thread in parallel. In our previous work, static frame subsets have been applied, restricting propagation of mapping information to be within individual subsets. This isolated refinement may produce undesired synthesis blocks in

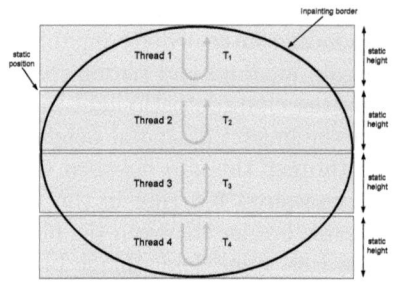 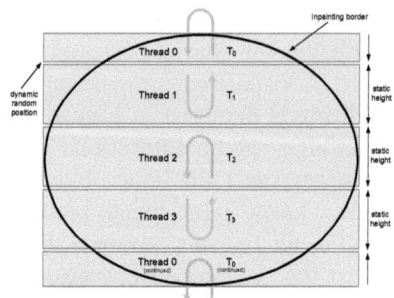

(a) Our previous multithreading approach as applied in [40] separating the entire inpainting region by static areas.

(b) Multithreading approach with dynamic offset position and threads working in opposite directions [48].

Figure 4.7: Scheme of the multithreading inpainting realization comparing our previous approach with the recent algorithm. The small gaps between the individual threads are added to improve visibility.

the final image as the mapping exchange between subsets is restricted to the subset borders. Further, damped propagation may reduce synthesis performance. Our current approach applies random subsets changing between forward and backward propagation while the subsets' size stays constant. Neighboring subsets propagate their mapping in opposite directions starting from a common start row. These start rows are optimized explicitly before any refinement iteration is processed, so that neighboring subsets have access to the same mapping information. Successive refinements toggle between forward and backward propagation, have changing target subsets, and start from common (already refined) rows. The random subsets have a significant impact on the final image quality and convergence performance as information propagation is applied to the entire synthesis mask, rather than limited to the sub-blocks. In Figure 4.7, a comparison between our previous and current approach is presented.

4.4 Initialization

Our algorithm is based on single pixel mappings and thus may be started on the first coarse pyramid layer without any remaining mask pixel. This coarse layer then provides initial visual information for mask pixels of the

4.4 Initialization

next finer layer. An explicit initialization is not imperative for our inpainting algorithm.

The more visual structures of the remaining image content preserved in the final image, the better the visual results of image inpainting. On coarse pyramid layers, tiny, thin, or filigree structures may not be visible due to reduced image resolution. If no explicit initialization is applied, iterative refinement of the mapping function f from (4.1) may get stuck in a local minimum not permitting preservation or the addition to structure information later becoming visible in finer pyramid layers. Proper initialization of the coarsest pyramid layer is decisive for speed of convergence and for overall quality of the synthesis.

In the following, three initialization strategies will be introduced, each of which has different characteristics regarding execution performance and the capability to recover important and filigree image structure. The strategies are:

1. **Randomized Erosion Filter**
   This strategy is based on an erosion technique and is not able to preserve significant structure information but can be processed very fast.

2. **Contour Mapping**
   Using the borders of the inpainting mask, this is slightly slower but is able to recover large regions of similar image content.

3. **Patch Initialization**
   This strategy is significantly slower than both other approaches but will allow reconstruction of complex and filigree image structures.

4.4.1 Randomized Erosion Filter

The first initialization strategy can be seen as the simplest form of a shrinking inpainting approach. The inpainting mask is iteratively reduced on the coarsest pyramid layer. A standard erosion filter [51] as we used in [40] calculates a value based on the adjacent pixels outside the inpainting mask for each pixel at the border of the mask (i.e., the area to be synthesized). Next, pixels at the new border are filled. The process is repeated until the mask is completely filled. This approach typically results in some artifacts (visible as triangle structures as depicted in Figure 4.8).

In this work, a randomized version of the standard erosion filter approach is applied. Rather than calculating the values for all border pixels, we randomly select a single border pixel and calculate its value based on pixels

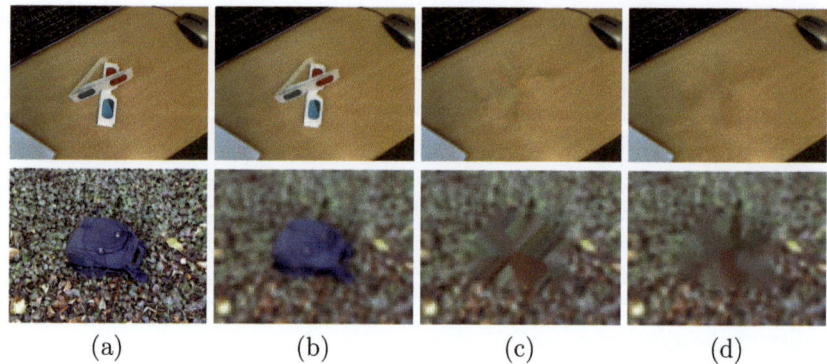

(a)   (b)   (c)   (d)

Figure 4.8: Comparison of the standard erosion filter and the randomized erosion filter for initialization. The approach works for homogenous backgrounds (top row) as well as for non-homogenous backgrounds (bottom row). a) original frame b) frame on the coarsest pyramid layer c) standard erosion filter result d) randomized erosion filter result

outside the border. This modifies the borderline, and the next pixel is then again drawn randomly from these new borderline pixels. This procedure is repeated until the entire mask is filled. Due to the randomized approach, the filter will create non-deterministic results each time it is applied. Further, the approach does not produce any artifacts. Figure 4.8 shows the improvements comparing the standard and the randomized erosion filter.

As a last step, the synthesized image content inside the inpainting mask is used to find an initial mapping. Simple visual appearance mapping is applied randomly, finding the best matching pixel from the remaining image content to each pixel inside the mask.

4.4.2 Contour Initialization

Image inpainting is often applied to objects covering a background that can be separated into obvious segments. For convincing synthesis of the background, it is important to preserve and reconstruct the borders of these segments. The borders between these segments are typically well approximated by straight lines if the image resolution is rather small (always the case in the coarsest layer) and the overall area to be filled is sufficiently small with regard to the entire image. Figure 4.10 shows such an image in which a person walking down a street is to be erased from the image. The background can be separated into four segments (the blue sky, the

4.4 Initialization

grass border, the street and the shoulder). Obviously, the blue sky must not exceed the green horizon-line in the synthesized image. A randomized erosion filter will fail as a proper initialization for this type of images. The contour of the defined synthesis mask can be separated into blocks covering the same background. If such a contour holds two blocks with almost the same appearance and size the probability is high that the two blocks should be connected during the inpainting.

We developed a novel initialization approach trying to find unique mappings between the object's contour pixels $P = \{p_1, p_2, \ldots\}$. The pixel correspondences found are used to create a rough initialization image by interpolation towards the mapping directions. Mapping is inspired by our synthesis mapping function f. The new contour mapping function $f_m : P \to P$ can be seen as a simplification of the original mapping function from 2D to 1D space. Again the mapping function is based on a cost measure separated into a spatial and an appearance impact:

$$contour_\beta(p, f_m)$$
$$= \beta \cdot contour_{spatial}(p, f_m) + (1 - \beta) \cdot contour_{appear}(p, f_m) \quad (4.20)$$

While the spatial impact $contour_{spatial}$ enforces neighboring source contour pixels to neighboring target contour pixels, the appearance impact $contour_{appear}$ ensures that the contour neighborhood between source and target pixels is almost similar. The control parameter $\beta \in [0, 1]$ allows balancing between both types of costs similar to the control parameter α in (4.3). As the contour is a ring, the neighborhood between source and target is inverted. For a 1D neighborhood N_m (specifying the pixel offsets within the contour ring), the spatial cost for a contour pixel p is defined by

$$contour_{spatial}(p, f_m) = \sum_{v \in N_m} d_m[f_m(p) - v, f_m(p+v)] \cdot \omega_m(v) \quad (4.21)$$

with weighting function $\omega_m(\cdot)$. Figure 4.9 shows that the ideal mapping of pixel p_{i+1} in relation to the neighbor contour pixel p_i is $f_m(p_{i+1}) = p_{h-1}$ and not p_{h+1} (as might be expected), if $f_m(p_i) = p_h$ is already assigned. The crossings between mappings are suppressed to ensure that segments remain separated during initialization. Simple mapping constraints are used to improve final initialization quality:

- No pixel on a Bresenham line [17] between a source contour pixel p and the target pixel $q = f_m(p)$ lies outside the synthesis mask (see Figure 4.9).

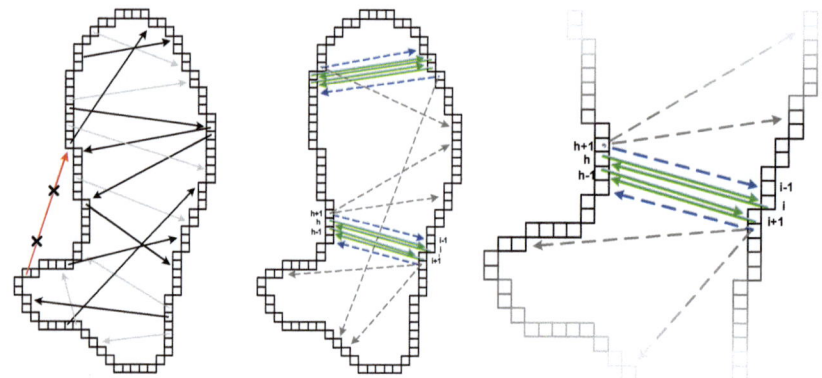

Figure 4.9: Left: Contour mapping with random initialization (black and gray arrow), mappings outside the mask are not allowed (red arrow). Center and Right: Mapping improvement and propagation, stable mappings (green), propagation (blue) and random improvements (gray arrows). The contour is taken from a real image as provided in Figure 4.10.

Figure 4.10: Contour mapping: from left to right: real image, final mapping, result after interpolation and final initialization after erosion.

- Target and source pixel must not be part of the mutual neighborhood.
- At the end of the algorithm all pixel mappings with cost exceeding a specified threshold are discarded. Pixels not having a convincing corresponding target pixel inside the contour are not used for the initialization process.

Similar to iterative refinement of the synthesis pipeline, contour mapping is improved during several randomized iterations and information is propagated to neighboring pixels in the contour and also proposed as back-mapping for the target pixels. Our algorithm starts with random contour mapping

4.4 Initialization

and stops after a few iterations (typically between 5 and 20 as discussed in Subsection 4.8). Figure 4.10 shows an example of the final mapping for an image with given contour. Determined pixel mappings are used to fill the synthesis mask by an interpolation between the source and target pixels (using a Bresenham line). Mask pixels belonging to more than one line are normalized afterwards. As some mask pixels might not be part of any Bresenham mapping line, the remaining small mask areas (typically isolated pixels) are removed by a small number of erosion filter iterations (see Figure 4.10). The interpolated image provides a basis for good initialization of the coarsest pyramid layer in the synthesis pipeline.

As already used for randomized initialization, a final appearance mapping is applied to determine the initial mapping f. In contrast to the randomized erosion initialization strategy, contour mapping creates an initial mapping not by shrinking the inpainting mask but by an approach directly and concurrently creating the entire image content. The contour mapping strategy is more related to a vanishing inpainting algorithm.

4.4.3 Patch Initialization

The previously introduced contour mapping initialization technique is suitable for backgrounds separable into unique segments not overlapping each other. This initialization approach is very fast due to the reduced data information and even provides acceptable results for images with crossing background segments. However, the more structure information present in the remaining background content, the more important a powerful initialization strategy becomes.

We investigated a shrinking approach able to recover important structure image content. The derivation of our entire image inpainting approach in Subsection 3.1 showed that a combination of shrinking and vanishing inpainting approaches may provide better visual results than the application of either approach alone. Patch initialization, as introduced in the following, will allow the combination of both inpainting strategies. The approach is inspired by recent powerful patch-based image inpainting algorithms as introduced in Subsection 2.1.2 and used by [24, 93, 34, 106]. These approaches have in common the application of a patch-based inpainting algorithm iteratively shrinking the inpainting area. All approaches provide strategies defining the inpainting order and use patches as inpainting units.

The mentioned approaches avoid the application of multiresolution layers and thus operate only on the original image dimensions. Instead, our approach applies initialization on the coarsest pyramid layer with significantly less visual information allowing much faster processing. The patch initialization approach is based on the following properties:

- Iteratively shrinking of the inpainting mask on a coarse pyramid layer
- A patch-based similarity measure between patches centered at the inpainting contour and all patches in the remaining image content
- Single pixels as inpainting unit (not using a patch, e.g., Criminisi et al.)
- Inpainting order according to visual structure, border orientation and confidence

Depending on the necessary performance or image quality, the performance characteristics can be tailored:

- Deterministic or heuristic search for best matching patches
- Search for best matching patches in the entire or in a narrowed image area
- One single initialization step, or several successive initialization steps

In the following, the detailed initialization approach is introduced. First, the patch similarity measure is investigated. The determination of the inpainting order is then presented.

The inpainting border separating the source area S and the target area T of the image $I = S \cup T$ will be denoted by ∂T. $\partial T \subseteq T$ is the subset of T holding target pixels with at least one neighboring source pixels.

4.4.3.1 Patch Similarity Measure

With only one initialization step, the inpainting mask will shrink iteratively until the target region is empty. If desired, a following (slightly modified) initialization step may be applied to refine the initialization result derived from the first step.

Let S^k be the intermediate source region and let T^k be the intermediate target region after k shrinking iterations so that

$$S^k \cup T^k = I \quad \wedge \quad S^k \cap T^k = \emptyset \qquad (4.22)$$

and

$$|T| - |T^k| = k \qquad (4.23)$$

4.4 Initialization

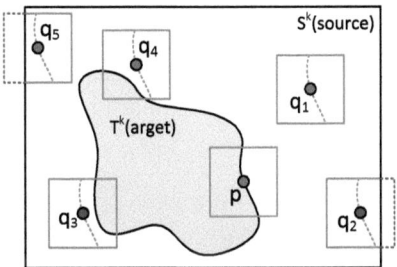

Figure 4.11: Patch similarity determination for patch initialization during the k-th shrinking iteration for a mask border point $p \in \partial T$. The candidate points q_1, q_4 and q_5 are valid. At least one weighting $w_i^1(\cdot)$ of a patch pixel for candidate q_2 and q_3 will invalidate the candidates.

holds for any $k \in [0, |T|]$. For the first iteration, the initial intermediate source and target regions S^0 and T^0 are initialized by

$$S^0 = S$$
$$T^0 = T \qquad (4.24)$$

During the k-th mask shrinking iteration, patch similarity $cost_{appear}^{init^1}(\cdot)$ between a patch centered at a point $p \in \partial T^k$ and any candidate point $q \in S^0$ is determined by

$$cost_{appear}^{init^1}(p,q) = \sum_{\substack{\vec{v} \in \{\vec{v} \in N_i \,|\, \\ (p+\vec{v}) \in S^k\}}} d_i(i(p+\vec{v}), i(q+\vec{v})) \cdot w_i^1(q+\vec{v}), \quad \forall q \in S^0$$
(4.25)

with neighborhood N_i holding relative vector offsets defining the patch to measure appearance similarity (comparable to the neighborhoods N_s and N_a as applied in (4.4) or (4.13)). The pixel intensity distance measure $d_i(\cdot)$ is comparable to $d_a(\cdot)$ applied for the appearance cost measure in (4.13). The weighting function $w_i^1(\cdot)$ ensures that any patch pixel $p_j = p + \vec{v}_j, \vec{v}_j \in N_i$ regarding to a point $p \in \partial T$ has a corresponding pixel $q_j \in S^k$:

$$w_i^1(q) = \begin{cases} 1, & q \in S^k \\ \infty, & \text{else} \end{cases} \qquad (4.26)$$

In Figure 4.11, the weighting of $w_i^1(\cdot)$ is visualized for several candidates.

If more than one initialization step is applied, a slightly different cost measure is used. This cost measure also uses visual information inside the inpainting mask, as this information has already been gathered during the previous initialization step. The patch similarity measure for the second and the following steps is defined by

$$cost_{appear}^{init^{2+}}(p,q) = \sum_{\substack{\vec{v}\in\{\vec{v}\in N_i \,|\\ (p+\vec{v})\in I\}}} d_i(p+\vec{v}, q+\vec{v}) \cdot \omega_i^{2+}(q+\vec{v}), \quad \forall q \in S^0 \qquad (4.27)$$

with

$$\omega_i^{2+}(q) = \begin{cases} 1, & q \in I \\ \infty, & \text{else} \end{cases} \qquad (4.28)$$

The slight modification between $cost_{appear}^{init^1}(\cdot)$ and $cost_{appear}^{init^{2+}}(\cdot)$ integrates patch pixels inside the inpainting mask for similarity determination and allows refinement and improvement of already initialized image content.

4.4.3.2 Determination of Inpainting Priority

Four criteria for the shrinking order of contour points $p \in \partial T$ have already been proposed in previous inpainting approaches, e.g., [25, 93, 106]:

1. Structured areas at ∂T are more privileged than homogenous areas.
2. Areas with a strong structure are more privileged than areas with a weak structure.
3. Structured areas perpendicular to the inpainting border are more privileged than structured areas not perpendicular to the inpainting border.
4. Areas with high confidence at ∂T (with a large number of neighboring source pixels) are more prioritized than areas with low confidence.

Figure 4.12 visualizes these four criteria.

The inpainting pixel $p \in \partial T^k$ with the highest prioritization in the k-th shrinking iteration is determined by the priority function $prior(\cdot)$:

$$prior(p) = |b(p) \cdot M_\times o(p)| \qquad (4.29)$$

with $b(\cdot)$ specifying the direction of the current mask border ∂T^k at contour pixel p and $M_\times o(\cdot)$ the skewed image orientation at position p. The position

4.4 Initialization

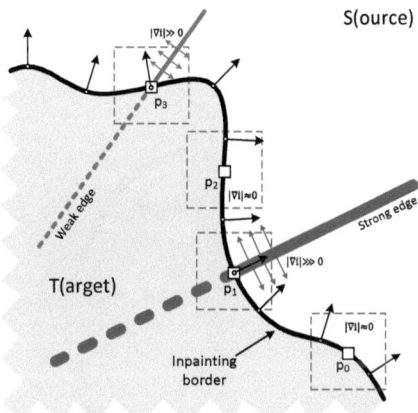

Figure 4.12: Inpainting priority of the patch mapping initialization strategy. Information within the neighborhood centered at four exemplary contour points $p_0, \ldots, p_3$ is used to determine the inpainting order. The neighborhood of p_0 and p_2 is homogenous outside the inpainting border and are assigned a low priority. In contrast, p_1 and p_3 are located at highly structured areas and have a higher priority. The priority of p_1 is higher than the priority of p_3, as at p_1 a stronger edge, more perpendicular to the contour border, is visible outside the target area. The confidence of pixel p_2 is lower than the confidence of p_0, as the latter has access to slightly more neighboring pixels outside the current inpainting mask.

$p \in \partial T^k$ with highest priority $prior(p)$ will be the pixel to be replaced in the k-th shrinking iteration.

As the image resolution on a coarse pyramid layer is low, determination of the inpainting border cannot reliably be found by the contour's derivative. We have to investigate a different approach providing a convincing border direction while remaining very efficient for coarse pyramid image resolutions. The contour direction $b(p)$ for a point $p \in \partial T^k$ is found by summing the vectors of the neighboring pixels lying outside the inpainting area T^k of the k-th iteration:

$$b(p) = \sum_{\substack{\vec{v} \in \{\vec{v} \in N_i \mid \\ (p+\vec{v}) \in S^k\}}} \vec{v} \cdot \omega_i^b(\vec{v}) \qquad (4.30)$$

with weighting function $\omega_i^b(\cdot)$ allowing the elements of N_i to be weighted individually, similar to $\omega_s(\cdot)$ in (4.4). As the sum of neighboring vectors in (4.30) is not normalized, the length of $b(\cdot)$ indicates the confidence of the

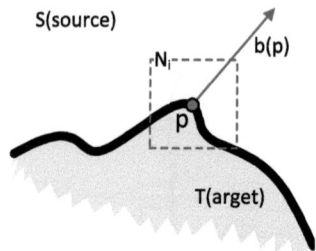

(a) Section of the inpainting mask. The border direction $b(p)$ at $p \in \partial T$ is determined by the neighborhood N_i. The length of $b(p)$ specifies the confidence of p.

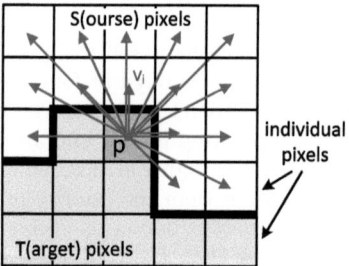

(b) The border direction is determined by summing all $v_i \in N_i$ pointing outside the inpainting mask T.

Figure 4.13: Determination of the direction of the inpainting border in a low resolution frame. b) depicts the zoomed area of the dashed neighborhood N_i from a).

inpainting pixel p. The larger the value of $b(\cdot)$, the higher the confidence of p and thus the higher the inpainting priority. Previous approaches integrated the confidence parameter into their inpainting priority so confidence was determined by explicitly counting the number of source pixels. Instead, our approach concurrently determines the border direction and position confidence. In Figure 4.13, the border direction determination $b(\cdot)$ and the confidence factor is depicted.

4.4 Initialization

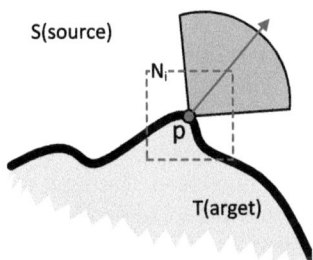

Figure 4.14: Area of interest for additional randomized searches. The blue circular sector starts at p and points towards the border direction $b(p)$. The visual content inside this sector has high probability to contain the best matching patch according to the inpainting pixel p.

Calculation of image content orientation during the k-th iteration at point $p \in \partial T^k$ is approximated by the application of the image gradient in the source region:

$$o(p) = \sum_{\vec{v} \in \{\vec{v} \in N_i \,|\, (p+\vec{v}) \in S^k\}} \tilde{\nabla} i(p + \vec{v}) \cdot \omega_i^o(\vec{v}) \quad (4.31)$$

with weighting function $\omega_i^o(\cdot)$ equivalent to $\omega_i^b(\cdot)$. Further, $\tilde{\nabla} i(p)$ maps the gradient $\nabla i(p)$ of image I at position p and the corresponding inverted gradient to the same value:

$$\tilde{\nabla} i(p) = \begin{cases} \nabla i(p), & \nabla i(p) \cdot (1,0)^\top \geq 0 \\ -\nabla i(p), & \text{else} \end{cases} \quad (4.32)$$

The skew symmetric matrix $M_\times$ allows creation of a perpendicular vector $\vec{v}_\times$ for any vector $\vec{v} \in \mathbb{R}^2$:

$$M_\times = \begin{pmatrix} 0 & -1 \\ 1 & 0 \end{pmatrix} \quad (4.33)$$

Since individual elements are based on simple pixel operations in a small neighborhood, equation (4.29) can be determined very efficiently

4.4.3.3 Heuristic Search for the Best Matching Patch

The best matching patch for a contour point p may be found by application of a deterministic (brute force) search or a heuristic (randomized) search. Even though the initialization step is applied on a coarse pyramid layer, a brute force search is still time intensive (see Table 4.1 for detailed Performance values). Even if the search area is narrowed to the inpainting contour pixel, a brute force search may violate the real-time capability of our approach on hardware with reduced computational power. The initialization approach additionally supports a heuristic execution mode allowing the process to be significantly accelerated. Therefore, the best matching patch candidates are selected randomly and compared to each other. Comparable to the approach for iterative refinement as described in Subsection 4.3, an information propagation of already determined neighboring contour pixels is applied to improve mapping quality. The border direction b is mainly used to preserve structured information of intersecting visual content. However, the border direction is further used to specify a region of interest for more intensive randomized searches. The region of interest is defined by a circular sector starting at the contour pixel $p \in \partial T^k$ to be replaced and pointing towards the border direction $b(p)$. Fang et al. [34] proposed a similar approach to reduce the search space for possible matching candidates. However, Fang used only the region of interest to find a best matching patch. Instead, our approach applies the region of interest as an additional criteria for a more concentrated randomized search. Figure 4.14 shows the region of interest for a significant improvement of mapping quality.

In contrast to other initialization techniques introduced above, patch matching initialization directly provides a unique initial mapping function f for each target pixel $p \in T$. Thus, the iterative inpainting approach from Subsection 4.3 may start directly on the same pyramid layer as used for the initialization, as an initial f is already known. In Figure 4.15, patch initialization for the *Pyramid* benchmark picture of Xu et al. [106] is presented. The patch initialization strategy first recovers structured information from the remaining image content. Then, the homogenous content is filled in. In Appendix A.2, the patch initialization is demonstrated on several images with individual image structures.

The patch initialization approach provides better and more reliable final image quality after the entire inpainting pipeline has been applied compared to the visual result from an approach with no initialization step. The final visual difference between non-initialized inpainting and patch-initialized inpainting increases with increasing complexity of the structure of the inpainting image. The randomized erosion initialization and the contour mapping strategy as described in Subsection 4.4.1 and Subsection 4.4.2, for the most part, cannot reach the overall quality of patch initialization but can be processed significantly faster (see Table 4.2 for a detailed performance comparison). Thus, these two initialization strategies are a good compromise

4.4 Initialization

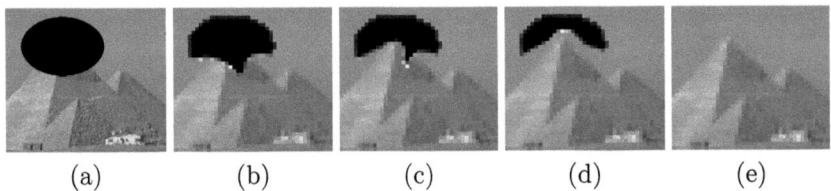

(a) (b) (c) (d) (e)

Figure 4.15: Patch initialization of the *Pyramid* image with given original. The original image has been taken from [106], kindly authorized by the author, ©2010 IEEE. (a) original image, (b-d) three intermediate results (white contour pixels have a high inpainting priority) and (e) the final initial mapping result with 310 inpainting mask pixels.

Table 4.1: Performance values of patch initialization for the *Bungee* image as also visualized in Figure 4.16. The initialization pyramid layer has 331 mask pixels to be initialized. The overall performance rate is the ratio between initialization time and overall inpainting time (including the initialization). A laptop Intel i7 Nehalem Core with 2.13 GHz running Windows 7 has been used for the performance measurements.

Mode	deterministic		randomized	
Number of iteration steps	2	1	1	1
SSD patch sampling	full	full	full	half
Initialization performance	88.2 ms	58.5 ms	14.7 ms	11.3 ms
Initialization fillrate	3.76 px/ms	5.66 px/ms	22.52 px/ms	29.30 px/ms
Overall performance rate	84.7 %	78.6 %	48.0 %	41.5 %

between image quality and overall processing time and may be applied whenever performance is more important than image quality. In Subsection 4.4.4, image quality and the performance of individual initialization strategies are compared and discussed in detail.

4.4.3.4 Performance Comparison of Individual Execution Modes

As previously described, patch initialization has been realized supporting individual execution modes. Patch matching can either be applied in a deterministic or heuristic mode. Several successive initialization steps iteratively improve an already initialized mapping. The similarity measure between image patches can be applied either by comparing each patch pixel or by comparing each second patch pixel. Undersampling the similarity measure allows faster execution while measurement quality stays acceptable.

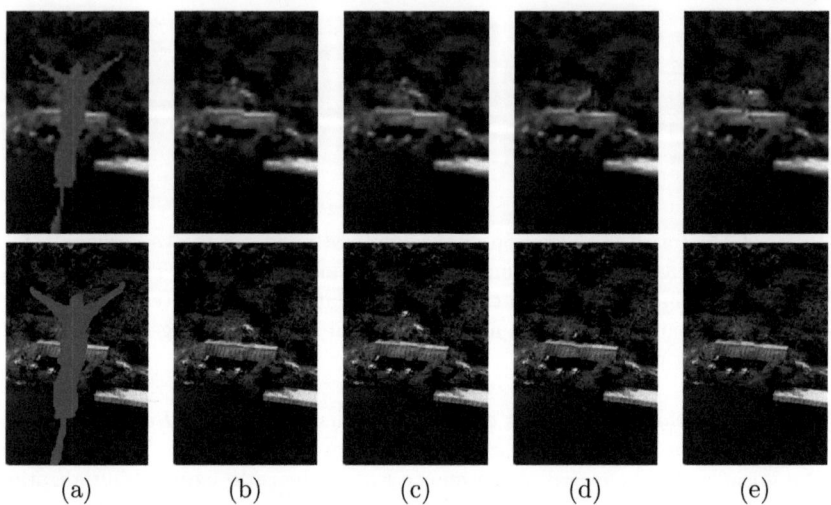

Figure 4.16: Comparison of individual patch initialization modes applied on the same image. Initialization results on the coarsest pyramid layer (top row) and final inpainting result (bottom row). a) original image with inpainting mask, b) deterministic mode with 2 iterations and full sampling, c) deterministic mode with 1 iteration and full sampling, d) heuristic mode with 1 iteration and full sampling, e) deterministic mode with 1 iteration and half sampling. The original image has been taken from Criminisi et al. [25], kindly authorized by the author, ©2004 IEEE.

Table 4.1 provides the performance values of four individual execution modes of the patch initialization approach. The performance values are determined for the *Bungee* image with 6,747 mask pixels in the finest image resolution and 331 mask pixels in the pyramid layer applied for the initialization process. The fastest execution mode needing 11.3ms is about eight times faster than the most accurate mode needing 88.2 ms.

The depicted combinations of execution modes (in Table 4.1) are a subset of the total number of possible combinations. Several other execution modes are possible and provide individual initialization results. In Figure 4.16, initialization results for the execution modes in Table 4.1 are visualized.

The quality of initialization results shown in Figure 4.16 corresponds with the time necessary for execution. The more time used for initialization, the better the intermediate initialization and thus the better the final image inpainting result. The overall execution time for image inpainting

4.4 Initialization

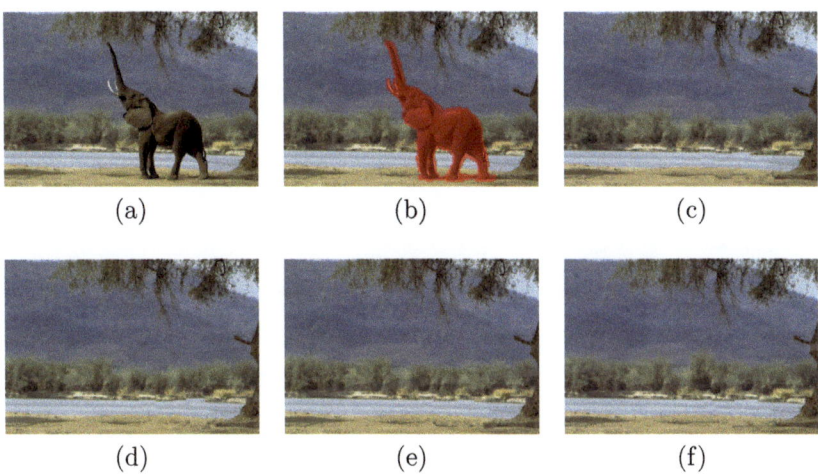

Figure 4.17: Initialization comparison for the *Elephant* image. a) original image, b) original combined with inpainting mask, c) no explicit initialization result, d) randomized erosion initialization result, e) contour mapping initialization, f) patch initialization result. The original image has been taken from Xu et al. [106], kindly authorized by the author, ©2010 IEEE.

in Figure 4.16b was 104.1 ms. The result shown in Figure 4.16e needed only 27.2 ms. The fastest execution mode for patch initialization allows a significant improvement of the overall inpainting performance.

Nevertheless, it should be mentioned that heuristic patch initialization modes rarely provide significantly worse results, as the approach is not deterministic. The performance factor between a fast and a slow patch initialization mode is less important for images with higher resolutions. The higher the image resolution, the more time necessary for mapping refinement of the core image inpainting approach as introduced above in Subsection 4.3.

4.4.4 Discussion

In this section the above introduced initialization approaches are compared to each other, using well known benchmark images with individual visual characteristics. The results are compared to an image inpainting without any explicit initialization, with randomized erosion initialization, with the contour mapping strategy, and with patch initialization.

(a)   (b)   (c)   (d)   (e)

Figure 4.18: Initialization comparison for the *Sign* image. a) original image combined with inpainting mask has been taken from Criminisi et al. [25], kindly authorized by the author, ©2004 IEEE; b) no explicit initialization; c) randomized erosion initialization; d) contour mapping initialization; e) patch initialization.

In Figure 4.17, the four initialization techniques are applied for the *Elephant* image of Drori et al. [30]. Individual initialization techniques result in almost the same visual image quality after the entire image inpainting is finished. The *Elephant* image has several individual (not filigree) image segments like the mountain in the background, the trees behind the river, the river, and the sand in the foreground. Intersections between two segments do not provide an absolute straight line or a regular geometric object. The appearance cost measure of our approach allows for sufficient image inpainting and thus no explicit guiding of structure information is necessary. Structures recovered by patch matching initialization do not differ from the results of other initialization strategies.

In contrast to the *Elephant* benchmark image, the images in Figure 4.18 and 4.19 show more differences between the final image inpainting results. Compared to the less important structure information in Figure 4.17, the *Sign* image as depicted in Figure 4.18 has a conspicuous and absolute straight line which must be reconstructed reliably to create a convincing result. Patch initialization creates a more ideal start for final inpainting refinement iterations and thus provides the best image quality. In Appendix A.3, more initialization comparisons are discussed.

Table 4.2 shows performance values of the above introduced initialization results. Performance values for patch initialization are determined for the slowest execution mode providing the best visual result. As the performance of the slowest patch initialization mode depends on the number of mask

4.4 Initialization

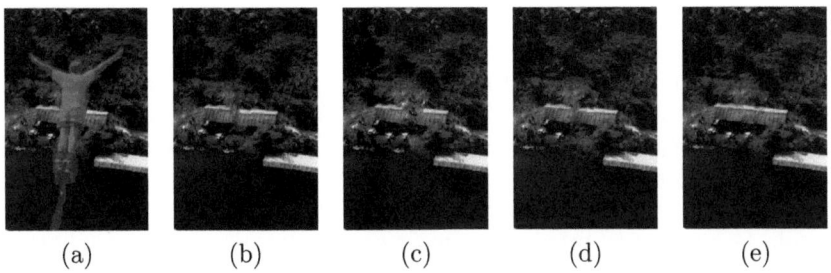

(a) (b) (c) (d) (e)

Figure 4.19: Initialization comparison for the *Bungee* image. a) original image combined with inpainting mask taken from Criminisi et al. [25], kindly authorized by the author, ©2004 IEEE; b) no explicit initialization; c) randomized erosion initialization; d) contour mapping initialization; e) patch initialization.

Table 4.2: Performance comparison of individual initialization approaches. The number of mask pixels are given for the coarse pyramid layer on that the initialization is applied. The values are determined for the Figures 4.17 - 4.18 and A.5 - A.9.

Image	Mask pixels	Randomized erosion filter	Contour mapping	Patch initialization
Elephant	138 px	0.4 ms	2.2 ms	39.3 ms
Sign	132 px	0.4 ms	1.9 ms	10.2 ms
Bungee	331 px	0.8 ms	4.4 ms	88.2 ms
Wall	183 px	0.5 ms	2.4 ms	20.2 ms
Biker	149 px	0.5 ms	2.3 ms	17.3 ms
Blobs	565 px	1.4 ms	4.5 ms	222.7 ms
Window	86 px	0.2 ms	1.0 ms	18.9 ms
Wood	60 px	0.1 ms	0.9 ms	2.6 ms

pixels and also on the number of remaining image pixels, the performance is not linear with the number of mask pixels. In contrast, the randomized erosion filter provides linear performance with the number of mask pixels. The table depicts that the *Blobs* image needs the most processing time. This fact can be explained by the size of the inpainting mask in the lowest pyramid layer. The inpainting mask is very thin even in the original image resolution. Therefore, the *Blob* image applies three pyramid layers only and thus has a larger inpainting mask on the lowest pyramid layer (compared to e.g. the *Wood* benchmark image). Table 4.2 also shows performance values for additional benchmark images that are presented in Appendix A.3.

Comparing individual initialization techniques, we note that for almost every test image, the patch initialization approach does produce equal or better results compared to other initialization approaches. However, as shown in Table 4.2, patch initialization is significantly slower than all other initialization strategies as this strategy bases on more computational effort. Considering the constraints regarding image quality and execution performance, a specific initialization strategy (or even no initialization) should be applied to provide the most optimal results for the application conditions. Please note that Table 4.2 does not provide any performance values if no explicit initialization strategy is applied, as obviously no time is necessary in this case.

4.5 Implicit Constraints

The applied image data space chosen is essential for the final inpainting result. Barnes et al. [8] and Wexler et al. [103] apply an L*a*b* color space [94], while in our previous work [40], we applied grayscale data of the image to reduce the amount of data. Usage of one third of the original image information speeds up appearance matching; however, important visual details not enclosed in the grayscale information may get lost. In Figure 4.20, our inpainting result for two data types is presented for an image with individual colored regions. The inpainting process applying only grayscale data during the mapping improvements integrates fragments from image regions not suitable in the final color result. A process using three color channels provides much better results. The approach developed in this work allows use of individual data formats on individual inpainting pyramid layers. If real-time performance has to be reached, the number of data channels has to decrease with increasing pyramid layer resolution. The lower the number of data channels on fine pyramid layers, the more CPU time can be saved.

As our approach does not blend or interpolate image patches, the approach is fast enough to use even more than three data channels and still performs faster than other inpainting techniques. This means other data channels can be added and fast performance still maintained. For example, for handling images with interleaved sharp and smooth regions, a fourth data channel is added that approximates the data frequency of the grayscale image. We found that a fast and sufficient approximation is represented by the Scharr filter response [84]. The additional channel represents a meaningful, but fast to determine, texture information, added to the image data. This additional texture channel is a significant simplification of texture vectors as often used

4.5 Implicit Constraints

(a) Original image.

(b) Original with inpainting mask.

(c) Inpainting applying one (grayscale) channel integrates fragments from the water region into the landscape region.

(d) Inpainting applying three color channels.

Figure 4.20: Inpainting with individual data formats. Image source: Marianne J. (photographer), kindly authorized by the author; pixelio.de (creative commons image database), viewed 20 August 2012.

in image segmentation [1] approaches. An explicit texture clustering can be avoided to increase performance while allowing distinguishing between image regions with individual frequencies. Figure 4.21 provides a comparison between our inpainting result using only color information and an inpainting result using an additional fourth Scharr filter texture channel.

As can be seen, the sharp and smooth image content is not mixed during iterative refinement steps if an additional texture channel is applied. The smooth image region is inpainted by smooth image information of the remaining image content, while the sharp foreground content is used to fill the inpainting mask surrounded by sharp image data.

(a) Original image combined with inpainting mask.

(b) Inpainting with three individual data channels.

(c) Inpainting with four individual data channels.

Figure 4.21: Inpainting with additional texture information for an image with interleaved sharp and smooth regions. Top row: entire frame with 1000 × 699 pixels, bottom row: zoomed area with 247 × 165 pixels. Image source: www.golfen-mv.de (photographer), pixelio.de (creative commons image database), viewed 20 August 2012.

4.6 Explicit Constraints

The above implicit constraints do not guide the inpainting algorithm according to user-specific decisions. The application of individual image formats only has an implicit implication for the final inpainting result. More advanced constraints may be used to guide the inpainting algorithm providing an improved visual result. Depending on the structure of the background or the desired and undesired visual elements, the final inpainting result may be tweaked with regard to the expectations of the users.

However, in a rigorous real-time video inpainting approach such as a Mediated Reality application, explicit user-defined constraints cannot be applied. The constraint definition itself needs a certain amount of time that would violate the real-time execution. Additionally, in a Mediated Reality application, users might not be willing to define several constraints guiding the inpainting algorithm in order to create better visual results.

4.6 Explicit Constraints

In general, the application of explicit user-defined constraints cannot be used for real-time video inpainting. Nevertheless, in the following, user-defined constraints will be introduced as:

- Video inpainting approaches that do not rely on real-time performance for post-processing tasks (and thus benefit from a better video quality).
- Live-video transmission broadcasted with a small time delay allowing the user to specify simple inpainting constraints in the interim.
- Simple structural constraints, e.g., lines or regular objects, which can be detected automatically in a real-time approach and therefore do not need to be specified by the user.

Our pixel mapping approach allows seamless integration of constraints into the synthesis pipeline by simply extending the cost measure from (4.3) by an additional constraint cost:

$$cost_{\alpha}(p,f) = \alpha_s \cdot cost_{spatial}(p,f)$$
$$+ \alpha_a \cdot cost_{appear}(p,f) \, , \quad p \in T \quad (4.34)$$
$$+ \alpha_c \cdot cost_{constr}(p,f)$$

with the new cost extension $cost_{constr} : T \times (T \to S) \to \mathbb{Q}$ and the weight control parameters $\alpha = (\alpha_s, \alpha_a, \alpha_c)$ with $\alpha_s, \alpha_a, \alpha_s \in [0,1]$, while $\alpha_s + \alpha_a + \alpha_s = 1$ must hold.

The cost constraint extension may be composed of several individual sub-constraints:

$$cost_{constr}(p,f) = constr_0(p,f) + constr_1(p,f) + \ldots, \quad p \in T \quad (4.35)$$

In the following, two constraints are introduced which simply allow improvement of the visual inpainting results.

4.6.1 Area Constraints

The most obvious form of inpainting constraints guide the algorithm to explicitly use or avoid image regions from the remaining image content. The algorithm is forced to use image content explicitly selected by the user, discarding content the user does not prefer. An inverse importance map $\overline{m} : S \to \mathbb{Q}$ over all elements (pixels) in S has to be defined to individually rate visual importance of image content.

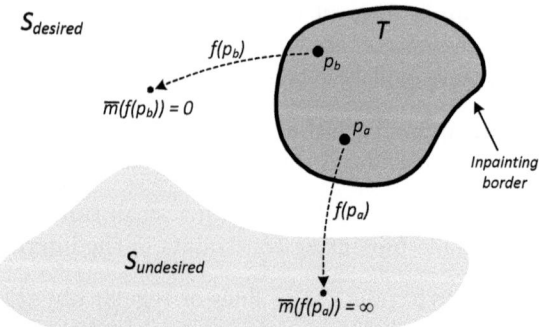

Figure 4.22: Inverse importance map of an area constraint separating the source area into two disjoint sets $S_{desired}$ and $S_{undesired}$.

A simple inverse importance map rates all undesired visual elements with an infinite high value while weighting the desired content with zero:

$$\overline{m}(q) = \begin{cases} 0, & q \in S_{desired} \\ \infty, & \text{else} \end{cases}, \quad \forall q \in S \qquad (4.36)$$

while $S_{desired} \subseteq S$ defines a set of visual elements in S appropriate for inpainting.

The scheme of such an inverse importance map is depicted in Figure 4.22. A map with a more detailed granularity clearly allows for more precise algorithm guidance.

The final area constraint $constr_A : T \times (T \to S) \to \mathbb{Q}$ is then directly given by the application of the inverse importance map $\overline{m}$:

$$constr_A(p, f) = \overline{m}(f(p)) \qquad (4.37)$$

In Figure 4.23, a comparison between an inpainting with and without an area constraint is provided. The inverse importance map provides an infinite cost for conspicuous elements. The inpainting result using the area constraint does not contain repetitions of these elements.

4.6 Explicit Constraints

(a) Original image.

(b) Original image combined with inpainting mask.

(c) Resulting inpainting picture with more than 30 % synthesized image content.

(d) Original image combined with area constraint. Blue pixels depict infinite constraint cost.

(e) Original image combined with inpainting mask and area constraint.

(f) Resulting inpainting image using area constraint.

Figure 4.23: Inpainting result for the *Ruin* image with dimension 2736 × 3648 and more than 3,000,000 inpainting pixels. Top row: our inpainting result without using an area constraint, bottom row: inpainting result using area constraint. Copyright for the original image: bbroianigo (photographer), kindly authorized by the author; pixelio.de (creative commons image database), viewed 3 October 2012.

4.6.2 Structural Constraints

Structural constraints may be used to explicitly preserve straight lines or strong borders during the inpainting process. Any number of individual structural constraints can be considered concurrently.

A set of arbitrary structural constraints $C_{cs} = \{cs_0, cs_1, cs_2, \ldots\}$ may be defined, characterizing the individual structural features of the current synthesis image I. Each structural constraint cs_i is composed of a 3-tuple $cs_i = (d_{cs}(\cdot), cs_{impact}, cs_{radius})$, combining individual spatial distance measures with two control parameters. This will be explained in more detail in the following.

The cost for all structural constraints $constr_S : T \times (T \rightarrow S) \rightarrow \mathbb{Q}$ for a given point $p \in T$ is specified by:

$$constr_S(p, f) = \frac{1}{\sum_{cs \in C_{cs}} g_{cs}(p, cs)} \cdot \sum_{cs \in C_{cs}} c_{struct}(p, cs, f) \cdot g_{cs}(p, cs) \quad (4.38)$$

with filter function $g_{cs}(p, cs)$ and structural constraint cost function c_{struct}. The individual cost for a constraint cs in combination with a position $p \in T$ is determined by $c_{struct} : T \times C_{cs} \times (T \rightarrow S) \rightarrow \mathbb{Q}$:

$$c_{struct}(p, cs, f) = |d_{cs}(p, cs) - d_{cs}(f(p), cs)|^2 \cdot \omega_{cs}(p, cs) \quad (4.39)$$

with spatial distance function $d_{cs}(p, cs) : I \times C_{cs} \rightarrow \mathbb{Q}$ between constraint cs and a given point p.

The weighting function $\omega_{cs}(p, cs) : T \times C_{cs} \rightarrow \mathbb{Q}$ weights constraint cost according to the distance between point p and constraint cs:

$$\omega_{cs}(p, cs) = cs_{impact} \cdot e^{-8\left(\frac{d_{cs}(p, cs)}{cs_{radius}}\right)^2} \quad (4.40)$$

The constant $cs_{impact} \in \mathbb{Q}$ specifies the overall impact of cs to the entire synthesis cost. This scalar factor allows distinct lines to be weighted stronger than weak lines. $cs_{radius} \in \mathbb{Q}$ shrinks the area of influence to a specific image sub-region. In Figure 4.24, the function graph of $\omega_{cs}(\cdot)$ is depicted. The smaller the distance between a target point $p \in T$ and the constraint $cs \in C_{cs}$ the higher the weighting $\omega_{cs}(\cdot)$ and directly implied, the higher the resulting constraint cost. Figure 4.25 visualizes the constraint cost determination for lines.

4.6 Explicit Constraints

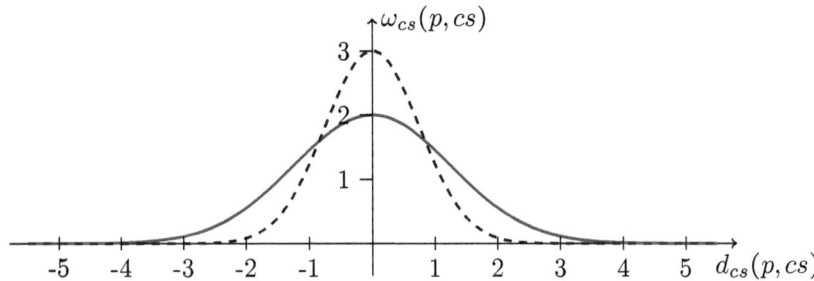

Figure 4.24: Function graph of the structural constraint weighting function $\omega_{cs}(p, cs)$ for two individual combinations of impact and radius parameters; red solid: $cs_{impact} = 2$, $cs_{radius} = 5$, blue dashed: $cs_{impact} = 3$, $cs_{radius} = 3$.

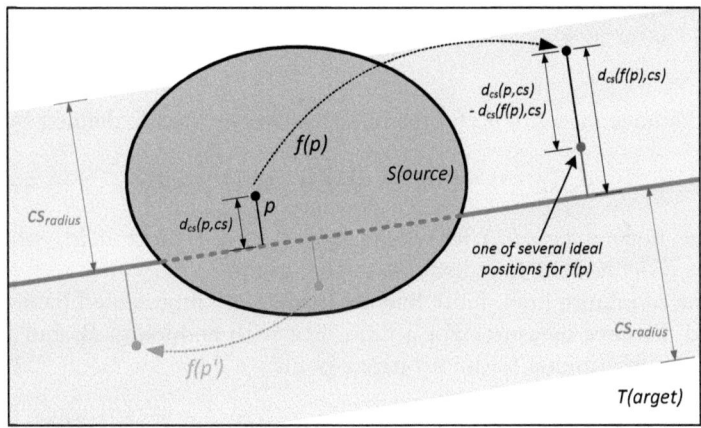

Figure 4.25: Determination of constraint costs for infinite lines. The constraint cost corresponds to the distance between the actual mapping position $f(p)$ and the projected ideal position for a given point p.

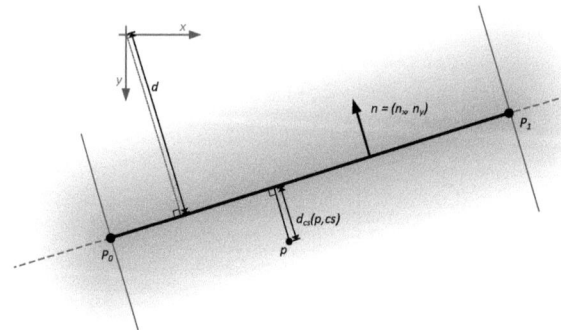

Figure 4.26: Determination of the distance between a point p and a finite line constraint cs specified by the line's end points P_0 and P_1. Points are separated into those projecting onto the finite line (blue area) and those violating the finite constraint (gray area).

The distance measure $d_{cs}(\cdot)$ for infinite straight lines is defined by:

$$d_{cs}(p, cs) = (n_x, n_y, d) \cdot (p_x, p_y, 1)^\top, \quad p \in I \qquad (4.41)$$

with line normal (n_x, n_y) for which $|(n_x, n_y)| = 1$ must hold, while the constant d defines the line distance to the origin.

Similar to infinite lines, finite line constraints are represented by a slightly modified distance measure. For a finite line with endpoints P_0 and P_1, the distance is determined for an arbitrary point $p \in I$ by:

$$d_{cs}(p, cs) = \begin{cases} (n_x, n_y, d) \cdot (p_x, p_y, 1)^\top, & 0 \leq (P_1 - P_0)^\top \cdot (p - P_0) \\ & \leq |P_1 - P_0|^2 \\ \kappa, & \text{else} \end{cases} \qquad (4.42)$$

with the penalty constant $\kappa \gg (n_x, n_y, d) \cdot (p_x, p_y, 1)^\top$ for points not projecting onto the finite line. The higher the penalty κ, the lesser the application of mapping positions outside the finite constraint. Thus, if κ is set to ∞, mappings positions projecting outside the finite line are rejected (see Figure 4.26). More complex structures such as splines and curves may be realized in the same manner as the distance function for straight lines.

4.6 Explicit Constraints

Finally, the constraint filter function $g_{cs}(p, cs)$ needs to be defined:

$$g_{cs}(p,cs) = \begin{cases} 1, & \omega_{cs}(p,cs) \geq \omega_{cs}(p,cs') \quad \forall cs' \in C_{cs} \smallsetminus \{cs\} \\ 0, & \text{else} \end{cases}, \quad p \in T \quad (4.43)$$

The filter function ensures that only the most relevant constraint for each pixel is considered in order to avoid race conditions in areas with several constraints. $g_{cs}(p, cs)$ selects the unique structural constraint cs with the highest influence value $\omega_{cs}(p, cs)$ for a point $p \in T$ as long as no two (or more) constraints exist with identical and maximal weight for the point p. Equation (4.38) has a normalization term to keep the overall constraint cost stable, even if more than one constraint has to be considered due to identical weights.

Barnes et al. explicitly change the mapping positions of pixels belonging to user-defined constraints after each optimization iteration by forcing them to lie on a straight line. The straight line is determined by a RANSAC [36] voting of all pixels belonging to the user-defined constraint.

Instead, our approach is more flexible. More complex constraints such as ellipsoids or splines can be easily supported due to the application of a universal distance function. Figure 4.27 provides a comparison for image inpainting with and without explicit user constraint. The randomized erosion initialization, as introduced in Subsection 4.4.1, has been applied for both inpainting results. In Appendix A.4, another image inpainting example using user-defined constraints is given in Figure A.20.

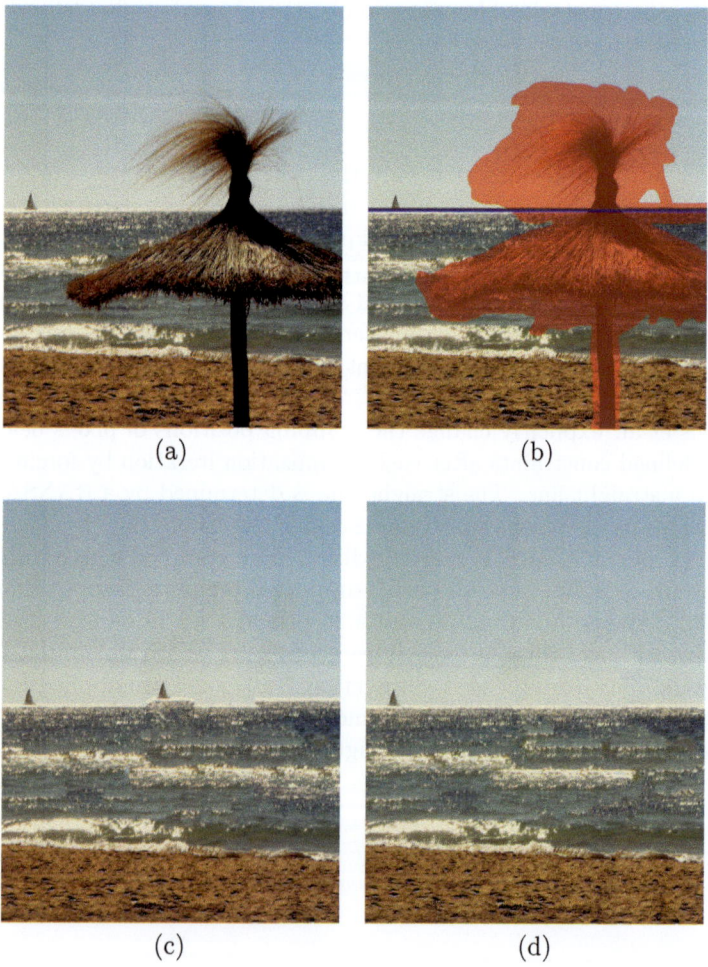

Figure 4.27: Constraint image inpainting example. a) original image with 845 × 1024 pixels, b) original image with inpainting mask and one infinite line constraints (the inpainting mask covers 35.6 % of the image), c) inpainting result without constraints, d) inpainting result with constraints. Original image source: Rainer Sturm / pixelio.de (creative commons image database), viewed 19 September 2012

4.7 Analysis

In this subsection, we will provide an analysis of the proposed inpainting approach. First, the convergence properties of our algorithm are investigated. Following, a complexity analysis of the approach is presented.

4.7.1 Convergence

The iterative approach of finding a cost minimum for the inpainting area needs to converge to a minimum ensuring that the visual result does not regress between two iterations. Using equation (4.2) and (4.3), the entire inpainting cost for a given image I with inpainting area T, remaining source area S, control parameter α and recent mapping function f is defined by

$$\begin{aligned} cost(\alpha, f) &= \sum_{p \in T} cost_\alpha(p, f) \\ &= \sum_{p \in T} [\alpha \cdot cost_{spatial}(p, f) + (1 - \alpha) \cdot cost_{appear}(p, f)] \quad (4.44) \\ &= \alpha \cdot \sum_{p \in T} cost_{spatial}(p, f) + (1 - \alpha) \cdot \sum_{p \in T} cost_{appear}(p, f) \end{aligned}$$

The optimization iteration converges if for any given mapping function $\hat{f}$ the algorithm results in a mapping function f while the convergence condition

$$cost(\alpha, f) \leq cost(\alpha, \hat{f}) \quad (4.45)$$

holds. The cost change between the two functions $\hat{f}$ and f is defined by:

$$\Delta cost(\alpha, \hat{f}, f) = cost(\alpha, f) - cost(\alpha, \hat{f}) \quad (4.46)$$

Thus, with (4.45) and (4.46) the convergence condition can be simplified by:

$$\Delta cost(\alpha, \hat{f}, f) \leq 0 \quad (4.47)$$

As directly derivable by (4.44), spatial cost and appearance cost do not interfere with each other and can be separated according to their cost impact. The entire cost of (4.44) is separated into a global spatial cost measure $cost_{spatial}(\cdot)$

$$cost_{spatial}(\alpha, f) = \alpha \cdot \sum_{p \in T} cost_{spatial}(p, f) \quad (4.48)$$

and a global appearance cost measure $cost_{appear}(\cdot)$:

$$cost_{appear}(\alpha, f) = (1-\alpha) \cdot \sum_{p \in T} cost_{appear}(p, f) \qquad (4.49)$$

Equivalent to (4.46), the spatial cost change $\Delta cost_{spatial}(\cdot)$ between two mappings $\hat{f}$ and f is defined by:

$$\begin{aligned}
&\Delta cost_{spatial}(\alpha, \hat{f}, f) \\
&= cost_{spatial}(\alpha, f) - cost_{spatial}(\alpha, \hat{f}) \\
&= \alpha \cdot \sum_{p \in T} cost_{spatial}(p, f) - \alpha \cdot \sum_{p \in T} cost_{spatial}(p, \hat{f}) \qquad (4.50) \\
&= \alpha \cdot \sum_{p \in T} \left[cost_{spatial}(p, f) - cost_{spatial}(p, \hat{f}) \right] \\
&= \alpha \cdot \sum_{p \in T} \Delta cost_{spatial}(p, \hat{f}, f)
\end{aligned}$$

with spatial cost difference for a single position $p \in T$:

$$\Delta cost_{spatial}(p, \hat{f}, f) = cost_{spatial}(p, f) - cost_{spatial}(p, \hat{f}) \qquad (4.51)$$

Corresponding to (4.50), the change of the appearance cost $\Delta cost_{appear}(\cdot)$ between two mappings $\hat{f}$ and f is defined by

$$\begin{aligned}
&\Delta cost_{appear}(\alpha, \hat{f}, f) \\
&= cost_{appear}(\alpha, f) - cost_{appear}(\alpha, \hat{f}) \\
&= (1-\alpha) \cdot \sum_{p \in T} cost_{appear}(p, f) - (1-\alpha) \cdot \sum_{p \in T} cost_{appear}(p, \hat{f}) \qquad (4.52) \\
&= (1-\alpha) \cdot \sum_{p \in T} \left[cost_{appear}(p, f) - cost_{appear}(p, \hat{f}) \right] \\
&= (1-\alpha) \cdot \sum_{p \in T} \Delta cost_{appear}(p, \hat{f}, f)
\end{aligned}$$

respectively. With appearance cost difference for a single position $p \in T$:

$$\Delta cost_{appear}(p, \hat{f}, f) = cost_{appear}(p, f) - cost_{appear}(p, \hat{f}) \qquad (4.53)$$

Iterative refinement of the mapping function, as described in Subsection 4.3, consecutively improves the mappings of the entire inpainting area in a scan-line order. Thus, the mapping optimization of $\hat{f}$ at any position $p \in T$ must be applied without violating the convergence condition (4.47). The local cost change caused by a modification of a single mapping position $p \in T$ in $\hat{f}$ has to be investigated in more detail.

In Chapter 7, proof is given that the global spatial cost change between $\hat{f}$ and f, resulting due to a modification of $\hat{f}$ at a single position $p \in T$, is

4.7 Analysis

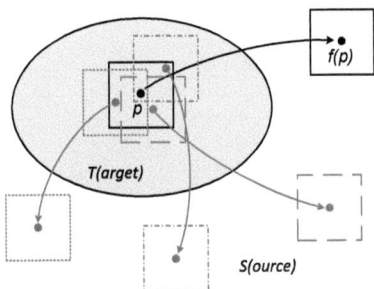

Figure 4.28: Appearance neighborhood for a given point $p \in T$ and the corresponding mapping point $f(p) \in S$. Exemplary, three neighbors of p with their own neighborhood and their own mapping positions are visualized.

twice as high as the local change of the spatial cost directly produced by the mapping. Thus,

$$\Delta cost_{spatial}(\alpha, \hat{f}, f) = 2\alpha \cdot \Delta cost_{spatial}(p, \hat{f}, f), \quad \forall p \in T$$

holds. It directly follows that any new single mapping at $p \in T$ with less spatial cost as compared to the previous mapping will directly reduce the entire global spatial cost by twice the local improvement. Further, a local mapping improvement at any $p \in T$ guarantees the spatial cost convergence. Thus,

$$\alpha \cdot \Delta cost_{spatial}(p, \hat{f}, f) < 0, \quad \forall p \in T \\ \Downarrow \\ \Delta cost_{spatial}(\alpha, \hat{f}, f) < 0 \tag{4.54}$$

holds.

In Chapter 8, proof is given that the global appearance cost change between $\hat{f}$ and f modified at a single position p is the sum of two parts. The first part $\Delta cost_{appear}(\cdot)$ is defined by the local change of the appearance cost directly produced by the mapping of p itself, while the second part $\Delta cost_{appear}^{N_a}(\cdot)$ is the sum of the appearance cost changes for all neighbors of p at their relative positions corresponding to p. Determination of the entire appearance cost change for one single position needs at most twice as much appearance distance calculations $d_a(\cdot)$ than that necessary for the determination of the direct appearance cost change. In Figure 4.28, the

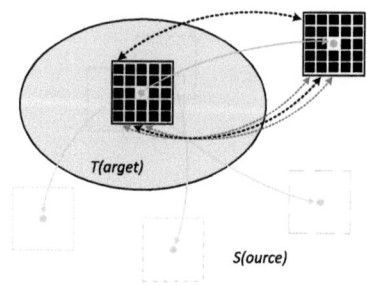 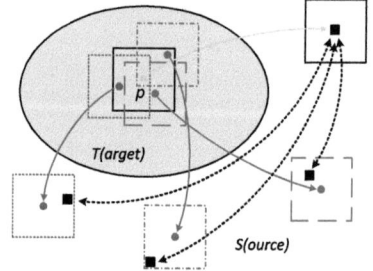

(a) Direct appearance cost produced by p itself (only four of the 24 connections are visualized).

(b) Indirect appearance cost produced by the neighbors of p.

Figure 4.29: Determination of the appearance cost difference at position $p \in T$ for a squared neighborhood with size 5×5. The appearance connections are visualized by dashed arrows, single pixels are represented by black squares.

scheme of the appearance neighborhood of a single point p is visualized, while in Figure 4.29, the corresponding two appearance costs are depicted.

Any single mapping at $p \in T$ with a lower appearance cost compared to the previous mapping (with respect to the direct cost $\Delta cost_{appear}(\cdot)$ and indirect cost $\Delta cost_{appear}^{N_a}(\cdot)$ as defined in (8.1)), will directly reduce the entire global appearance cost by the same amount. Thus,

$$(1-\alpha) \cdot \left[\Delta cost_{appear}(p,\hat{f},f) + \Delta cost_{appear}^{N_a}(p,\hat{f},f)\right] < 0, \quad \forall p \in T$$
$$\Downarrow$$
$$\Delta cost_{appear}(\alpha, \hat{f}, f) < 0$$
(4.55)

holds, with $\Delta cost_{appear}^{N_a}(p,\hat{f},f)$ representing the indirect appearance cost as defined in (8.46).

Finally, both cost changes have to be investigated concurrently to allow a convergence statement of the overall cost covering spatial and appearance distances. From the spatial convergence statement (4.54) and the appearance

4.7 Analysis

convergence statement (4.55) it directly follows that $\forall p \in T$ and for any two mappings $\hat{f}$ and f that only differ at the single point p, the following holds:

$$\begin{array}{c}\alpha \cdot \Delta cost_{spatial}(p,\hat{f},f)\\ +(1-\alpha)\cdot\left[\Delta cost_{appear}(p,\hat{f},f)+\Delta cost_{appear}^{N_a}(p,\hat{f},f)\right] < 0\\ \Downarrow\\ \Delta cost(\alpha,\hat{f},f) < 0\end{array} \quad (4.56)$$

Therefore, the convergence of our iterative refinement algorithm as presented in Subsection 4.3 guarantees to converge. Thus, the algorithm can be applied to iterative pixel mapping optimization for image inpainting. In Subsection 4.8, the convergence behavior of the iterative refinement approach is visualized in Figure 4.40.

4.7.2 Complexity

Independent of the convergence behavior as investigated above, we now analyze the complexity of our algorithm. As a heuristic optimization approach is applied during pixel mapping, our approach is much faster than other pixel-based approaches based on applying a brute-force or graph labeling optimization like that of Pritch et al. [81]. For each pixel to be removed, our algorithm tries to find a better matching pixel using several random seeks. This optimization iteration is repeated several times for each pyramid layer. Each layer with n pixels to be removed has a run-time complexity of:

$$\mathcal{O}(ik \cdot n) \quad (4.57)$$

while i is the number of improvement iterations and k is the number of random seeks on each layer. If i and k are static independent of the pyramid layer, the entire complexity over all layers l is given by:

$$\mathcal{O}\left(\sum_{t=1}^{l} ik \cdot n \left(\frac{1}{s}\right)^{t-1}\right) \quad (4.58)$$

with n the number of mask pixels in the finest pyramid layer and with the shrinking factor s. As the shrinking factor s is larger than 1 (a factor of $s = 4$ means that the horizontal and vertical frame dimensions are bisected at

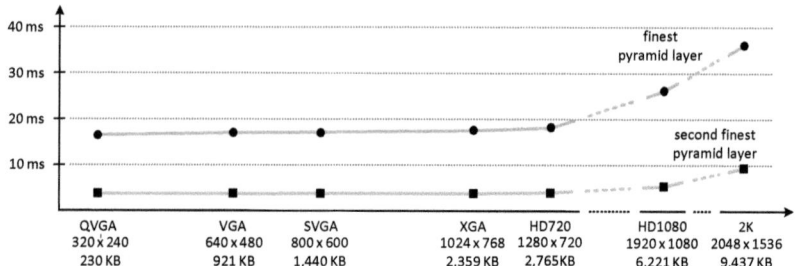

Figure 4.30: Performance comparison of an inpainting image with individual frame dimensions for the two finest pyramid layers. In each test the inpainting mask has the constant size of 10,000 pixels.

each coarser layer), the geometric series converges to $\frac{s}{s-1}$. Thus, the upper bound of the algorithm complexity is

$$\mathcal{O}\left(ik \cdot \frac{s}{s-1} \cdot n\right) \qquad (4.59)$$

As the number of iterations i, random seeking repetitions k and shrinking factor s are constants, the overall complexity can be estimated by

$$\mathcal{O}(n) \qquad (4.60)$$

Figure 4.30 depicts the optimization performance of our algorithm applied to the same image with individual frame resolutions. The image completion mask has a constant size of 10,000 pixels in each inpainting execution. Performance stays constant up to an image resolution of 1280×720. However, for images with higher frame resolutions, the inpainting process shows performance loss. This loss solely results from the insufficient size of the CPU cache as the overall number of random seeking iterations remains constant, while the computational time for SSD calculations increases. The test has been performed on a laptop Intel i7 Nehalem Core with 2.13 GHz and 8 MB L3 cache.

In contrast to Figure 4.30, Figure 4.31 shows the performance graph for one unique image with constant frame resolution of 640 × 480 pixels with changing number of inpainting mask pixels. The graph depicts that the computation time has an almost linear gain related to the number of pixels to be removed in each frame.

4.8 Implementation Issues

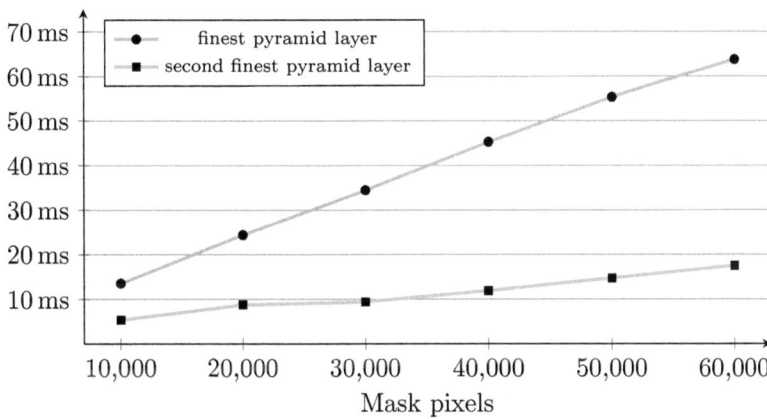

Figure 4.31: Performance comparison of an inpainting image with individual inpainting mask for the two finest pyramid layers. In each test, the same image has been applied with a dimension of 640 × 480 pixels.

4.8 Implementation Issues

In the following section implementation issues regarding the static image inpainting algorithm are discussed.

In order to achieve the fastest inpainting pipeline possible, our implementation applies minor optimizations to the above presented inpainting algorithm, allowing faster overall performance. We apply two individual modifications with respect to the spatial distance cost measure and the appearance cost measure. Although these two modifications will violate the convergence guarantee as discussed in Subsection 4.7.1, we found that the visual result does not change significantly but processing is several times faster than the original algorithm.

In detail, the spatial cost measure from (4.4) is modified not summing up all spatial distances but instead taking only the minimal distance:

$$cost_{spatial}^{min}(p,f) = \min_{\substack{\vec{v} \in \{\vec{v} \in N_s \,|\, \\ (p+\vec{v}) \in T\}}} \left(d_s[f(p) + \vec{v}, f(p+\vec{v})] \cdot \omega_s(\vec{v}) \right), \quad p \in T \quad (4.61)$$

The modification between (4.4) and (4.61) forces ideal mapping to at least one neighboring pixel in the neighborhood N_s. Further, (4.4) allows for much faster calculation and even avoids cost determination for mappings during the propagation steps, as the spatial cost for propagated mapping is zero due to (4.61).

Further, we approximate the determination of the appearance cost difference at a single position $p \in T$. The appearance cost impact of direct neighboring mappings of p regarding to N_a is not investigated and thus the determination of $\Delta cost_{appear}^{N_a}(\cdot)$ from (4.55) is discarded to reduce computational time. Although the number of SSD calculations is cut in half by discarding the indirect appearance cost, the computational time can commonly be reduced by more than a factor of two. We found that an average speedup factor of up to one magnitude can be achieved, as scattered memory lookups at individual image areas are significantly slower than the SSD calculations in a joint image block.

During the iterative optimization steps, a new mapping position between $\hat{f}$ and f at position $p \in T$ is accepted whenever

$$\alpha \cdot \Delta cost_{spatial}^{min}(p, \hat{f}, f) + (1 - \alpha) \cdot \Delta cost_{appear}(p, \hat{f}, f) < 0 \qquad (4.62)$$

holds. $\Delta cost_{spatial}^{min}(\cdot)$ comparable to (4.51), is determined by:

$$\Delta cost_{spatial}^{min}(p, \hat{f}, f) = cost_{spatial}^{min}(p, f) - cost_{spatial}^{min}(p, \hat{f}) \qquad (4.63)$$

As already mentioned above, the approximated optimization criteria from (4.62) cannot mathematically guarantee that the iterative refinement algorithm will converge. However, we found that in practice, the approximated algorithm generally converges although in the in-between stage, it may temporarily fall slightly back to a higher overall cost before decreasing again. Intensive measurements have been applied for individual inpainting images to verify that the approximated algorithm still tends to find a minimum.

In Figure 4.32, the number of changed mapping modifications is visualized for the *Elephant* image of Drori et al. [30]. The number of changed modifications are separated for each pyramid layer and depicted for the first 20 optimization iterations. The control parameter $\alpha = 0.2$ from (4.62) provides the best visual results for almost all inpainting images. The graphs show that the entire number of mapping modifications mainly decreases with almost every iteration on each pyramid layer. In Figure 4.33, the ratio between mask pixels and modified mapping positions is depicted. Independent of the pyramid layer, it can be seen that after five iterations, less than 10% of the mask pixels receive a modified mapping. After ten iterations, even less than 3% of all mappings change. A similar behavior can be observed for all inpainting images.

4.8 Implementation Issues

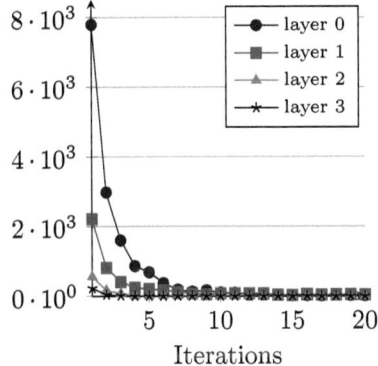
(a) Number of optimized mappings for consecutive iterations with $\alpha = 0.2$.

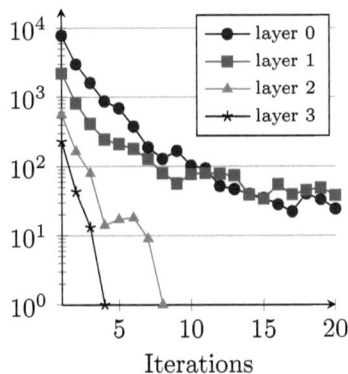
(b) Logarithmic scaled visualization of the same data set as in a).

Figure 4.32: Convergence of the number of optimized mappings during consecutive inpainting optimization iterations. Four inpainting pyramid layers of the *Elephant* image (Figure 4.42) with a moderate spatial weighting $\alpha = 0.2$ are visualized. The individual layers have the following dimensions (with mask pixels in brackets): layer 0: 384×256 (13,048); layer 1: 192×128 (3,532); layer 2: 96×64 (960); layer 3: 48×32 (271).

The same convergence behavior as in Figure 4.32 is visualized in Figure 4.34 and 4.35. Properties are depicted here for two different control parameters $\alpha = 0.05$ and $\alpha = 0.8$. One control parameter is an example for an extreme low value, the other provides an extreme high impact of the spatial cost constraint. The control parameter α is directly related to the convergence behavior of the number of modified mappings of f. The higher the control parameter and thus the higher the impact of the spatial cost in relation to the appearance cost, the faster the convergence of the number of mapping changes. The graphs show that the absolute number of mapping changes is related to the control parameter α. The higher the spatial weighting, the lower the absolute number of changed mapping positions in f.

In Figure 4.36 and 4.37, a direct comparison between three individual control parameters applied on identical pyramid layers is provided. For the finest pyramid layer in Figure 4.36, the difference between the number of mapping changes according to the applied control parameter amounts to almost one magnitude. In Figure 4.37, it can be seen that this significant difference gets smaller on the coarser pyramid layers. The distinct conver-

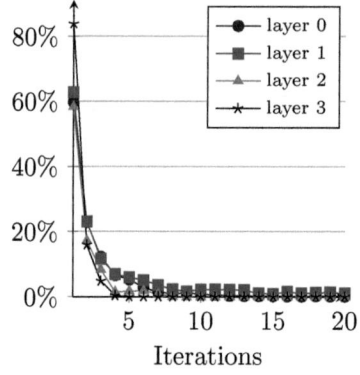 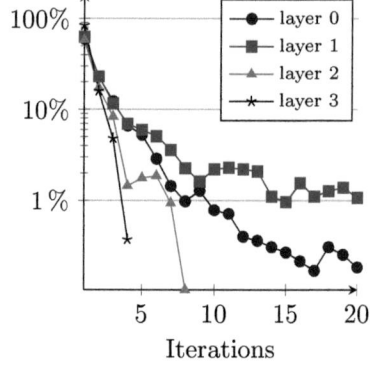

(a) Ratio between the number of optimized mappings and the number of mask pixels for consecutive iterations with $\alpha = 0.2$.

(b) Logarithmic scaled visualization of the same data set as in a).

Figure 4.33: Convergence of the ratio between the number of optimized mappings and the number of mask pixels with the same data set as in Figure 4.32.

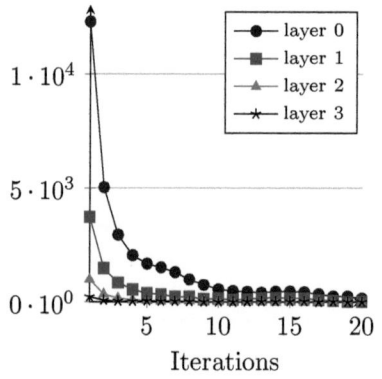 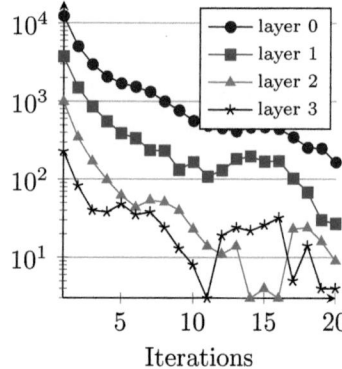

(a) Number of optimized mappings for consecutive iterations with a weak spatial weighting.

(b) Logarithmic scaled visualization of the same data set as in a).

Figure 4.34: Convergence of the number of optimized mapping during consecutive inpainting optimization iterations with a weak spatial weighting $\alpha = 0.05$. Four inpainting pyramid layers of the *Elephant* image (Figure 4.42) are visualized.

4.8 Implementation Issues

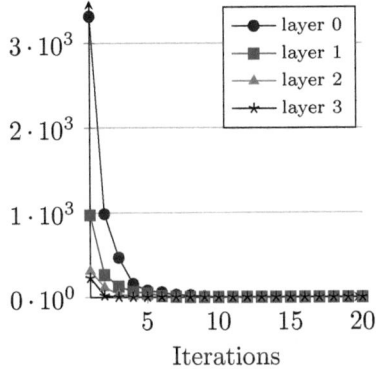

(a) Number of optimized mappings for consecutive iterations with a strong spatial weighting.

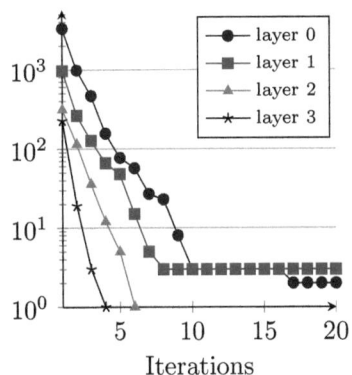

(b) Logarithmic scaled visualization of the same data set as in a).

Figure 4.35: Convergence of the number of optimized mapping during consecutive inpainting optimization iterations with a strong spatial weighting $\alpha = 0.8$. Four inpainting pyramid layers of the *Elephant* image (Figure 4.42) are visualized.

gence behavior relative to strong spatial weightings is independent of the pyramid layer. The spatial weighting behavior has been visualized above in Figure 4.6. The inpainting result has been created with the approximated cost measure showing that spatial cost weighting has a direct influence on the resulting size of the joint pixel blocks.

The ratio between the entire initial inpainting cost and the entire cost after each optimization iteration is depicted in Figure 4.38. The graph shows the ratio separately for individual pyramid layers. The entire inpainting cost tends to converge to a minimum cost as shown in the graph.

The ratio between the inpainting mask pixels and changed mappings in f for individual inpainting images is shown in Figure 4.39. The ratio is depicted for the first 20 optimization iterations on the finest pyramid layer. Again, for each of the inpainting images, the ratio of mapping changes tends to converge. The graph shows that the visual complexity of the inpainting images is related to the number of mapping changes. The simpler the image content, the fewer the number of mapping changes. For example, the *Blobs* image (Figure 4.45) has two identical regular objects with two individual colors. This image has less than 10% modified mappings in the first optimization iteration and almost none after three iterations. In contrast, the *Outlook* image (Figure

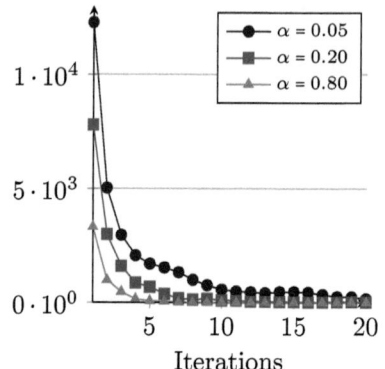 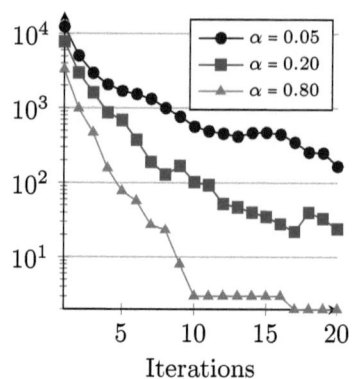

(a) Comparison of mapping changes for the layer 0 (384 × 256) with 13,048 mask pixels for three individual spatial weightings.

(b) Logarithmic scaled visualization of the same data set as in a).

Figure 4.36: Direct comparison of individual spatial weightings with $\alpha = 0.05$, $\alpha = 0.2$ and $\alpha = 0.8$ for the finest inpainting pyramid layer of the *Elephant* image (Figure 4.42).

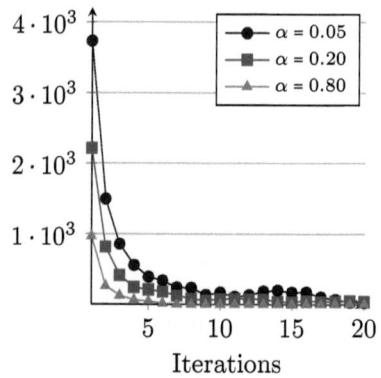 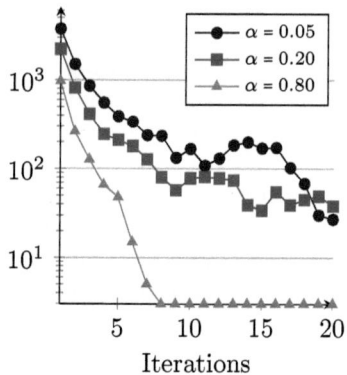

(a) Comparison of mapping changes for the layer 1 (192 × 128) with 3,532 mask pixels for three individual spatial weightings.

(b) Logarithmic scaled visualization of the same data set as in a).

Figure 4.37: Direct comparison of individual spatial weightings with $\alpha = 0.05$, $\alpha = 0.2$ and $\alpha = 0.8$ for the second finest inpainting pyramid layer of the *Elephant* image (Figure 4.42).

4.8 Implementation Issues

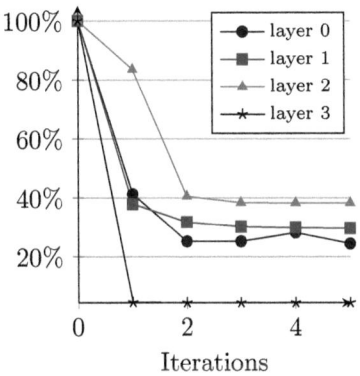

(a) Graph for the first five iterations.

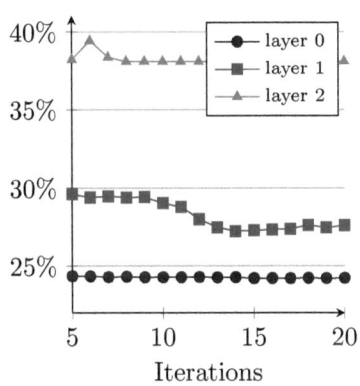

(b) Graph beginning with the fifth iteration (for better visualization, layer 3 has been omitted).

Figure 4.38: Ratio between the entire cost after the optimization steps and the entire cost before the first optimization step for four inpainting pyramid layers of the *Elephant* image (Figure 4.42) with $\alpha = 0.2$. The individual layers have the following dimensions: 384×256 (layer 0), 192×128 (layer 1), 96×64 (layer 2), 48×32 (layer 3).

4.44) provides far more complex elements and therefore shows a significantly higher mapping change ratio during all iterations.

In Figure 4.40, the cost ratio for the exact cost function is depicted, not for an approximated ratio. For this graph, a new mapping position is accepted according to the exact convergence condition (4.56) not according to the approximated convergence condition (4.62). The ratio is determined for each pyramid layer individually. If the exact cost measure is applied for image inpainting, the cost monotonously converges and finally ends in a minimal overall cost.

A visual comparison between the exact and the approximated inpainting approach is presented in Figure 4.41. Both inpainting results provide almost comparable image quality. However, the approximated cost function can be determined several times faster than the exact one.

Although the approximated cost determination from (4.62) does not guarantee convergence while the exact cost determination from (4.56) does, the approximation is well suited. We found that in practice, the approximated algorithm mainly converges, although in the in-between stage it may fall

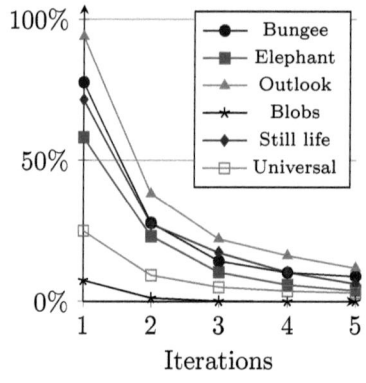 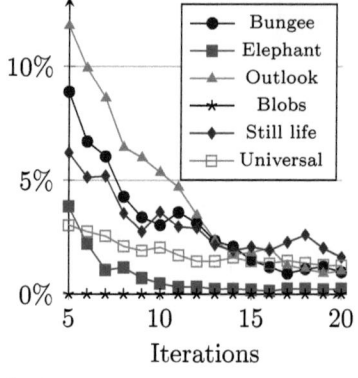

(a) Graph for the first five iterations.

(b) Graph beginning with the fifth iteration.

Figure 4.39: Ratio between the number of mapping changes and the number of mask pixels during the optimization in the finest pyramid layer for seven individual inpainting images. *Bungee* (Figure 4.43), *Elephant* (Figure 4.42), *Outlook* (Figure 4.44), *Blobs* (Figure 4.45), *Still life* (Figure A.14), *Universal Studios* (Figure A.13).

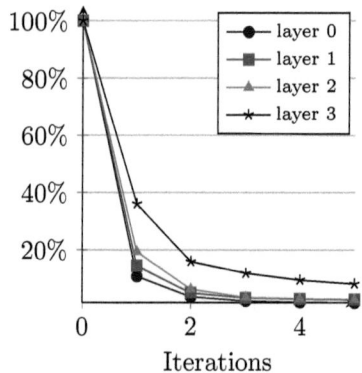 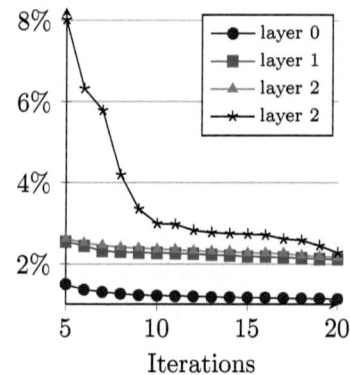

(a) Graph for the first five iterations.

(b) Graph beginning with the fifth iteration.

Figure 4.40: Ratio between the entire cost after the exact optimization steps and the entire cost before the first optimization step for four inpainting pyramid layers of the *Elephant* image (Figure 4.42) with $\alpha = 0.2$. The individual layers have the following dimensions: 384 × 256 (layer 0), 192 × 128 (layer 1), 96 × 64 (layer 2), 48 × 32 (layer 3).

(a) Application of the exact spatial and appearance cost function.

(b) Application of the approximated spatial and appearance cost function.

Figure 4.41: Visual comparison between the exact and the approximated cost measures for the *Elephant* image. Both inpainting qualities are almost the same. The Figures 4.38 and 4.40 provide the corresponding inpainting costs during the inpainting process. The original image has been taken from Xu et al. [106], kindly authorized by the author, ©2010 IEEE.

slightly back to a higher overall cost before decreasing again and it is significantly faster than the more expensive cost determination. If real-time performance is necessary, e.g., for video inpainting, the approximated cost function may especially provide high quality results while the processing time can be reduced. A compromise between accuracy and performance has to be applied to allow the real-time execution of algorithmic problems typically not real-time capable on current computer hardware.

4.9 Results

In this section, the visual results of the static image inpainting approach are presented. Our inpainting results using well known benchmark images are compared to the results of related approaches.

In the following, if not mentioned explicitly, all inpainting images have been created by application of the patch initialization approach as introduced in Subsection 4.4.3. Patch initialization applies a fast heuristic execution mode as already discussed in Table 4.1. The iterative optimization steps use three data channels on each pyramid layer except for the finest layer. On the finest layer, a grayscale image with one data channel is used. To allow for a reliable comparison of performance values between our approach and related image inpainting approaches, the performance measurements of the related algorithms have to be rated according to the computational power of the individual test devices. As computational power increases with each new hardware generation, we apply an estimated performance factor for related approaches. In Appendix A.7, the detailed description of the performance translation factor is given.

We apply all performance measurements on a laptop Intel i7 Nehalem Core with 2.13 GHz released in 2010. We estimate the performance increase factor Θ of a related approach that has been proposed in year y by:

$$\Theta(y) = 1.39^{(2010-y)} \qquad (4.64)$$

We wish to emphasize that the factor Θ is merely an estimation allowing a rough performance comparison. However, it is precise enough to show significant performance differences between our approach and related approaches.

In Figure 4.42, we compare our result for the well known *Elephant* picture. The iterative mapping refinement approach as developed in this work provides visual results comparable to the approach of Drori et al. [30] and Xu et al. [106]. The individual visual elements of the image, such as the river or the forest in the background, are recovered reliably. Our approach needs about 16.5 ms for the entire image inpainting pipeline. In detail, our algorithm needs 1.5 ms to create the image pyramid, requires 6.2 ms for the randomized patch initialization step, and finally needs 8.8 ms for the iterative mapping refinement of all pyramid layers. In contrast, Drori et al. claimed that they needed 83 minutes for the inpainting in 2003. Even with the application of performance increase $\Theta \approx 10$, the algorithm of Drori would need more than 8 minutes on our test hardware today. In Table 4.3, a detailed performance comparison between our approach, Drori et al. and the approach of Xu et al. is given. It can be seen that our approach is more than 10,000 times faster than the algorithm of Xu et al. and more than 20,000 times faster than that of Drori et.al. Please note that Xu et al. did not provide a unique performance value for the *Elephant* image but provided a fillrate for a different image instead.

We found that the often used *Bungee* image is one of the most challenging images to provide a convenient quality comparison, as related approaches use individual image dimensions and inpainting masks. The final inpainting result depends significantly on the image quality and the applied inpainting mask. In Figure 4.43, we compare our result to four other approaches. Criminisi et al. [25] needed 18 seconds in 2004 (equivalent to about 2.5 seconds on our i7 CPU with a correction factor $\Theta = 7.2$) for an image

4.9 Results

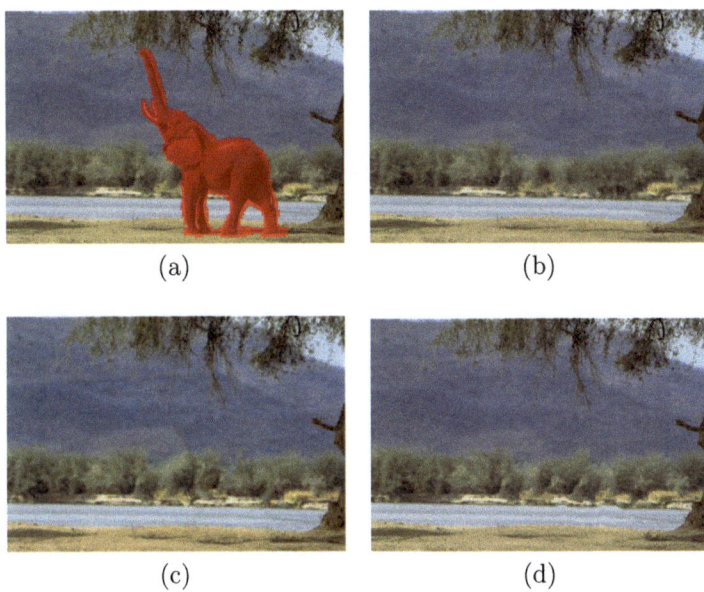

Figure 4.42: *Elephant* image from Drori et al. [30] compared using two related approaches: a) Original image with inpainting mask b) result by Drori et al. [30] c) result by Xu et al. [106] d) our result. The reference images have been taken from [106], kindly authorized by Drori and Xu, ©2010 IEEE

Table 4.3: Performance comparison for the *Elephant* image from Figure 4.42 with resolution 384 × 256. The inpainting mask has 13,048 pixels and thus covers about 13.3 % of the original image.

	Our approach with i7 X940	Drori et al. 2003 [30] original in 2003	Drori et al. 2003 [30] on i7 X940 (with Θ = 10)	Xu et al. 2010 [106]
Total	16.5 ms	83 min	$\approx$ 8 min 18 s	
Fillrate	790.8 px/ms	$2.6 \cdot 10^{-3}$ px/ms	$\approx 2.6 \cdot 10^{-2}$ px/ms	$\approx 5.2 \cdot 10^{-2}$ px/ms
Speedup	1	> 300,000	> 30,000	> 15,000

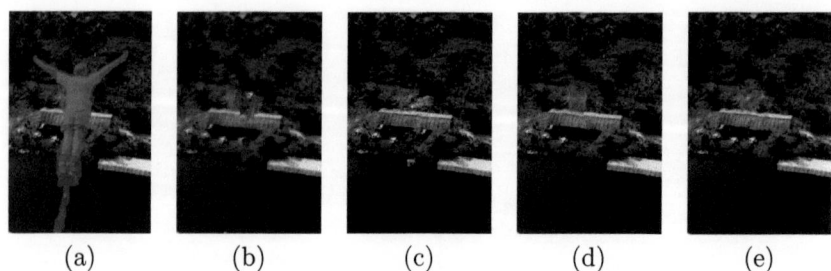

(a) (b) (c) (d) (e)

Figure 4.43: Result comparison for the *Bungee* image using four different approaches. a) Original image with inpainting mask (notice that the mask does not cover the small gray area behind the man's chest) b) result by Criminisi et al. [25] c) result by Shen et al. [85] d) result by Kwok et al. [65] e) our result. The reference images have been taken from [25], [85] and [65], kindly authorized by the authors. ©2004 - 2010 IEEE.

Table 4.4: Performance comparison for the *Bungee* image from Figure 4.43 with resolution 186 × 279. The inpainting mask has 6,747 pixels and thus covers about 13.0% of the original image.

	Our approach with i7 X940	Criminisi 2004 [25] on i7 X940 (with Θ = 7.2)	Shen 2007 [85][1] on i7 X940 (with Θ = 2.7)	Kwok 2010 [65][2]
Total	21.5 ms	≈ 2.5 s	≈ 24.0 s	0.9 s
Fillrate	313.8 px/ms	≈ 2.7 px/ms	≈ 0.3 px/ms	7.5 px/ms
Speedup	1	> 100	>[1] 900	>[2] 40

[1] with image size 206 × 308 and 7,997 inpainting pixels
[2] with a GPU implementation

with size of 186 × 279 and 6,747 inpainting pixels. Shen et al. [85] used a benchmark image with slightly different dimensions and created the final result within 64.8 seconds in 2007 (24 seconds on our i7 with a Θ = 2.7). The GPU implementation of Kwok et al. [65] is significantly faster, needing only about 0.9 seconds for the image inpainting. Our approach needed 21.5 ms, while providing equal or even better image quality than all other approaches. Thus, our approach is more than 100 times faster than the fastest CPU implementation and still more than 40 times faster than the Kwok's GPU implementation. In Table 4.4, an performance overview is provided for our and the related approaches. In Appendix A.4, a further comparison for the *Bungee* image is provided.

4.9 Results

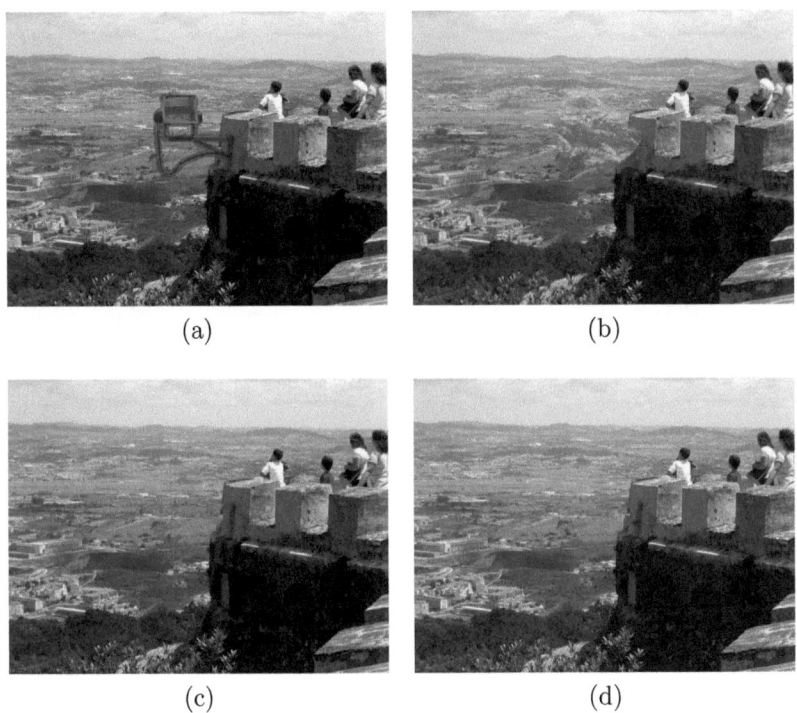

Figure 4.44: Result comparison for the *Outlook* image introduced by Hays et al. a) Original image with inpainting mask b) result by Hays et al. c) result by Bugeau et al. d) our result. The images are taken from [21] ©2010 IEEE and [39] ©2007 ACM, kindly authorized by the authors.

Table 4.5: Performance comparison for the *Outlook* image from Figure 4.44 with resolution 750 × 563. The inpainting mask has 11,668 pixels and thus covers about 2.8 % of the original image.

	Our approach with i7 X940	Bugeau et al. 2010 [21] slow[1]	fast[2]
Total	21.1 ms	25 min	15 min
Fillrate	553.0 px/ms	$7.8 \cdot 10^{-3}$ px/ms	$1.3 \cdot 10^{-2}$ px/ms
Speedup factor	1	> 70,000	> 40,000

[1] with coherence transport diffusion
[2] with Laplacian diffusion

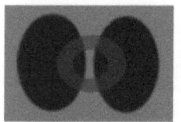 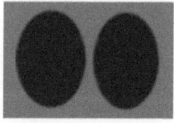   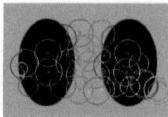

(a) Bertalmio et al. provides blurred regions at the synthesized blob boundaries.

(b) The result by Drori et al. seems to be convincing although the result has not been provided without sampling information.

 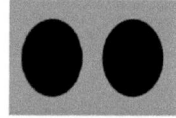    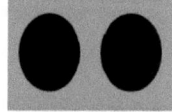

(c) The result by Criminisi et al. shows tiny edges.

(d) Xu et al.'s result shows small convexities.

Figure 4.45: Result comparison for the *Blobs* image. The individual inpainting masks (left) are depicted with their individual inpainting results (right). The images are taken from [13] ©2000 ACM, [30], ©2003 ACM, [25] ©2004 IEEE and [106] ©2010 IEEE, kindly authorized by the authors.

In Figure 4.44, a comparison between our approach and that of Bugeau et al. [21] is presented for the *Outlook* image. Our approach needs 21.1 ms. The approach of Bugeau needed between 15 and 25 minutes in 2010 (see Table 4.5). Although our approach is more than 40,000 times faster than that of Bugeau, a significant difference between the results is not observable. Figure 4.44 further shows the result of Hays et al. creating the image by an image database with more than one million images. The process needed about one hour to find the best matching image content from the database. It has to be mentioned here that Hays et al. presented this test image as failing for their algorithm.

The inpainting result for an artificial picture is given in Figure 4.45 and 4.46. Although, the blobs seem to be a simple inpainting benchmark image, the regular shape of the blobs directly reveals even tiny inpainting errors. A unique comparison between our inpainting approach and all related approaches cannot be given as all related approaches use their own inpainting images and own inpainting masks. However, the individual images are almost similar which allows a basic impression of the algorithmic performance and the resulting image quality to be determined. The Figures 4.45 and 4.46

4.9 Results

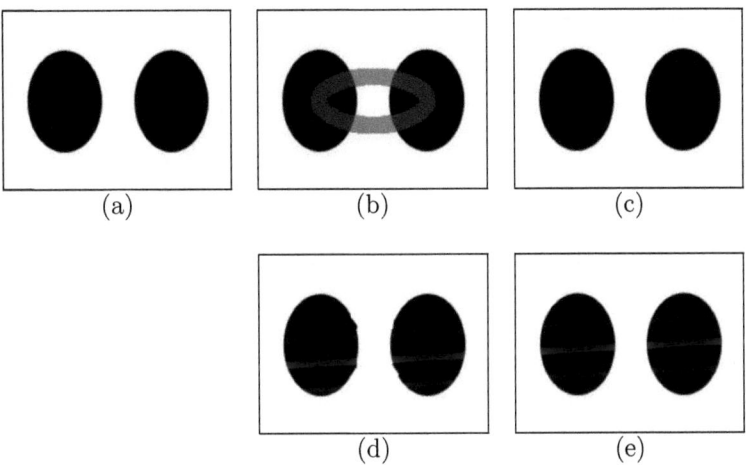

Figure 4.46: Result comparison for the *Blobs* image of Kwok et al. a) Original image b) original image with inpainting mask c) the almost perfect visual result by Kwok et al. d) our approach with randomized patch initialization, e) our approach with brute-force patch initialization. The images are taken from [65] ©2010 IEEE, kindly authorized by the author.

Table 4.6: Performance comparison for the *Blobs* image from Figure 4.45 with resolution 326 × 243. The inpainting mask has 10,474 pixels and thus covers about 13.2 % of the original image.

	Our approach		Kwok et al.	Xu et al.
	heuristic[1]	deterministic[2]	2010 [65]	2010 [106]
Total	36.8 ms	161.1 ms	1.8 s	
Fillrate	284.6 px/ms	65.0 px/ms	5.8 px/ms	≈ $5.2 \cdot 10^{-2}$ px/ms
Speedup	1	> 4	>[3] 50	> 5,000

[1] with heuristic patch initialization
[2] with deterministic patch initialization
[3] with a GPU implementation, (0.67 s for a resolution of 200 × 150 pixels)

show that the approach of Bertalmio et al. [13], and the approach of Xu et al. [106] provides tiny but noticeable blurring effects or convexities. Our approach using the fast randomized patch initialization method (Figure 4.46c) also does not produce a convincing result. However, the slower but accurate deterministic execution mode of the patch initialization strategy (see Table 4.1) allows the creation of an absolute perfect inpainting result

(a) (b) (c) (d) (e)

Figure 4.47: Result comparison for the *Sign* image. a) Original image with inpainting mask as used in the approach by Criminisi et al. b) result by Criminisi et al. c) original image with inpainting mask as used in the approach by Pritch et al. d) result by Pritch et al. e) our result (applying the mask of Pritch et al.). The images are taken from [25] ©2004 IEEE and [81] ©2009 IEEE, kindly authorized by the authors.

(Figure 4.46d). In Table 4.6, the performance values of our and related approaches are presented.

An inpainting image with a straight and clearly defined edge is depicted in Figure 4.47. Our inpainting approach provides the resulting synthesized image after 10.1 ms. Unfortunately, none of the related works cited provide performance values for this image. Pritch et al. only claim that the algorithm needs between 0.5 and 30 seconds. Our result as depicted in Figure 4.47e reliably recovers the stick of the sign. In Table 4.8, the detailed performance values for our recent approach are given.

In Figure 4.48, a benchmark image used by Criminisi et al. [25] and Kwok et al. [65] is depicted. This is the largest image (with the largest inpainting mask) that has been inpainted by Kwok. The performance comparison in Table 4.7 shows that the speedup factor of our approach compared to the algorithm of Kwok et al. gets larger with an increasing number of inpainting pixels (see also Table 4.4 and 4.6). Kwok et.al. apply a discrete cosine transformation (DCT) to reduce the data amount. The result shows undesired pixel blocks, well-known with image compression algorithms applying a DCT (see Figure 4.48c). Unfortunately, Criminisi et al. do not provide any performance measurements for this benchmark image.

4.9 Results

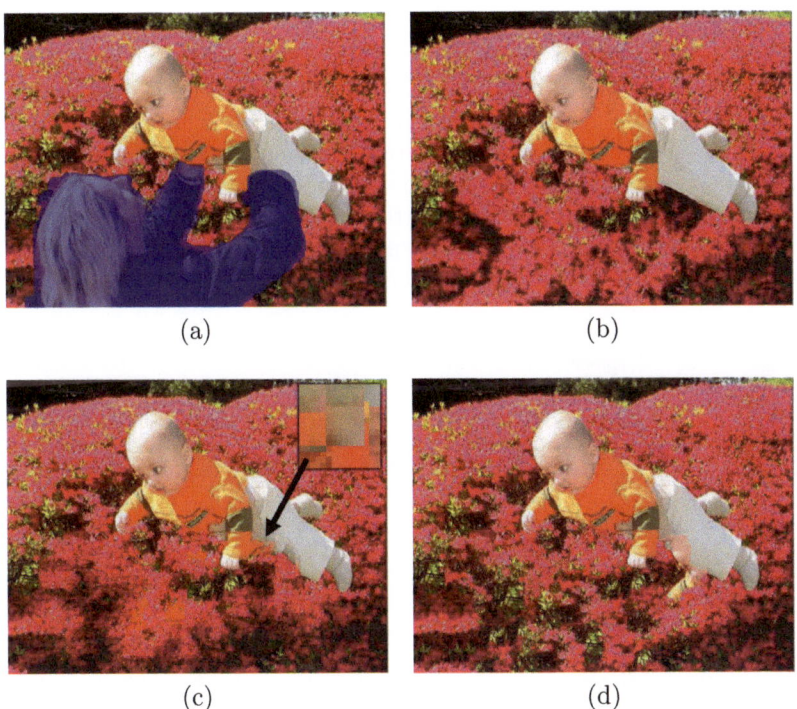

Figure 4.48: Result comparison for the *Baby* image. a) Original image with inpainting mask, b) result by Criminisi et al. [25] (with slightly different inpainting mask), c) result by Kwok et al. [65], d) our result. The images are taken from [25] ©2004 IEEE and [65] ©2010 IEEE, kindly authorized by the authors.

Table 4.7: Performance comparison for the *Baby* image (Figure 4.48) with resolution 538 × 403. The inpainting mask has 58,573 pixels and thus covers about 27.2 % of the original image.

	Our approach	Kwok et al. 2010 [65]
Total	27.0 ms	11.56 s
Fillrate	2,169.4 px/ms	5.1 px/ms
Speedup factor	1	>[1] 400

[1] with a GPU implementation

Traditionally, benchmark images for image inpainting are very small due to the low performance of related image manipulation approaches. Most pictures are even smaller than a VGA resolution. Figures 4.49 and 4.23 explicitly provide image inpainting results for significantly larger image dimensions. The *Wall* picture has a resolution of more than 7 megapixels, more than 1 megapixels are inpainted. Our approach needs less than half a second to provide the final inpainting result. Table 4.8 shows that the patch initialization strategy has a minor impact on the overall execution time as the initialization is only applied on the coarsest pyramid layer.

(a) Original image with inpainting mask.   (b) Resulting inpainting image.

Figure 4.49: Inpainting result for the *Wall* image with 3416 × 2237 pixels and almost 1,000,000 inpainting pixels. ©2012 Paul Träger kindly authorized by the author.

4.9 Results

Table 4.8: Detailed performance values of our image inpainting approach for individual inpainting benchmark images.

Image	Resolution	Mask size	Pyramid	Initial-ization	Refine-ment	Overall fillrate
Ruin (4.23)	2736×3648	3,110,235 px; 31.2 %	54.5 ms	7.8 ms	1,396.3 ms	2,227 px/ms
Elephant (4.42)	384×256	13,048 px; 13.3 %	1.5 ms	6.2 ms	8.8 ms	790 px/ms
Bungee (4.43)	186×279	6,747 px; 13.0 %	1.9 ms	14.1 ms	5.5 ms	313 px/ms
Outlook (4.44)	750×563	11,668 px; 2.8 %	2.2 ms	5.4 ms	13.5 ms	553 px/ms
Blobs[1] (4.45)	326×243	10,474 px; 13.2 %	1.1 ms	23.9 ms	11.8 ms	284 px/ms
Blobs[2] (4.45)	326×243	10,474 px; 13.2 %	1.1 ms	151.7 ms	8.3 ms	65 px/ms
Sign (4.47)	87×169	2,444 px; 16.6 %	0.5 ms	6.6 ms	3.0 ms	242 px/ms
Baby (4.48)	538×403	58,573 px; 27.0 %	1.4 ms	3.6 ms	22.0 ms	2,169 px/ms
Wall (4.49)	3416×2237	997,852 px; 13.1 %	30.6 ms	8.6 ms	367.9 ms	2,451 px/ms
Window (A.11)	473×334	7,017 px; 4.4 %	1.7 ms	9.1 ms	8.2 ms	369 px/ms
Wood (A.12)	192×128	4,608 px; 18.8 %	0.7 ms	5.4 ms	10.3 ms	281 px/ms

[1] with heuristic patch initialization
[2] with deterministic patch initialization

A large amount of pixels have been inpainted in the *Ruin* picture (Figure 4.23a-c). The inpainting algorithm as developed in this work synthesizes more than 3 megapixels (more than 30 % of the entire image information) within 1.5 seconds. Thus, more than 2,000 pixels are synthesized within one millisecond. By comparison, the recently developed method of Bugeau et al. [21] is able to inpaint about 10,000 pixels within 15 minutes. Even the GPU implementation of Kwok et al. [65] would need more than one minute for the inpainting, since our CPU implementation is estimated to be more than 50 times faster than their GPU implementation.

In Appendix A.4, more image results are discussed showing that our approach provides similar image quality compared to other inpainting approaches.

4.10 Limitations

The static image inpainting approach presented in Chapter 4 is able to create a high image quality for several benchmark images. In Subsection 4.9, a wide variety of test images have been presented and compared with the results of state-of-the-art approaches.

Nevertheless, the inpainting algorithm may still be improved. In specific situations, the final image result is not able to fool observes at all. In the following, the major issues limiting our static inpainting approach will be discussed.

4.10.1 Pixel-based Inpainting of Homogenous Content

The image inpainting approach as developed in this work uses single pixels as the inpainting unit and does not interpolate or blend between neighboring pixels. This allows us to create a high quality result in real-time without blurring artifacts. However, the final inpainting result may show minor visual borders between joined pixel regions if the remaining image content is almost homogenous with a smooth color gradient distributed over the entire image region. For example, in Figure 4.50, four inpainting results are provided. Two inpainting images are used. One image has a smooth diagonal gradient, the other has a smooth horizontal gradient. Both images are inpainted with two individual inpainting masks; a small mask, and a large mask covering almost half the gradient image. The small inpainting mask provides a sufficient inpainting result for the diagonal gradient image as well as for the horizontal gradient image. The large inpainting mask

4.10 Limitations

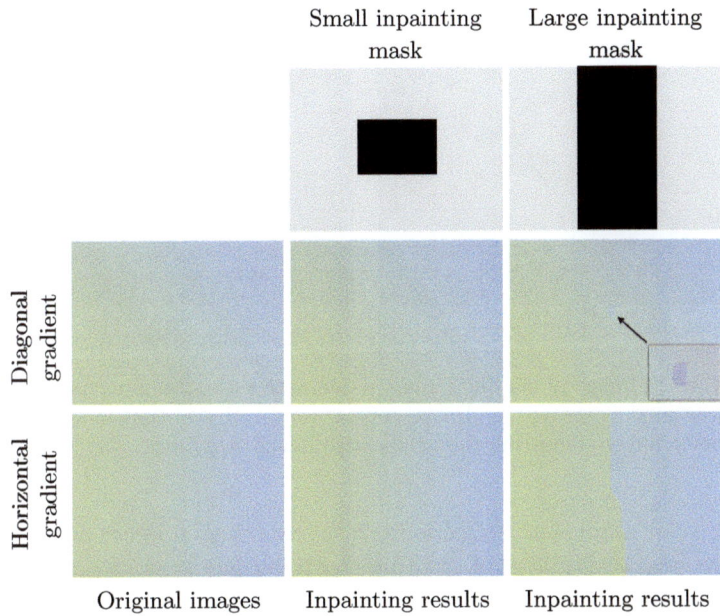

Figure 4.50: Pixel-based image inpainting with a soft color gradient background. An image with a horizontal and a diagonal gradient is inpainted with two individual inpainting masks. The small inpainting mask provides enough remaining image content to allow a convincing gradient image to be reconstructed. However, the algorithm fails to synthesize a sufficient result for the large inpainting mask as a significant amount of visual gradient information is missing.

covers the entire image content with intermediate gradient color, so the pixel-based inpainting approach fails to recover a smooth gradient image. Therefore, neither the pixel-based approach of Demanet et al. [29] nor the algorithms of Pritch et al. [81] or Bugeau et al. [21] are able to provide a convincing inpainting result.

Even patch-based algorithms like that of Criminisi et al. [25] or Barnes et al. [8] (creating synthesized images by blending image patches) cannot provide a sufficient image quality as those approaches are mainly driven by exemplary based inpainting algorithms. Image information that does not exist in the remaining image content cannot be reconstructed during the inpainting process. The blending of image patches commonly creates (at least slightly) blurred image results that are more suited for images with

Figure 4.51: Image inpainting in an environment with strong perspective distortion. a) original image with undesired content (drain) b) real-time image inpainting result not reliably recovering the perspective image structure

smooth color gradients. In Section 6.2, future research issues are discussed to overcome the problem of creating sharp borders in homogenous image regions.

4.10.2 Perspective Image Inpainting

Similar to almost all related non-real-time capable approaches, our (real-time capable) approach also fails to reliably recover perspective image fragments. Figure 4.51 shows an example of a perspective image inpainting. A comparison between perspective and non-perspective image inpainting for an artificial image is given in Figure 4.52. The inpainting result for the non-perspective image is perfect. Contrarily, the result for the perspective inpainting image shows undesired artifacts.

The application of a warping-free neighborhood during the determination of appearance cost in Section 4.2 allows the image inpainting approach to be able to handle perspective distortion up to a specific degree. As the approach developed in this work targets real-time application, an advanced (perspectively transformed) neighborhood that still performs fast enough cannot be considered using current computer hardware. In Section 6.2, several future research aspects with regard to the current image inpainting algorithm will be discussed, eventually allowing for image inpainting of e.g., images with perspective complexity.

4.11 Discussion

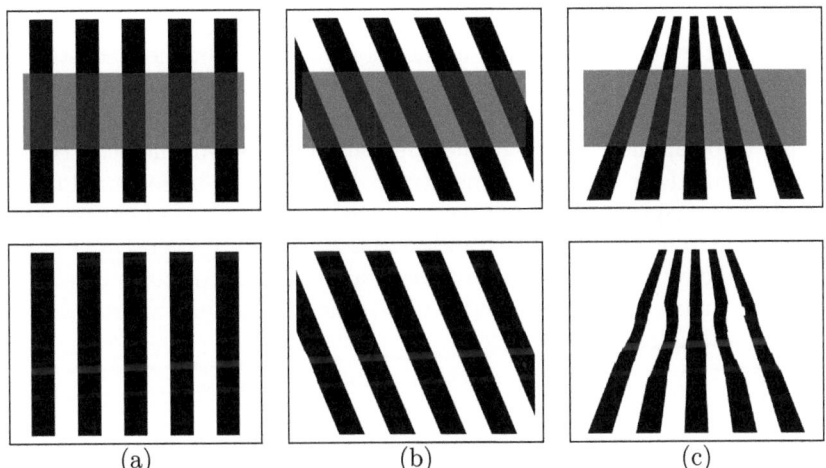

Figure 4.52: Inpainting of an individually transformed artificial image. Top row: original images with identical inpainting mask, bottom row: inpainting results. a) no transformation, b) rotational transformation, c) perspective transformation.

4.11 Discussion

In this chapter, the static inpainting algorithm of our work has been introduced. Detailed performance values and a comparison regarding the image quality have been provided, and the limitations of our approach have been discussed.

As shown in Section 4.9 and also in Appendix A.4, our image manipulation approach, using only the CPU, creates final image results comparable to all state-of-the-art approaches introduced in Section 2.1 and does so between two and four magnitudes faster. The manipulation of images with inpainting masks larger than 10,000 pixels show especially significant performance differences. Only the GPU implementation of Kwok et al. [65], applying a data reduction by application of a DCT, approaches the performance of our approach, and even this is between one and three magnitudes slower than our method. However, the larger the images to be manipulated, the slower the approach of Kwok 2010 et al. and the image quality does not reach the inpainting results of other state-of-the-art approaches, as the DCT causes undesired pixel blocks.

The inpainting approach of Sun et al. [93] seems to provide slightly better image quality than our preprocessing-free approach. However, their algorithm is based on explicit user-defined constraints describing important visual structure information and it does not work without these constraints since simple texture synthesis algorithms for inpainting of textured image content are applied. Our image manipulation approach has to be fast enough to be applied in a real-time application, so user-defined constraints cannot be used for live video inpainting. As developed in Section 4.6, our pixel mapping approach also allows for seamless integration of explicit user-defined constraints. These constraints violate the real-time constraint of our objective, however, comparable to Sun et al., constrained image inpainting allows for manipulation of images with salient structure information as depicted in Figure 4.27 and A.20.

5 Video Inpainting

In this chapter, the real-time video inpainting approach presented in Subsection 3.2 is introduced.

The video inpainting algorithm combines continuous image inpainting iterations with a reference model to provide a coherent video stream. An image inpainting process is applied to each video frame to create high quality image results. Similar to image warping strategies used in several previous video manipulation approaches, the reference model guides the inpainting algorithm, creating a visual stream with high coherence accuracy. The combination of image inpainting and image warping has not been applied in any of the related approaches introduced in Subsection 2.2. No previous approach exists that is able to use either of both strategies in real-time. However, in this work, continuous image inpainting is combined with a reference model and processed in real-time. The derived image inpainting approach is fast enough to be able to be applied to each video frame. Therefore, our approach provides an accurate video coherence while creating better image quality than related approaches.

However, live video inpainting cannot be accomplished solely just by using a visual manipulation algorithm. Object selection and the tracking approach are just as important as the image manipulation itself. The more accurate and reliable a previously unknown object can be tracked in an unknown environment, the better the final overall results of the video inpainting approach. Like the synthesis algorithm, the selection and tracking technique also has to be real-time capable to allow manipulation of a live video transmission.

The video inpainting pipeline has to provide a coherent video stream without visual artifacts or undesired blurring for homogenous as well as for heterogeneous backgrounds. An almost homogenous background allows the simplified creation of a coherent video stream, while the creation of a coherent video stream in heterogeneous environments is more sensitive to visual errors.

A homogenous background further allows simpler segmentation between the desired and undesired video content and thus faster object tracking. However, detection of camera movement in homogenous environments is more difficult and error prone than in heterogeneous environments. This is because homogenous backgrounds do not provide enough visual features that can be reliably tracked, e.g., Harris Corners [38], FAST [82], SIFT [72] or SURF features [10]. Feature detectors cannot be applied to determine camera motions in an arbitrary video stream. A heterogeneous video stream allows simpler and more precise detection of camera motion, but the synthesis of visual content is more challenging. A homogenous video stream allows simpler creation of the visual content, while the detection of camera motion is more complex. In the following sections, a real-time solution will be introduced allowing tracking of an undesired object in almost any unknown environment.

Our approach to real-time object selection is introduced in Section 5.1. In 5.2, the object tracking algorithm providing the basis for real-time video inpainting of complex objects with homogenous and heterogeneous backgrounds will be discussed. In Section 5.3, the propagation of the transformation function f is introduced for two successive video frames. Section 5.4 describes the entire video inpainting pipeline. The creation of a reference model for video stream coherence is introduced in Section 5.5. Section 5.6 discusses an additional appearance cost measure allowing visual results to be partially guided by the reference model, ensuring a coherent video stream. The results of our video inpainting approach are presented in Section 5.7. Performance issues and visual quality as well as an extensive user study will be discussed in that section. Limitations and restrictions of the video inpainting pipeline will be presented in Section 5.8. In Section 5.9, we conclude with a discussion summarizing our approach for video inpainting.

5.1 Object Selection

Interactive object selection for static image inpainting is a rather trivial task. The synthesis mask can be defined by the user applying common selection techniques such as polygon or lasso tools. The closer and the more accurate the object to be removed is selected (including e.g., areas shadowed by the object), the better the final synthesis result. Object selection and image segmentation for static frames has been the focus of research for several decades. The most sophisticated approaches include combinations of graph, mean shift, scribble and painting based techniques as in the work of Ning et al. [76], Rother et al. [83], Li et al. [70], Levin et al. [68], and Arbelez et al. [1] or the progressive paint selection of Liu et al. [71]. Although segmentation results for arbitrary objects may achieve high accuracy, these approaches do

5.1 Object Selection

not provide real-time performance. The majority of approaches need at least several seconds for processing of each single frame. Further, these approaches often require several iterative adjustments by the user and never include image areas shadowed by the objects to be removed. Existing selection and segmentation approaches for video streams are even slower, i.e. the approaches of Tong et al. [96] or Bai et al. [6].

In our previous work [40], a simple active contour algorithm [56] has been applied to detect and track objects exhibiting a noticeable boundary with almost homogenous backgrounds. This approach allowed users to roughly select previously unknown objects and track them during successive video frames. Although our previous approach benefits from improved usability as well as better selection and tracking performance, the boundary constraint and the necessary homogenous background limits the number of areas of application. Typically, the background of an undesired object is not homogenous and does not provide a uniquely visible boundary. Our previous object selection and tracking approach failed in such environments.

Therefore, we now combine the rather rough selection technique of our previous approach with a more complex segmentation approach allowing non homogenous backgrounds and blurred object contours. As state-of-the-art segmentation approaches are not yet real-time capable, we developed a new algorithm based on the following three assumptions:

- Objects to be removed are entirely visible in the video frame and do not intersect with the frame boundaries in successive frames.

- The image area to be removed is directly enclosed by image content apparently different from the undesired area.

- The enclosed image content itself may be textured and may change along the object boundary.

In Figure 5.1, it can be seen that these three conditions hold for several individual environments. The figure also shows that image areas covered by the direct neighborhood of the rough user selection are visually different from the content of objects to be selected. The approach is designed to detect image content visually not matching the characteristics of the rough user selection.

Figure 5.1: Real-time selection results for our fingerprint segmentation approach for individual objects and backgrounds. Top row: original with rough user-defined selection, Bottom row: selection result. a) object with a noisy background b) object with a large shadow and a homogenous background c) two-colored object and an almost homogenous but two-colored background d) three background regions e) highly but regularly textured background f) tree with frayed borders g) non-homogenous object h) highly individually textured background.

In detail, the selection approach is based on several fingerprints $U = \{U_{p_1}, U_{p_2}, \ldots, U_{p_n}\}$ storing the appearance of the frame at n equally distributed positions $p_1, p_2, \ldots, p_n$ spread on the roughly defined object contour. Each fingerprint U_{p_i} is determined by a function $\phi(p_i) : I \to \mathbb{Q}^m$ defining the most important visual characteristics of a point $p_i \in I$. A fingerprint U_{p_i} is composed of m individual components defining disjoint fingerprint characteristics:

$$U_{p_i} = \{u_1, u_2, \ldots, u_m\} \tag{5.1}$$

5.1 Object Selection

The n fingerprints are compared to the entire image content inside the rough user-defined contour and tested for similarity. A dissimilarity map M_D is determined separating roughly selected content into desired and undesired elements. The binary dissimilarity map M_D is calculated for each pixel p inside the rough contour by:

$$M_D(p) = \begin{cases} 1, & \sum_{k=1}^{|U|} d_\phi(\phi(p), U_k) \geq |U| \cdot \gamma \\ 0, & \text{else} \end{cases} \quad (5.2)$$

where γ defines the amount of fingerprint dissimilarities necessary to consider the pixel p undesired, and d_ϕ measures the dissimilarity between two fingerprints U_k and U_j by

$$d_\phi(U_k, U_j) = \begin{cases} 0, & \tilde{d}_\phi(u_{k_i}, u_{j_i}) \leq v_i, \quad u_{k_i} \in U_k, u_{j_i} \in U_j, \\ & \quad v_i \in V, \forall i \in [1, m] \\ 1, & \text{else} \end{cases} \quad (5.3)$$

while $\tilde{d}_\phi$ measures the component-wise distance between the corresponding components of two individual fingerprints. The distances are rated according to reference thresholds $v_i \in V = \{v_1, v_2, \ldots, v_m\}$.

The cost measure $\tilde{d}_\phi$ is defined as the one dimensional Euclidean distance:

$$\tilde{d}_\phi(u_{k_i}, u_{j_i}) = |u_{k_i} - u_{j_i}| \quad (5.4)$$

while the corresponding thresholds v_i are adapted to the deviation of U. Instead of using the entire deviation of all fingerprints U, we separate U into b disjoint fingerprint clusters:

$$C = \{C_1, C_2, \ldots C_b\} \quad (5.5)$$

with

$$C_1 \cup C_2 \cup \ldots \cup C_b = U \quad \wedge \quad C_i \cap C_j = \emptyset, \quad \forall i, j \in [1, b] : i \neq j \quad (5.6)$$

with $b \ll n$. Thus, C is the set of fingerprint clusters.

The maximal deviation from all b clusters is taken as a reference threshold. Thus, each $v_i \in V$ is calculated by:

$$v_i = \max_{j \in [1,b]} \sqrt{\mathbb{E}\left[C_j{}^2\right] - (\mathbb{E}\left[C_j\right])^2} \quad (5.7)$$

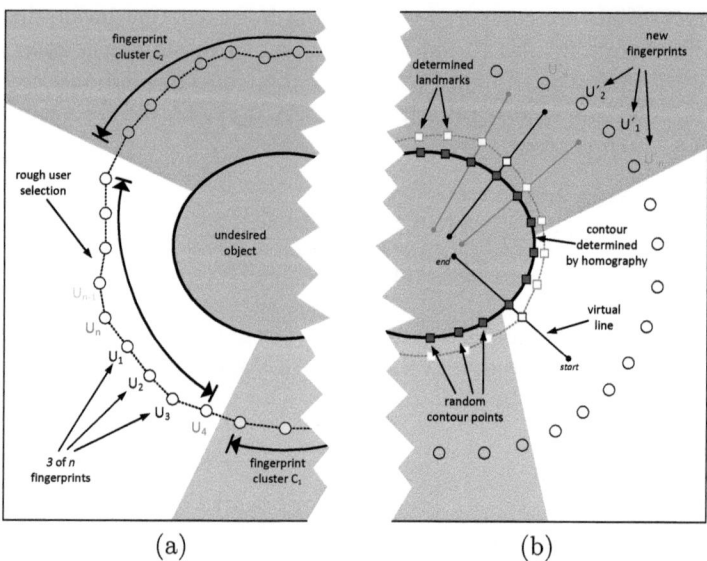

Figure 5.2: Object selection and tracking scheme. a) Object segmentation by the application of fingerprints distributed along the rough user-defined selection. Fingerprints are clustered into disjoint sets. b) Adjustment of the contour by homography - solid (red) squares: randomly selected contour points with perpendicular virtual lines; white squares: resulting landmarks; dashed (blue) line: resulting accurate and final contour.

Without clustering, application of the deviation would be useless for background images represented by more than one visual characteristic. Figure 5.2a depicts a selection situation with individual background areas illustrating the necessity of data clustering.

Cluster calculation has to be investigated. A wide variety of clustering algorithms exist providing individual clustering accuracies and run-time complexities as hierarchical, k-means, or distribution-based clustering approaches. In view of the real-time requirement, we decided to apply a very simple but (for our needs) adequate clustering algorithm:

1. One fingerprint is randomly selected and defined as the center of the first cluster.

2. Remaining fingerprints are assigned to the new cluster if their distance is close enough to the cluster's center.

5.1 Object Selection

3. If there are still fingerprints left, again, one of the remaining objects is randomly selected, taken as the center of a new cluster and the algorithm is restarted with 2).

This algorithm is repeated several times and the clustering result with lowest maximal deviation within all clusters is finally accepted. The clustering method is very efficient, we found the result accurate enough for our needs. For about 200 fingerprints we measured a clustering performance of less than one millisecond on our evaluation hardware. Another benefit is that the number of clusters does not have to be defined in advance such as the case with, e.g., k-means algorithms. The more variations within the fingerprints, the higher the number of final clusters. Rough user-defined selection in Figure 5.1a produced one fingerprint cluster, while selection in 5.1h) ended with 17 clusters.

We defined $\gamma = 0.95$ to detect undesired pixels if at least 95 % of the fingerprints reject the corresponding pixel. As data base, we use the color image with three channels. Several individual fingerprint functions $\phi(\cdot)$ have been evaluated, we found that a simple Gaussian filter with large kernels provides sufficient results. For performance reasons, however, we apply a modified mean filter with one large and one small kernel in combination with an integral image. This optimized mean filter only needs eight integral image lookups and performs much faster than a Gaussian filter while providing sufficient results.

The entire fingerprint segmentation is combined with a multiresolution approach reducing computational effort. The approach starts on the coarsest image resolution and forwards the result to the next finer layer. On this layer, only border pixels are investigated according to their fingerprint dissimilarity. Next, a dilation filter is applied to the dissimilarity map M_D to remove possible tiny gaps. All pixels considered undesired build the binary synthesis mask M as introduced in Subsection 4.19. A corresponding synthesis contour directly enclosing this mask is determined and used afterwards in the tracking process.

In Subsection 5.7.1, we provide performance results showing segmentation and tracking time in detail. Dependent on the available processing time, performance and accuracy of the approach can be tailored easily by adding or removing contour fingerprints or visual characteristics u_i (e.g., color and texture channels). The more information used to determine dissimilarities, the better the selection result.

We found that the application of fingerprints with three elements, one for each image color channel, is a good compromise between segmentation accuracy and application speed. However, if accuracy is more important than computational time or if computational hardware is powerful enough, we use a fourth fingerprint element by default. The fourth fingerprint element represents a simple texture property determined by averaging the Scharr [84] response for grayscale image information.

5.2 Object Tracking

Once found, the determined object contour has to be tracked in successive video frames. Recent approaches able to track almost arbitrary objects are inspired by mean shift approaches like that of Comaniciu et al. [23]. Although mean shift algorithms can be applied for interactive frame rates, the approaches only provide a rough guess of the tracking object. The image manipulation approach needs by far the most computational time in the entire video inpainting pipeline (between 10 ms and 50 ms - see Subsection 5.7.1 for a detailed performance analysis). An application of a mean shift algorithm would require additional time, further reducing the amount of time available for visual manipulation of the video stream. Therefore, a significantly faster approach for object tracking will be applied in this work.

Object tracking is realized by a two phase contour tracking approach. In the first phase, homography based contour tracking is used. In the second phase, the new contour is refined and adjusted with respect to the undesired object area. A sole contour tracking approach without the following refinement step would accumulate small drift errors over time.

In the first phase, a heterogeneous background will allow more reliable tracking than a homogenous background. In the second phase, a homogenous background will allow simpler and faster distinguishing between background and undesired object and vice versa. An environment that is ideal for both tracking phases obviously does not exist. However, a wide variety of environments is able to be handled by the tracking approach introduced below.

As defined in the objective in Subsection 1.1, our algorithm is designed for almost planar environments in the direct neighborhood of the undesired object. The remaining environment may be arbitrary and thus may be non-planar. In this work, an adaptive contour tracking has been realized applying three individual tracking sub-algorithms. A scheme of the tracker is depicted in Figure 5.3, showing the three sub-algorithms and their technical interactions.

5.2 Object Tracking

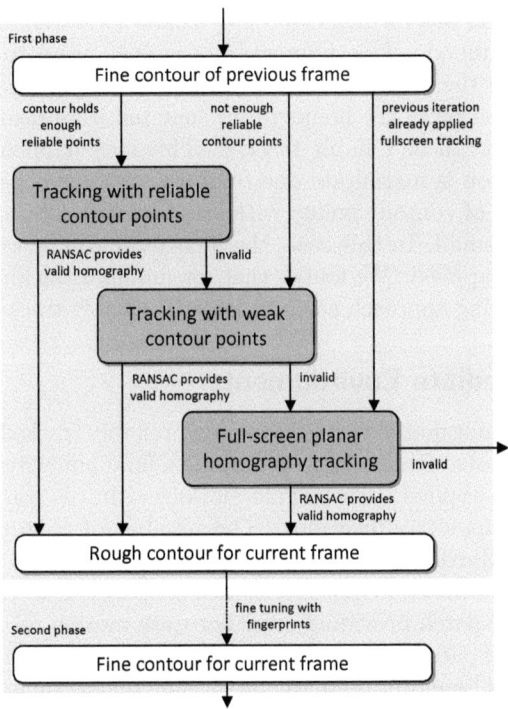

Figure 5.3: Contour tracking scheme showing the tracking (first) and refinement (second) phase. The first phase is composed of three sub-algorithms (blue) to determine a homography for a rough contour.

5.2.1 Heterogeneous Environments

Typically, an inpainting contour of an object to be removed with heterogeneous background can be reliably tracked by motion detection of the contour points. As these points are almost planar, the relation of a set of tracked contour points between two consecutive frames can be described by determination of a homography [94]. For cases with non-planar backgrounds, motion between two frames can be expected to be very small. Even for these cases, determining the homography may provide a good approximation of the contour's movement. For homography determination, only the strongest contour points are tracked between two video frames using pyramid based motion detection [11]. The response of a Harris corner filter [38] distinguishes between contour points with good and bad motion tracking properties. Within several RANSAC [36] iterations, a reliable homography H can be determined. This homography is then used to transform the contour points of the previous video frame to contour points of the current frame. Determination of the homography may fail if an insufficient number of contour points can be reliably tracked. This may happen if detection of the contour motion is inaccurate due to almost homogenous image content or if the number of contour points with strong votes determined by Harris detection is too small. In this case, the next least robust contour tracking sub-algorithm is applied. We found, that for minimal tracking performance, our contour tracking approach needs at least 15 reliably tracked image points.

5.2.2 Intermediate Environments

If the object contour does not provide enough reliably tracked contour points or if the first sub-algorithm fails to determine a final homography, the second sub-algorithm is applied. The second sub-algorithm is comparable to the first one with minor modifications. The number of contour points to be tracked and the Harris corner strength factor is weakened to receive a larger number of candidates for RANSAC iterations. Motion detection is applied to a larger image patch providing more accurate motion results. The larger the applied image patch, the lesser the probability for ambiguities of tracked contour points. Therefore, the patch area is increased by a factor of about 10 for this sub-algorithm allowing to achieve a significantly more reliable tracking result. The second sub-algorithm is slower than the first one as more processing time is necessary for motion detection, RANSAC execution and homography calculation.

5.2.3 Homogenous Environments

If neither the first nor the second sub-algorithm determines a valid homography, the background of the undesired object is expected to be almost homogenous and thus the contour's neighborhood cannot be used for contour tracking. As a fall back, the remaining image content may be expected to be almost homogenous, or at least almost planar. The third sub-algorithm uses the entire image information to provide a final tracking result. Scattered feature points with highest Harris votes are selected by separating the video frame into a virtual grid. All Harris corners are tracked by the same motion algorithm as already applied and a global homography H is determined and validated with RANSAC.

It should be mentioned that application of the third sub-algorithm (the fullscreen planar homography tracking) is a backup and thus used very seldom. However, it allows reliable tracking e.g., on single-colored backgrounds with bad lighting conditions, or other complex environments.

5.2.4 Contour Refinement

In the second phase for contour tracking we adjust the new contour positions (determined by homography) more precisely to the real contour of the object. To do this fingerprint dissimilarity is used again. This time, reference fingerprints are automatically defined outside the new contour (equally distributed) in the current frame. To ensure the required performance, contour adjustment is only performed for a randomly selected subset of the new contour points. For each random point, a virtual line perpendicular to the new contour starting outside and ending inside the new contour is defined. For each pixel covered by this virtual line, fingerprint dissimilarity is determined. To avoid the influence of fingerprints at the opposite side of the contour, only new fingerprints in the direct neighborhood are investigated. The first pixel on the virtual line identified as undesired and followed by at least two successive undesired pixels defines a contour landmark for the virtual line. Thus, the correct object contour is determined as single scattered undesired pixels are not considered as candidates for a contour landmark. All contour points extracted in the first tracking phase are adjusted according to contour landmarks in their neighborhood (see Figure 5.2b). The adjusted positions define the final and accurate contour.

5.2.5 Discussion

We wish to emphasize that the homography H is calculated in the first tracking phase. The final synthesis mask is determined in the second phase. The homography is based on strong correspondences between contour points, the mask is based on the actual object border. This separation is important as the homography determined will be used later to ensure visual coherence of subsequent frames for non-linear camera movements. In contrast to the active snake approach of our previous work [40], improved object tracking provides unique correspondences for contour points between successive video frames.

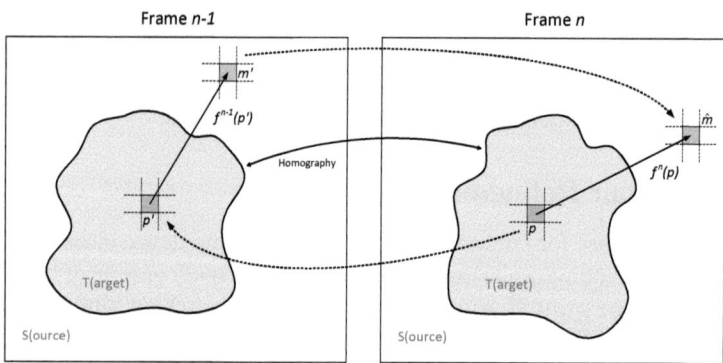

Figure 5.4: Mapping forwarding by application of the determined homography. The transformation function of the previous frame is represented by f^{n-1}, the new transformation function is denoted by f^n.

5.3 Mapping Propagation

In the case of a given mapping function for the previous synthesis frame, the number of optimization iterations for the new frame (to find a transformation function minimizing the cost measure as defined in 4.2) can be reduced by a factor of four. An initial mapping for each mask pixel is determined from the corresponding pixel in the previous image by application of the associated mapping. The already determined homography H is applied as depicted in Figure 5.4. An arbitrary mask pixel p in the frame n is translated to the corresponding pixel p' in the frame $n-1$ by application of the homography H determined between the frame $n-1$ and n by:

$$p' = Hp \qquad (5.8)$$

The previous mapping in frame $n-1$ at point p' is given by:

$$m' = f^{n-1}(p') \qquad (5.9)$$

with f^{n-1} representing the previously found mapping function. A sufficiently precise prediction of this mapping for the current frame n can be calculated by applying the inverse homography:

$$\hat{m} = H^{-1}m' \qquad (5.10)$$

The initial mapping prediction $\hat{m}$ of an arbitrary mask point p in frame n is approximated by:

$$\hat{m} = \hat{f}^n(p) = H^{-1}(f^{n-1}(Hp)) \quad (5.11)$$

Finally, in general, a guess of an initial transformation function $\hat{f}^n$ is defined by:

$$\hat{f}^n = H^{-1} f^{n-1} H \quad (5.12)$$

Please note that the application of the inverse homography H^{-1} usually will not result in precise mapping for the current frame. This is due to the determination of the homography from the object contour, only providing exact estimations for totally planar contours. Non-planar contours and environments will introduce a certain inaccuracy that depends on the volume and the size of the undesired object. However, as the change in content between two successive video frames is low, this inaccuracy is negligible. It will be adjusted in subsequent cost minimization iterations as described in Subsection 4.3.

5.4 Inpainting Pipeline

First, the user selects those image parts to be replaced. Based on this selection, a precise contour is calculated and a static image synthesis is invoked. The synthesized image is provided to the observer and stored as key frame I_K. For the following video frames, the homography and the contour are determined as described above. The key frame, the current binary synthesis mask M_n, and the calculated homography define a reference model I_R corresponding to the video frame I_n for the n-th video frame. Current frame pixels $p \in I_n$ are copied directly for all desired image regions with $M_n(p) = 1$, while undesired pixels with $M_n(p) = 0$ are replaced by interpolated information from the key frame I_K. This interpolation is defined by a concatenation of homographies $(\ldots \cdot H_{n-2} \cdot H_{n-1} \cdot H_n) = H_K$ determined since the key frame has been changed:

$$I_R(p) = \begin{cases} I_n(p), & M_n(p) = 1 \\ I_K(H_K \cdot p), & M_n(p) = 0 \end{cases}, \quad \forall p \in I \quad (5.13)$$

The reference model I_R will be slightly modified to compensate changing lighting conditions, however, the main pipeline stays the same. Additional modifications of the reference model will be described in detail in the next Subsection 5.5.

The synthesis module then replaces all undesired mask pixels p with $M_n(p) = 0$ of the current frame with pixels of the remaining image data creating a visual result almost identical to the given reference model I_R. As described for the static inpainting approach, a current mapping f is determined having minimal overall costs for the current frame. The mapping found for the previous frame is adjusted as the initial guess to improve quality and to speed up convergence (see the previous Subsection 5.3). In contrast to static image synthesis, the appearance costs are extended and additionally measured between the synthesis result and the reference model (see Subsection 5.6). This extension ensures that sufficient coherence between successive video frames will be exhibited. Synthesized image content is blended with the original frame at the synthesis border to avoid mask border effects like semi-sharp transitions. Bisectioning tests revealed that a blend border of 3 – 5 pixels is typically sufficient. Depending on the key frame's age, it might be replaced by the final synthesis result. The number of key frame replacements has to be carefully balanced to avoid visual drifts during synthesis. We apply a homography decomposition and replace the key frame any time the concatenated rotation extends an angle of 45 deg. Afterwards, the synthesis pipeline restarts with the new video frame.

5.5 Compensation of Ambient Lighting Changes

The reference model I_R is created by concatenated homographies as described in the previous subsection. However, the reference model as described above is not able to compensate changing lighting conditions as long as the key frame I_K stays untouched. To handle changing illumination conditions during the lifetime of a key frame, the reference model I_R needs an additional modification for each individual video frame.

Our approach allows for compensation of ambient lighting changes. Inpainting contour points $B = \{b_1, b_2, b_3, \ldots\}$ of the current frame are transformed to the corresponding points $B' = \{b'_1, b'_2, b'_3, \ldots\}$ in the key frame I_K by application of the gathered homographies. In Figure 5.5, the relationship between the corresponding contour points b_i and b'_i is depicted. For all pairs of contour points, the color differences $\Delta b_i = b_i - b'_i$ between the current frame and the key frame are stored individually for each image channel. A sparse virtual grid G is defined covering the entire inpainting mask of the current frame. The nodes of the grid $G = \{g_1, g_2, g_3, \ldots\}$ receive approximated color

5.5 Compensation of Ambient Lighting Changes

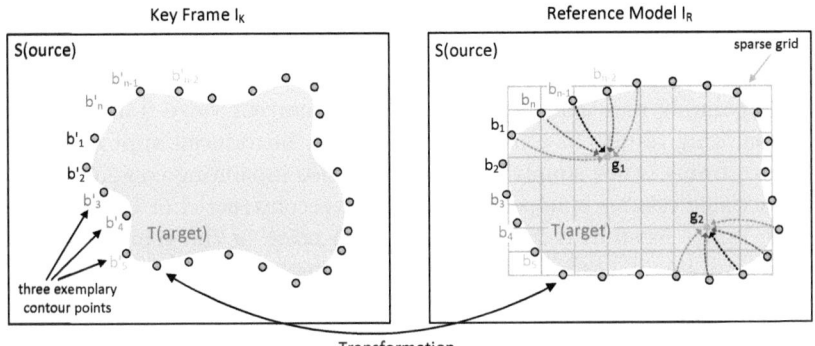

Figure 5.5: Lighting compensation between the key frame I_K and the reference frame I_R. The sparse grid receives the approximated correction values Δb_i by an interpolation. The interpolation is depicted for two exemplary grid points g_1 and g_2. Afterwards, the individual gird nodes are used to modify the reference frame I_R by a bi-linear interpolation of the grid values.

corrections by interpolation of the gathered contour differences Δb_i. Thus, for a grid node $g_i \in G$ the approximated color correction $\mu(g_i)$ is determined by

$$\mu(g_i) = \frac{1}{\theta(g_i)} \sum_{k=1}^{|B|} (b_k - b'_k) \cdot e^{-\sqrt{|g_i - b_k|}} \tag{5.14}$$

while $\theta(g_i)$ represents a simple normalization factor:

$$\theta(g_i) = \sum_{k=1}^{|B|} e^{-\sqrt{|g_i - b_k|}} \tag{5.15}$$

The virtual grid G is then used to correct the reference frame I_R according to the illumination changes between the current and key frame. Each image pixel p that has been interpolated from the key frame is corrected by a bi-linear interpolation of the four nearest grid nodes. An application of the Poisson equation [79] may provide more accurate results than the proposed approximation. However, we found that the interpolation allows for compensating the most important lighting changes while processing in less than 1 ms, which is several magnitudes faster than, e.g., a Poisson related approach.

Application of the reference frame is comparable to image warping algorithms of related video inpainting approaches as introduced in Subsection 2.2. However, our reference frame is used only for coherence guiding as the video inpainting uses image information of the current video frame to create the inpainting result. In contrast to previously introduced approaches, the reference frame is not simply used as final video inpainting content but provides a visual reference model that has to be reconstructed or approximated by the image inpainting algorithm. Visual noise of the remaining video content will be adopted by the video inpainting approach while a coherent video stream is synthesized. Further, zooming camera movements can be supported as more detailed visual content may be introduced by the guiding capabilities of the reference model.

The compensation of lighting changes creates a reference model matching the illumination conditions of each current video frame. In Figure 5.6, a comparison between reference models with and without illumination correction is provided. Obviously, the reference model with lighting compensation will result in more convincing image quality than a reference model that does not compensate for changing lighting conditions.

5.6 Extended Appearance Cost

When compared to static image synthesis, video inpainting must additionally provide a coherent video stream. The inpainting algorithm will create a visual result partially from the remaining image content of the current video frame and partially guided by the reference model. The appearance cost from (4.13) is extended to measure not only the cost between synthesized data and remaining image information but also the cost between synthesized data and the reference model I_R as refined in the previous subsection. While the standard appearance cost ensures coherence inside the frame itself, the additional appearance cost ensures visual coherence between successive synthesized frames. The cost is extended by the coherence cost term $cost_{cohere} : T \to \mathbb{Q}$:

$$cost_{cohere}(p) = \sum_{\vec{v} \in N_a} d_c[i(p+\vec{v}), r(p+\vec{v})] \cdot \omega_c^1(\vec{v}) \cdot \omega_c^2(p+\vec{v}) \quad (5.16)$$

with $r(p)$ holding the image pixel value of the reference model I_R at image position $p \in I$ and an own distance function d_c and weighting functions ω_c^1 and ω_c^2. The distance measure as well as the weighting functions may be

5.6 Extended Appearance Cost

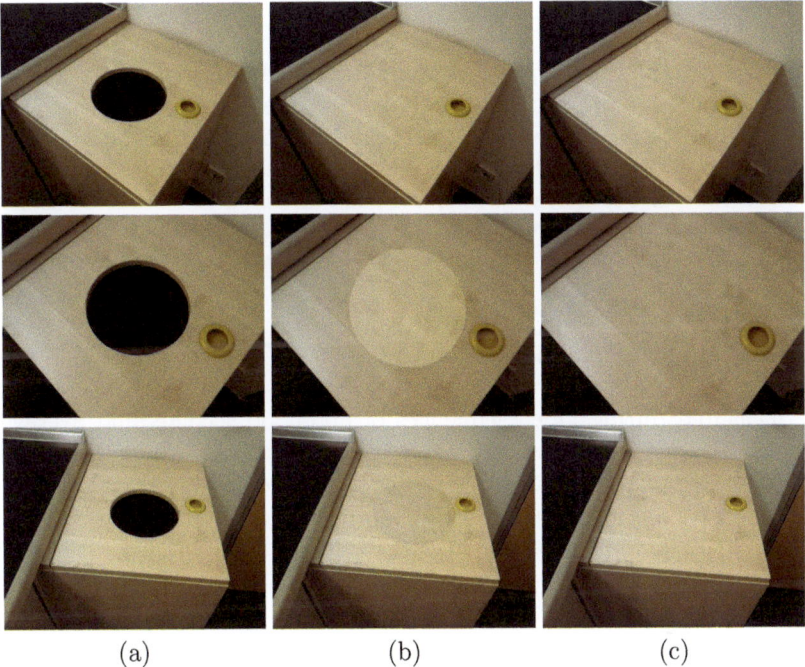

(a) (b) (c)

Figure 5.6: Comparison between a default and a corrected reference model regarding illumination changes. a) original video frames b) corresponding reference models without correction c) corresponding reference models with lighting compensation. Top row: second 1, center row: second 14, bottom row: second 25 of the video sequence. The reference model without lighting compensation shows a synthesized block with invalid content brightness after several seconds.

identical to d_a, ω_a^1 and ω_a^2 from (4.13). The extension of the appearance cost allows application of any appropriate cost measure, e.g., a zero-mean SSD.

The video inpainting approach does not directly apply the appearance cost measure from (4.13) but extends this measure. The entire appearance cost function of the video inpainting approach is defined by $cost_{xappear}$: $T \times (T \to S) \to \mathbb{Q}$:

$$cost_{xappear}(p, f) = cost_{appear}(p, f) + cost_{cohere}(p), \quad p \in T \qquad (5.17)$$

5.7 Results

The results of the video inpainting approach that has been developed in this work will be introduced in this section. First, performance values for the entire inpainting pipeline are provided in detail. Following, visual results are presented showing that a high quality video stream with accurate coherence can be achieved. Further, we will present and discuss a user study measuring the resulting image quality.

5.7.1 Performance Issues

Object selection and tracking performance have been measured for individual objects and backgrounds with a video resolution of 640 × 480. The values are measured during video sequences of about 30 seconds and averaged afterwards. Table 5.1 shows the detailed results separated according to the individual pipeline components. Once an object is reliably selected, object tracking needs between an average of 4.62 ms and 6.31 ms for each frame as shown in the table. Frame filtering for the fingerprint function (with three color components) is also necessary, requiring an average of 2.92 ms. Even in worst case, object tracking finishes in less than 10 ms for each frame.

Compared to static image inpainting, manipulation of an entire video sequence is more complex. The creation of a convincing coherent stream cannot be achieved by the sole application of image inpainting iterations in each independent video frame. As our previous approach showed, the sole inpainting application allows only linear and smooth camera movements and requires an almost homogenous background in order to produce a coherent video stream. Our previous approach [40] still showed noticeable artifacts

Table 5.1: Performance of fingerprint selection and tracking approach for four individual video sequences with frame dimension 640 × 480. From left to right: video sequence, averaged resulting mask size in number of pixels, time for object selection in the first frame; for successive frames: averaged processing time of contour point tracking, homography determination and contour adjustment.

Sequence	Mask	Initialization	Tracking	Homography	Adjustment
Figure 5.21	26,486 px	19.78 ms	0.85 ms	2.02 ms	2.47 ms
Figure 5.22	60,503 px	24.25 ms	0.41 ms	1.62 ms	3.68 ms
Figure A.22	55,422 px	22.77 ms	0.82 ms	1.96 ms	3.53 ms
Figure A.23	12,758 px	13.43 ms	0.79 ms	2.05 ms	1.78 ms

5.7 Results

Table 5.2: Performance of the video inpainting for four individual video sequences with frame dimension 640 × 480. From left to right: video sequence, averaged mask size in pixels, averaged ratio between mask pixels and entire frame pixels, averaged reference frame preparation time, averaged inpainting time, the resulting pixel fillrate corresponding to the ratio between mask pixels and inpainting time.

Sequence	Mask size	Mask ratio	Reference	Inpainting	Fillrate
Figure 5.21	26,419 px	8.6 %	5.47 ms	21.38 ms	1,238.8 px/ms
Figure 5.22	60,518 px	19.7 %	6.45 ms	53.37 ms	1,133.7 px/ms
Figure A.22	55,296 px	18.0 %	6.32 ms	48.21 ms	1,149.6 px/ms
Figure A.23	12,902 px	4.2 %	4.60 ms	11.16 ms	1,143.2 px/ms

and undesired flow effects whenever the camera moved around the undesired objects.

Our current approach applies the combination of image inpainting and homography detection to allow improved coherence. We measured performance and quality results of our approach for individual objects and different backgrounds. We further compared our current approach with the previous video inpainting approach applying the same video data. The comparison confirmed the significant coherence improvements of our current approach compared to our previous results. The result for a non-homogenous background is depicted in Figure 5.21. The object is removed reliably during the entire video sequence. Almost no disturbing coherence errors are visible. We measured performance for video synthesis applying the same video sequences already used for the evaluation of tracking performance. Again, the same video resolution of 640 × 480 pixels was applied. Table 5.2 provides detailed performance values showing the linear dependency between performance and the amount of pixels to be removed in each frame (see Subsection 4.7.2 for a detailed complexity discussion).

The entire Diminished Reality pipeline performance including tracking and video inpainting lies between 43.43 ms for the example from Figure 5.1b and 65.53 ms for the example from Figure 5.1g. On each pyramid layer, three image data channels are used for appearance measurements during iterative refinement of the inpainting approach. Our laptop Intel i7 Nehalem Core with 2.13 GHz system reaches between 15 and 23 fps, providing the visual quality result depicted in Figure 5.21. As discussed in Subsection 4.7.2, our image processing approach behaves linear with the number of mask pixels. Therefore, the performance values for the identical video sequences with a quarter image resolution (320 × 240) increase by a factor of almost four (as the number of mask pixels are reduced by a factor of four). An equivalent performance decrease can be observed for video sequences with higher image resolutions.

In Appendix A.5, further video inpainting results are provided showing the high image quality of each individual video frame. If reduced quality is acceptable, the inpainting performance can be improved by reducing the number of optimization iterations and map seeking repetitions as discussed in Subsection 4.7.2. The number of applied color data channels may also be reduced on finer pyramid layers to significantly speed up computation of the appearance measure (see Subsection 4.5).

5.7.2 User Study

The performance values in the previous section impressively demonstrated the real-time capability of our approach. In this section the perceived quality issues of our video inpainting algorithm will be discussed. For the analysis of image quality, we asked test subjects whether they were able to recognize if a video sequence had been manipulated or not. We applied a randomized controlled trial to receive measurements with maximal impact. First, the methodology of our cross-sectional study is introduced, then the study results are presented.

5.7.2.1 Methodology

The video inpainting approach, as introduced in this chapter, is mainly designed for planar backgrounds. Therefore, we focused on planar environments in our analysis and created several test videos capturing individual environments with planar backgrounds. The video sequences captured include a table top in an office, a regularly patterned carpet, and several individual sheets of gift wrapping paper. The sheets of wrapping paper have individual visual characteristics and, for the most part, patterns with a regular structure (see Figure 5.8 or Figures A.30 - A.34). We enriched some backgrounds with one or two objects such as smartphones or sunglasses to create video sequences with additional visual points of interest. These points of interest are intended to reflect the fact that video manipulations will mainly not be applied in the focus of video streams. The observers of videos do not know that the video has been manipulated and so will not search for manipulations. Thus, it was necessary to place these additional visual elements to distract the test subjects.

For the quality analysis, 12 different backgrounds $B = \{B_0, \ldots, B_{11}\}$ were selected and for each background, two individual video sequences were

5.7 Results

captured $B_i = (O_i, M_i)$. We created an original video sequence O_i that captured the original environment without any further manipulation. For the second video sequence M_i, a live video inpainting of an undesired object was applied using the same background. For each evaluation background, we inpainted 4 almost identical video sequences in real-time and finally selected the sequence with best visual result. Overall, 24 short video clips were created, half of them without manipulation and the other half with live manipulation:

$$B = \{(O_0, M_0), (O_1, M_1), \ldots, (O_{11}, M_{11})\}$$

All video sequences were captured with the same webcam with an image resolution of 640×480 pixels. We placed the camera on a tripod that allowed the rotation of the camera around one fixed axis. The camera had a static translation offset between sensor and rotation axis of about 20 cm. For each video sequence, a forward and backward panning shot was captured. The camera was rotated by an angle of about 60 degrees. Both panning shots were applied with almost the same speed of movement. Each evaluation video had a length between 5 and 7 seconds. In Appendix A.6, the manipulated evaluation video for one exemplary background (B_2) is depicted in Figure A.35.

We realized a test application that showed a subset of the created video sequences. The application showed only one test video of each evaluation background. The test videos were selected randomly with the constraint that 6 original and 6 manipulated video sequences were chosen. Our application created a random permutation or the randomly selected subset of evaluation videos. Such a test permutation P_{rand} might look like the following randomly generated one:

$$P_{rand} = \{M_6, O_{10}, M_7, M_1, O_2, M_9, O_0, O_5, M_{11}, O_3, O_8, M_4\}$$

The permutation guaranteed an individually determined order of the evaluation videos displayed. Thus, the order of the video sequences could not influence the ratings of the test subjects.

Each video was displayed one after another and a three second countdown was displayed before each video started. When an evaluation video ended, it was immediately hidden and the test subjects were asked to provide a rating. We asked the test subjects whether they noticed a manipulation in the video sequence or whether they thought that the video sequence had not been manipulated and thus was original. The test subjects had to make a decision

Table 5.3: The five values the test subjects could select as rating answer.

Value	Meaning
−2	obviously manipulated
−1	might be manipulated
0	undecidable
1	might be not manipulated
2	obviously not manipulated

with a granularity level of five. In Table 5.3, the bipolar rating scale with the individual answer possibilities and their corresponding measurement values (not provided to the test subjects) are given.

Directly at start of the application, the test persons were asked about their gender, age and whether they had knowledge about Diminished Reality. The test persons that stated to know Diminished Reality knew the research topic from previous lectures or previous live demonstrations (not in the context of our user study). Contrarily, all test persons stating not to know Diminished Reality, were not aware of the possibility to remove real objects in live video streams. Our application provided an additional introduction video for each second test participant. The introduction video showed an original video sequence following by a manipulated video and a short explanation describing some differences between an original and a manipulated video sequence. Therefore, half of all test subjects received a detailed briefing before they had to rate the evaluation videos. In the following, a test person with *knowledge* denotes a participant that stated having knowledge about Diminished Reality. All subjects that saw the introduction video will be denoted as *briefed*. *Nonbriefed* test persons did not see the introduction video.

We used one laptop computer to run our test application. All test subjects performed the study on the same device to guarantee that we can eliminate correlations due to individual display resolutions and brightness settings.

5.7.2.2 Sample

For the study, 101 student volunteers were collected, all enrolled at Ilmenau University of Technology. 53 female and 48 male students attended the user study. In Figure 5.7, the age distribution of the test subjects is visualized. The ages of the students were between 17 and 32. The diagram shows that most students have an age of 22 or 23 years.

5.7 Results

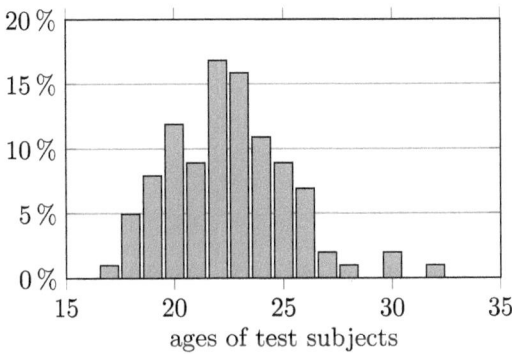

Figure 5.7: Age distribution of the 101 test subjects.

Table 5.4: Distribution of the test subjects. The values provide the absolute number of participants.

	knowledge	no knowledge	sum
briefed	13	37	50
nonbriefed	14	37	51
sum	27	74	101

50 test persons were briefed with the introduction video, 51 persons had to rate the evaluation videos without the briefing. Only 27 of the 101 students stated knowing Diminished Reality. The majority of our test persons, 74 students, did not know DR in advance. In Table 5.4, the detailed distribution of our test subjects is given.

5.7.2.3 Analysis

In the following, we will provide an analysis of our study and we will discuss the results in detail. Figure 5.8 depicts the ratings of all test subjects for two pairs of the twelve evaluation backgrounds. The diagram in Figure 5.8a) shows that the test persons did not have a unique opinion regarding background B_0. Almost half of the subjects identified the manipulated test video as original or undecidable, the other half identified the test sequence as manipulated. A similar disagreement can be observed for the original test sequence. Contrary, the second background B_1 provided a more unique result. The majority of all test subjects identified the original test video as well as the manipulated video as an original video stream. In Appendix A.6,

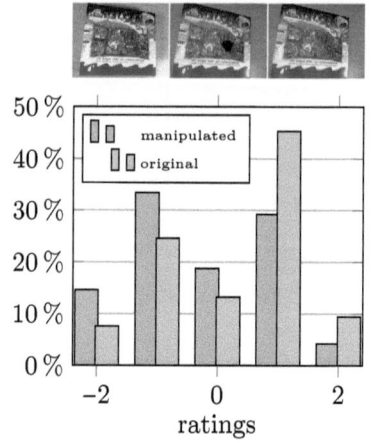
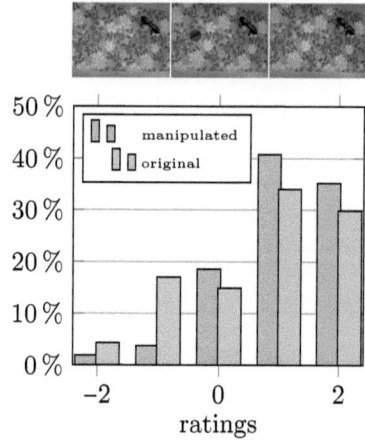

(a) Rates for the original and manipulated video of background B_0.

(b) Rates for the original and manipulated video of background B_1.

Figure 5.8: Test subject rates for evaluation background B_0 and B_1. Top (from left to right): screen shot of original video test sequence, original video sequence that will be manipulated, manipulated video sequence, bottom: corresponding ratings of test persons.

the rates of the test persons for the remaining evaluation backgrounds are given.

In Figure 5.9, the accumulated ratings of the test subjects are presented. The ratings for the manipulated test videos and the ratings for the original video sequences have been averaged. Further, two diagrams are presented splitting the results into a female and a male group. All three diagrams show that the test persons could not provide a unique rating for the manipulated test videos. On average, the participants identified the manipulated test videos as original as well as manipulated to almost the same extent. The original test videos provided a slightly more sharpened rating. Only a few of the test subjects rated some of the original video sequences as *obviously manipulated* (-2).

The ratings for the individual backgrounds $B = \{B_0, B_1, \ldots, B_{11}\}$ are given in Figure 5.10 and 5.13. The diagram for the ratings of the manipulated video sequences (Figure 5.10) shows that only three of the twelve test videos were identified as manipulated. On average, the majority of the test subjects

5.7 Results

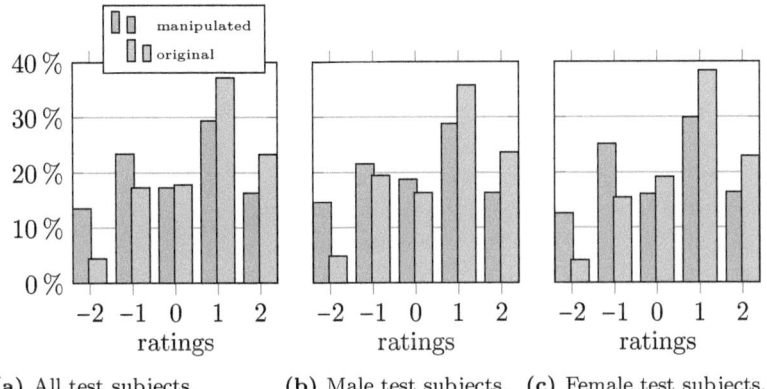

(a) All test subjects. (b) Male test subjects. (c) Female test subjects.

Figure 5.9: Averaged ratings for all backgrounds.

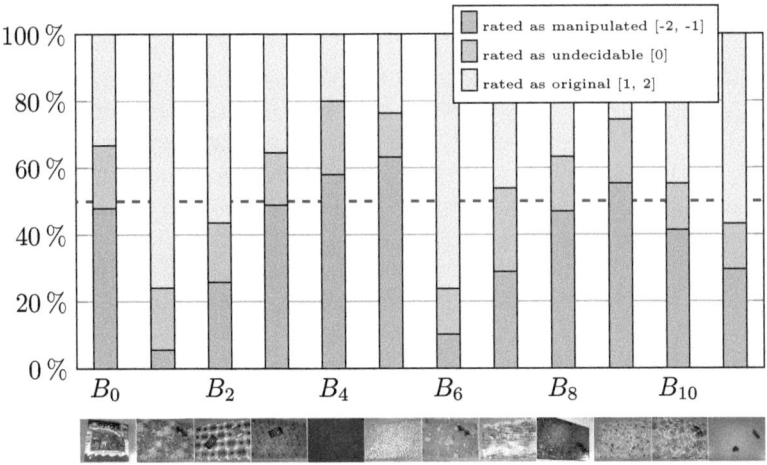

Figure 5.10: Test subject ratings for all twelve manipulated video sequences. The corresponding video backgrounds are depicted below the individual ratings.

rated the backgrounds B_4, B_5 and B_9 with a value lower than 0. Thus, nine of the twelve manipulated test videos were exposed as manipulated video information. Especially for background B_1 and B_6, our live video inpainting algorithm seems to provide an almost perfect image quality.

In Figure 5.11, we focused on all participants that rated the manipulated evaluation videos as manipulated (with a value of -2 or -1). Three groups of test subjects are depicted. We compared the amount of all participants with the amount of participants that were briefed by an introduction video. The amount of participants that did not see the introduction video is also provided. The introduction video improved the ratings for seven of the twelve test backgrounds significantly (the t-test determined $P = 0.0003$ for these seven backgrounds). On average, more test subjects of the briefed group rated the (manipulated) videos as manipulated compared to the group of nonbriefed subjects. Thus, more correct ratings were given for these seven backgrounds.

In Figure 5.12, we provide the same rating as in Figure 5.11. However, the ratings are compared between the subset of test persons that knew Diminished Reality already and the subset of test persons that did not know DR in advance. On average, more test subjects of the group knowing DR rated the (manipulated) videos as manipulated compared to the group of test subjects not knowing DR.

The briefing had a negative influence for three manipulated videos sequences (B_2, B_6 and B_7). On average, more participants of the briefed group rated these three (manipulated) videos as non-manipulated compared to the group of nonbriefed subjects. Almost no changes in rating can be observed for the backgrounds B_1 and B_{10}. The diagram shows that the majority of the nonbriefed participants did not identify not even a single manipulated videos. Even the group of briefed test subjects did not identify more than half of the manipulated videos.

In Figure 5.13, the diagram for the ratings of the original video sequences is depicted. The majority of the test subjects identified nine of the twelve test videos as original video content. Only three backgrounds (B_4, B_8 and B_{10}) were not rated as original by a majority of the participants.

A more detailed comparison for the original evaluation videos is given in Figure 5.14. Again, the amount of participants that rated the original video sequences as original image content is separated into three groups. The diagram shows that the introduction video improved the ratings for seven backgrounds. For these seven (original) video sequences, more test subjects decided to rate the videos as original. Thus, more correct ratings have been given for these test videos.

In Figure 5.15, the equivalent rating results are provided for the group of test subjects knowing Diminished Reality and the group of test subjects not knowing DR in advance.

The introduction video had a negative influence on three of the backgrounds (B_2, B_7 and B_8). Thus, less correct ratings have been given by the group of nonbriefed test participants for these three backgrounds. For

5.7 Results

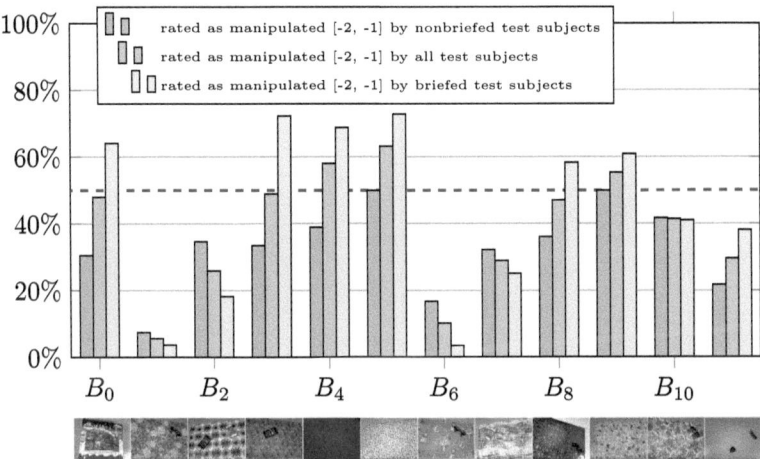

Figure 5.11: Comparison of ratings of test subjects that identified the manipulated videos as manipulations. The comparison is provided between the results of all test subjects, the results of the subset of briefed test persons, and the subset of nonbriefed test subjects. The corresponding video backgrounds are depicted below the individual ratings.

two backgrounds (B_3 and B_{10}), no noticeable difference between briefed and nonbriefed test subjects can be observed.

In Figure 5.16 the average ratings for individual groups of test subjects is provided. The participants were separated into seven groups:

- **all:** This group includes all participants without any filtering.
- **nonbriefed:** This group covers the subjects that did not see the introduction video (briefed subjects are not part of this group).
- **briefed:** All subjects that were briefed with the introduction video.
- **no knowledge:** All test persons that have no knowledge about Diminished Reality (subjects with knowledge about DR are not part of this group).
- **knowledge:** The group of test persons that know Diminished Reality.
- **nonbriefed & no knowledge:** The group of participants that were not briefed with the introduction video and that have no knowledge about Diminished Reality in advance.
- **briefed & knowledge:** The group of participants that were briefed with the introduction video and have knowledge about Diminished Reality in advance.

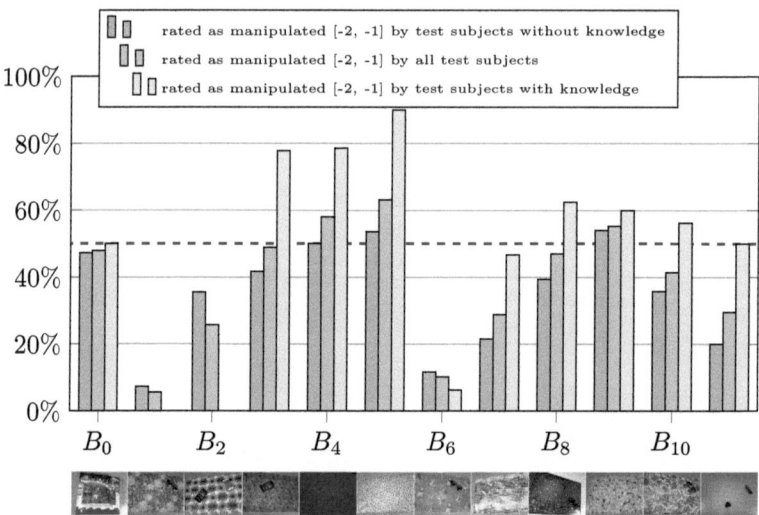

Figure 5.12: Comparison of ratings of test subjects that identified the manipulated videos as manipulations. The comparison is provided between the results of all test subjects, the results of the subset of test persons with knowledge, and the subset of test subjects without knowledge. The corresponding video backgrounds are depicted below the individual ratings.

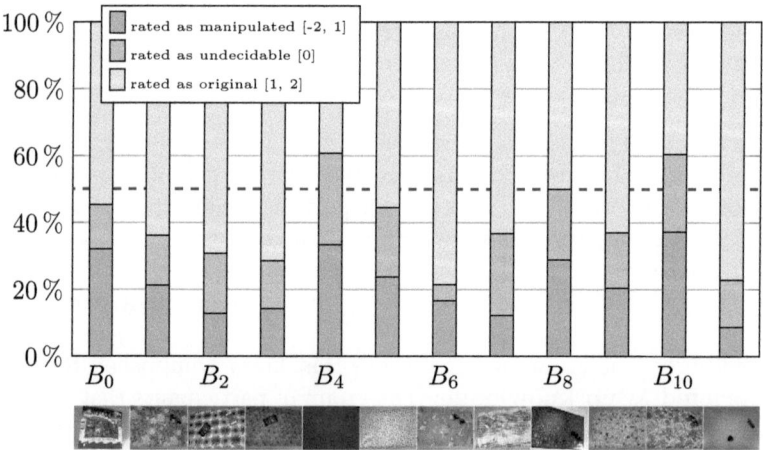

Figure 5.13: Test subject ratings for all twelve original video sequences. The corresponding video backgrounds are depicted below the individual ratings.

5.7 Results

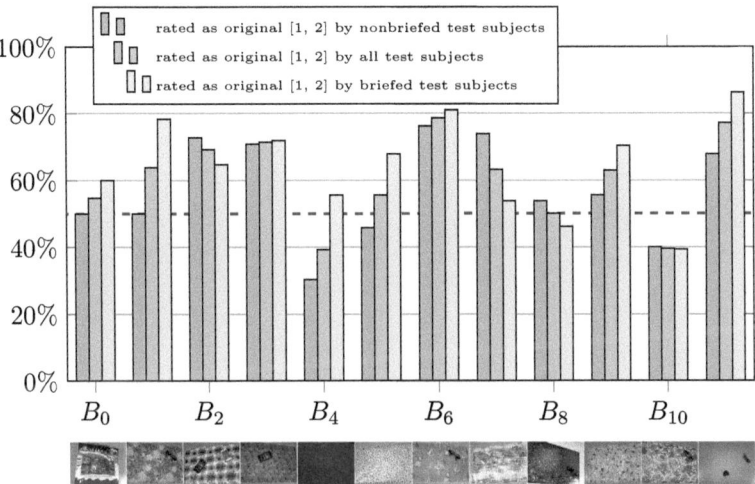

Figure 5.14: Comparison of ratings of test subjects that identified the original videos as originals. The comparison is provided between the results of all test subjects, the results of the subset of briefed test persons, and the subset of nonbriefed test subjects. The corresponding video backgrounds are depicted below the individual ratings.

The diagram in Figure 5.16 shows that the ratings of the test subjects becomes more correct the more a priori information the participants have. The average rating of our test persons that did not know Diminished Reality and that were not briefed by the introduction video is almost identical for the manipulated and original video sequences. This specific group of test persons decided an average rating of $\bar{x} = 0.266$ (with standard deviation $s = 1.161$) for the manipulated evaluation videos. An average rating of $\bar{x} = 0.279$ (with standard deviation $s = 1.187$) was given for the original videos. Obviously, on average, the test subjects could not observe a difference between the manipulated and the original evaluation videos.

In contrast, the group of test subjects that already knew Diminished Reality and that saw the introduction video provided a more correct rating. The manipulated video sequences have been rated by $\bar{x} = -0.256$ in average (with standard deviation $s = 1.480$). An averaged rating of $\bar{x} = 0.846$ (with standard deviation $s = 0.975$) has been provided for the original evaluation videos. In Figure 5.17, the ratings of the two groups of test subjects are visualized in two diagrams. It can be seen that the rating distribution for

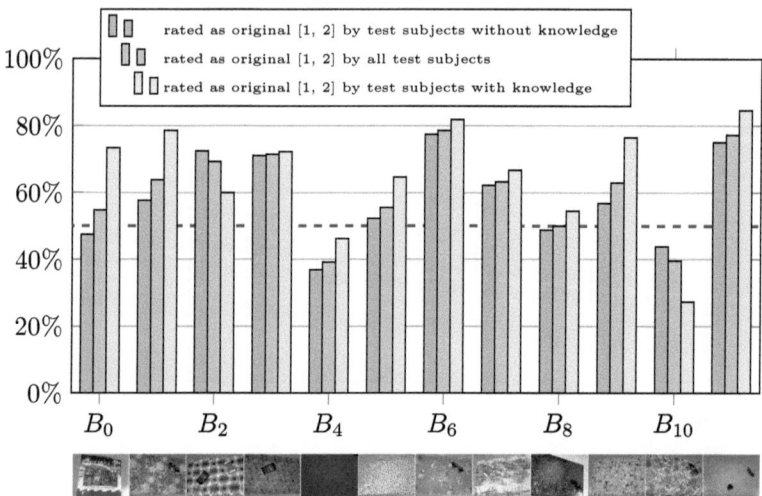

Figure 5.15: Comparison of ratings of test subjects that identified the original videos as originals. The comparison is provided between the results of all test subjects, the results of the subset of test persons with knowledge, and the subset of test subjects without knowledge. The corresponding video backgrounds are depicted below the individual ratings.

the group without a priori information is almost similar for the manipulated and the original evaluation videos.

The detailed ratings for the individual groups of test subjects and the individual deviation of the data set is given in the appendix in Table A.1. In Figure 5.18, the averaged ratings for the individual evaluation backgrounds is provided for the subset of test persons the did not know Diminished Reality and that did not see the introduction video. In Figure 5.19, the averaged ratings of the subset of test persons that knew DR already and that saw the introduction video is depicted.

We performed a t-test for all evaluation backgrounds to determine whether a significant difference between the ratings for the original and manipulated video sequences may be observed. For the test, the different ratings of the test subjects (as provided in the Figures 5.8 and A.30 - A.34) have been used. In Table 5.5, the mean values $\bar{x}$, the corresponding standard deviation s and the resulting P value for all twelve evaluation backgrounds are provided. We found no significant difference for six of the twelve evaluation backgrounds. The user ratings for the backgrounds B_0, B_1, B_2, B_6, B_8 and

5.7 Results

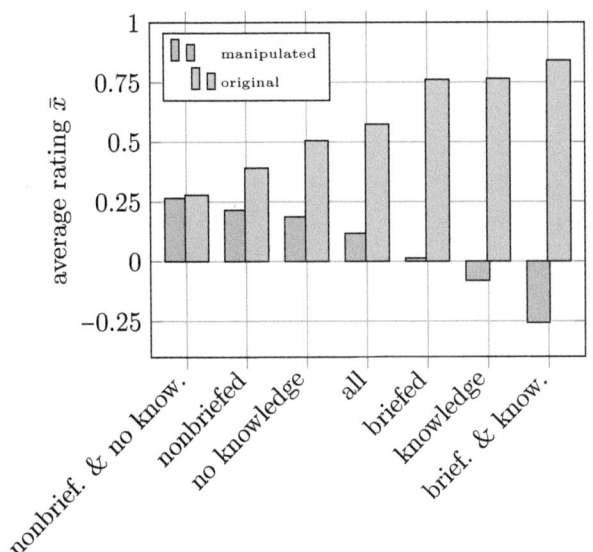

Figure 5.16: Average rating $\bar{x}$ of the test subjects for all evaluation videos for individual groups.

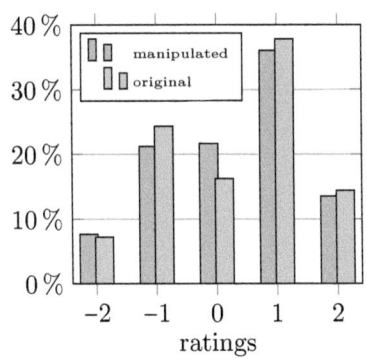

(a) 37 nonbriefed participants without knowledge.

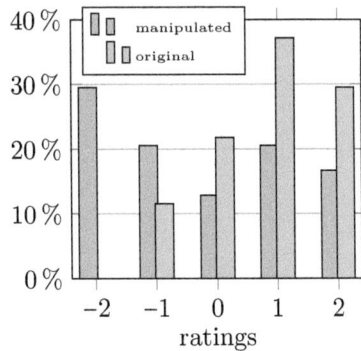

(b) 13 briefed participants with knowledge.

Figure 5.17: Comparison of averaged ratings for all backgrounds for two individual groups of test persons.

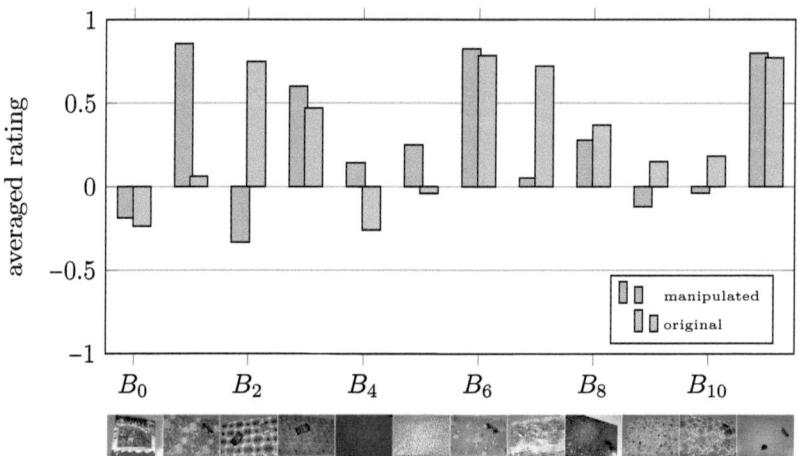

Figure 5.18: Comparison of the averaged ratings between original and manipulated video sequences. Ratings for nonbriefed test persons without knowledge about DR are depicted only.

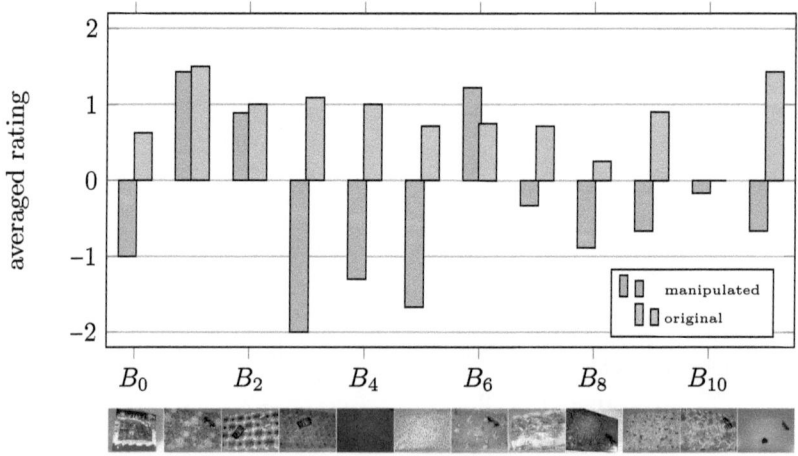

Figure 5.19: Comparison of the averaged ratings between original and manipulated video sequences. Ratings for briefed test persons that know DR are depicted only.

5.7 Results

Table 5.5: T-test analyzing the differences of user ratings for all evaluation backgrounds. $\bar{x}$ determines the mean user ratings, s provides the standard deviation.

Background	Manipulated videos $\bar{x}$	s	Original videos $\bar{x}$	s	t-test P
B_0 (Figure 5.8a)	-0.25	1.16	0.25	1.16	0.034
B_1 (Figure 5.8b)	1.04	0.93	0.68	1.20	0.103
B_2 (Figure A.30a)	0.45	1.29	0.79	1.03	0.143
B_3 (Figure A.30b)	-0.24	1.45	0.84	1.04	0.000
B_4 (Figure A.31a)	-0.66	1.26	0.10	1.15	0.002
B_5 (Figure A.31b)	-0.47	1.25	0.49	1.18	0.000
B_6 (Figure A.32a)	0.95	1.02	0.93	1.16	0.927
B_7 (Figure A.32b)	0.15	1.13	0.71	1.00	0.009
B_8 (Figure A.33a)	-0.10	1.26	0.25	1.20	0.155
B_9 (Figure A.33b)	-0.49	1.20	0.67	1.12	0.000
B_{10} (Figure A.34a)	0.05	1.16	0.02	1.03	0.897
B_{11} (Figure A.34b)	0.48	1.36	1.14	1.03	0.008

B_{10} show no statistical relevant differences in the user ratings. Contrarily, for the remaining evaluation backgrounds B_3, B_4, B_5, B_7, B_9 and B_{11} we determined a significant difference between the ratings of the test subjects for the manipulated and the original video sequences. The t-test shows that the test persons provided an individual rating for all evaluation backgrounds with regular and filigree patterns. The ratings for all backgrounds without regular pattern show no significant difference between manipulated and original video sequences.

Further, we applied a t-test to analyze the difference between the averaged ratings for manipulated and non-manipulated video sequences for the entire group of test subjects. The test revealed that statistically a significant difference between the averaged ratings exists. Thus, the entire group of test subjects provided different ratings for the manipulated and original video sequences.

In Figure 5.20, the amounts of undecidable ratings (sequences rated by 0) are depicted for each evaluation background and a direct comparison between manipulated and original video sequences is provided. We performed a paired two-tail t-test to analyze whether a significant statistical difference can be determined between manipulated and original evaluation videos. The test provided that no significant difference can be found in the sample (with $P = 0.772$). Thus, the same amount of test persons could not provide a unique decision regarding the original or the manipulated video sequence for

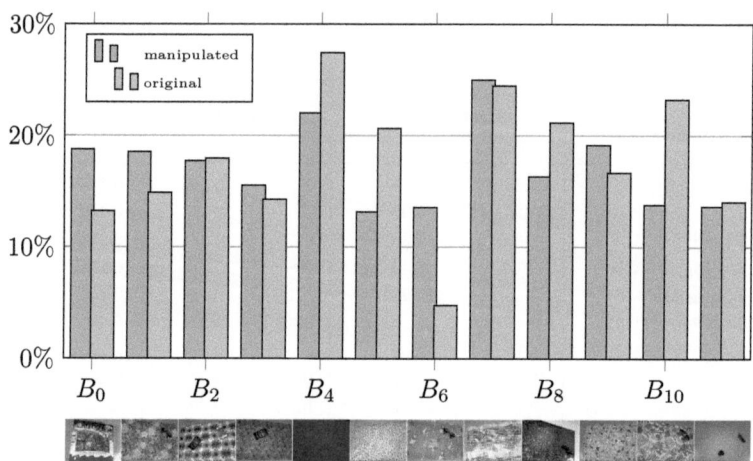

Figure 5.20: Comparison of the amount of undecidable ratings (all ratings with value 0) between original and manipulated video sequences. The corresponding video backgrounds are depicted below the individual ratings

all evaluation backgrounds. Further, the test showed that in average almost each fifth test person ($\bar{x} = 17.27\,\%$ for manipulated videos and $\bar{x} = 17.73\,\%$ for original videos) could not provide a specific rating regarding the video content.

5.7.2.4 Limitations

The above presented quality analysis of our video inpainting approach has some limitations that have to be discussed. Our study can only provide a quality statement regarding short video sequences with standard webcam image resolutions. Our sample was composed of only students at a University of Technology. The study cannot make a generalization about persons without or with less technical background.

Further, the majority of our evaluation videos captured non-natural video backgrounds (gift wrapping paper). We mounted the camera device on a tripod to guarantee comparable evaluation results between original and manipulated video sequences. Our study did not integrate videos captured with a hand-held camera.

After each test video, we asked the subjects whether they have noticed a manipulation in the video content, so emphasis was directly placed on the issue of manipulation. The study cannot reflect the fact that observers of videos normally do not expect manipulation and thus do not seek for manipulation. We tried to accommodate this issue by limiting the duration of the evaluation videos to a range of length between 5 and 7 seconds.

Future studies should investigate a comparison between short and long video sequences. An evaluation of the influence of the image resolution has to be applied to measure the differences between low resolution and high resolution video streams. Test persons should provide more detailed feedback regarding their classifications. Our study did not measure whether the participants identified the correct video elements as manipulated or whether they distrusted original image content in the evaluation videos. Test persons should be asked to highlight the manipulated image regions to create more detailed measured results about the correct identification of original and manipulated video sequences.

5.7.3 Visual Results

In Figure 5.21, the original video sequence, real-time object selection and real-time video inpainting results are depicted by individual frames of an entire video sequence. In the video sequence, an undesired object, a black smartphone, is reliably removed from the video stream. The undesired object and the background environment do not share similar visual content. Our real-time segmentation approach is able to distinguish between object and background fragments. Although the background is heterogeneous, the fingerprint approach allows for object segmentation and tracking during the entire video sequence.

The inpainting result shows a blur-free video stream with high coherence. The final video inpainting result does not reconstruct the real background information, as this information is not available in the video stream. The results match the remaining image content. As claimed in the objective of this work, and as discussed in the previous Subsection 5.7.2.3, observers not knowing that the video stream has been manipulated probably will not identify any irregular visual artifacts or visual content.

The background of the video sequence as depicted in Figure 5.21 is absolute planar and thus is a perfect match for the homography based tracking approach as developed in Subsection 5.2. In Appendix A.5, more video inpainting results are presented that do not have an absolute planar background environment. The approach developed in this work is suitable for several types of video streams with different types of environments.

In Figure 5.22, a coat of arms has been removed in a video sequence of more than 400 frames. The image has a resolution of 640 × 480 pixels. The sequence has been captured with a hand-held camera that has been moved around the undesired object. The direct environment of the coat of arms has a 3D structure and thus is not strictly planar. This video sequence is an ideal example of the video inpainting approach not attempting to create the final video sequence by the application of a multi-view approach (see Subsection 2.3.2.2), but by an application creating plausible image content. As the coat of arms is integrated in the wall, a multi-view approach could use an arbitrary number of cameras, but no camera could provide a view behind the object for sufficient matching. The approach as presented in this work overcomes this problem as video content is synthesized from the remaining image content. The Figure 5.22 depicts several screenshots of the resulting live inpainting result showing a coherent video stream with high image quality.

In Appendix A.5, several additional video sequences with undesired objects and individual background characteristics are given.

5.7 Results

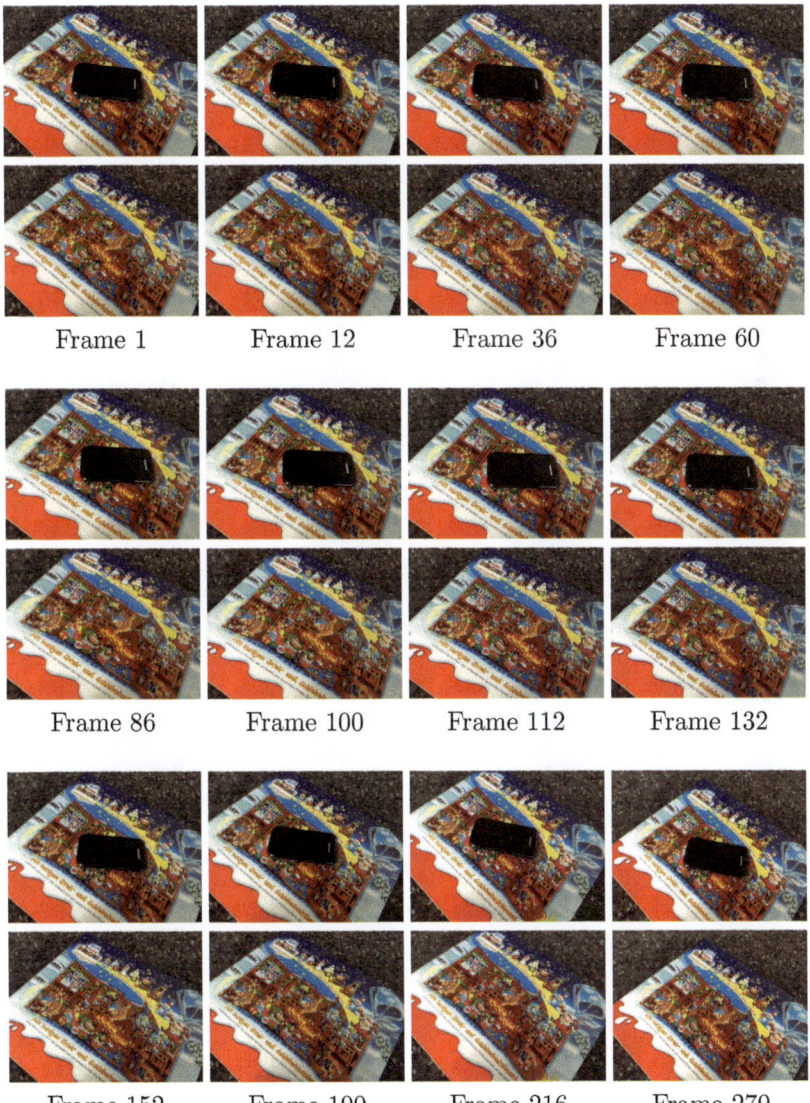

Figure 5.21: Real-time video inpainting for an undesired object lying on a planar and heterogeneous background. The video has been captured with a hand-held camera and moved without constraints. Top rows: original video input, bottom rows: resulting live video inpainting result.

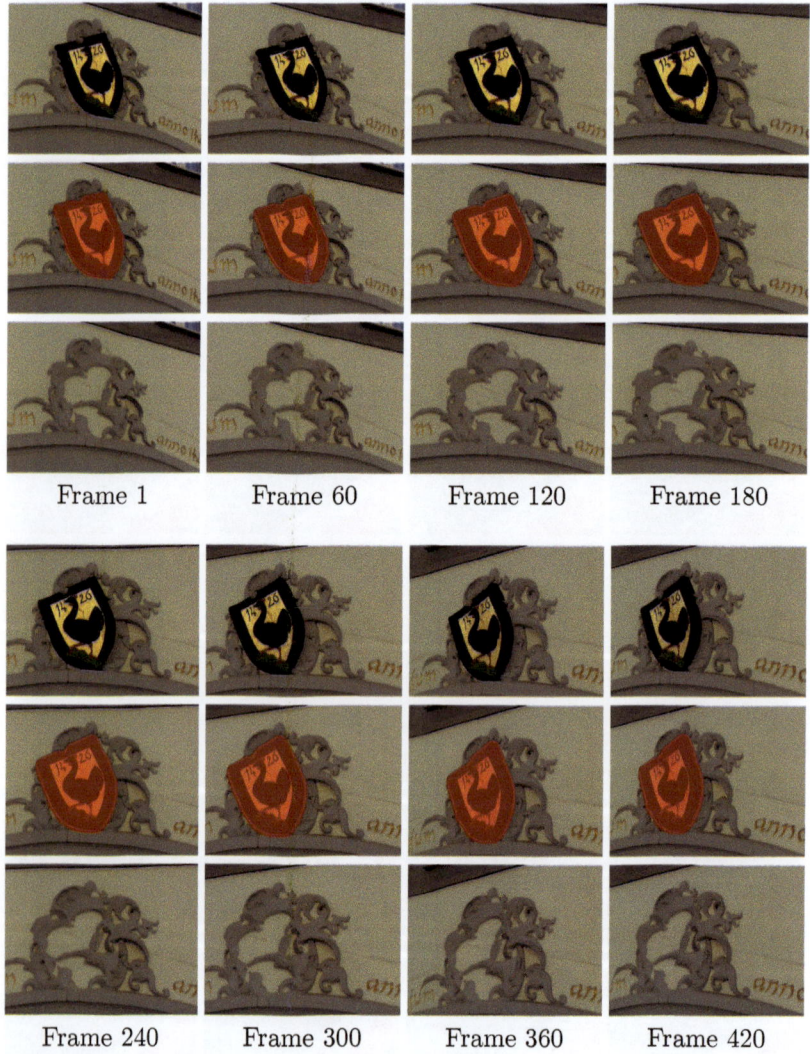

Figure 5.22: Real-time video inpainting of a coat of arms in a video with an image resolution of 640 × 480 pixels. The video has been captured with a hand-held camera that has been moved around the coat of arms. The resulting video stream seems to be plausible as the flourishes of the remaining image content are automatically reconstructed. Corresponding performance values are discussed in Table 5.1 and 5.2.

5.8 Limitations

Limitations and restrictions of the video inpainting pipeline developed in this work will be discussed in this chapter.

5.8.1 Object Selection and Tracking

As depicted in Figure 5.1, our fingerprint based object selection approach is a significant improvement compared to our previous approach [40]. However, object selection may still fail because of the complex appearance of the undesired object or the background environment. The more individual characteristics the object and the background exhibit, and the smaller the difference between the object and the background characteristics, the more difficult a reliable selection becomes. Figure 5.23 shows two examples our real-time selection approach is not able to handle in a sufficient manner. The first example misses significant visual differences between the fingerprints of the rough user-defined contour and the visual characteristics of the stone. A wrong area is selected, not as intended by the user. Selection in the second example fails for a small part of the object. The area of the car's hatchback is not included as selected by the user. The rough contour fingerprints scattered at the gray sky are almost identical to the visible characteristics of the hatchback due to the reflection of the sky on the hatchback.

5.8.2 Video Inpainting

The presented video inpainting system is able to provide a coherent high quality result for a hand-held camera with dynamic translations and rotations. Homography determination of the object's contour requires a static object with almost planar background. However, if the camera is rather static or the movements limited, a coherent video stream can be provided even for non-planar backgrounds.

While our approach supports real-time video inpainting applications with a camera moving around a rather static object to be removed, it does not yet cover scenarios where the object moves around or where both camera and object are dynamic. Our approach currently does not sufficiently cover situations where a previously unknown background becomes visible later on. These situations may occur if an object with significant volumetric expansion (perpendicular to the surface) in combination with dynamic camera movements has to be removed. A previously synthesized image area is then replaced by the real image content. In order to realize a coherent view,

(a) The stone cannot be uniquely separated from the environment.

(b) Although the main parts of the car are sufficiently determined, the algorithm fails to identify parts of the hatchback

Figure 5.23: Real-time selection results of the fingerprint segmentation approach with fingerprints using three color data channels only; top row: original image with rough user-defined selection, bottom row: selection result.

additional fading mechanisms will be required. However, as a real-time video inpainting system does not have any information about future video frames (in contrast to removing objects from a pre-recorded video), a trivial solution for this problem does not exist. In Figure 5.24, the video inpainting results of two individual video sequences are depicted. After several seconds, object tracking fails to reliably identify the undesired object. Minor fragments of the undesired object become visible in the synthesized live video result. The contour refinement step as described in Subsection 5.2.4 needs a larger impact to compensate for movement of a volumetric object, as the contour movement of such undesired objects cannot be approximated sufficiently by a homography. A larger impact of the contour refinement may provide

5.8 Limitations

(a) (b) (c)

Figure 5.24: Video inpainting of a volumetric object. a) original video frame, b) inpainting result after a few seconds, c) video frame after the camera has moved around the volumetric object.

undesired tracking results for video sequences without volumetric objects. A sketch of an enhanced tracking approach able to support volumetric objects is given in Subsection 6.2.

As discussed in the introduction in Section 1.1, the approach developed in this work focuses on real-time video manipulation for static objects captured by a camera with unconstrained motions. In contrast, most previous video inpainting approaches, as presented in Subsection 2.2, focused on a non-real-time capable approach for moving objects with almost stationary cameras.

Currently, the applied real-time tracking approach of this work does not allow manipulation of dynamic objects like walking people. Contour tracking and application of homography determination between successive video frames expect a static inpainting object. Due to the tracking approach, a coherent video stream cannot be produced. In contrast to previous approaches, our approach proves successful for live video streams and thus does not need the entire video sequence as a priori information. An enhanced tracking algorithm as discussed in the next chapter will provide the basis to concurrently support the inpainting of static and dynamic objects while still allowing unconstrained camera motions.

5.9 Discussion

Our real-time capable video inpainting approach as developed in this work has been presented in this chapter in detail. First, the object selection and tracking approach able to separate desired from undesired video pixels in real-time performance has been presented. Creation of manipulated video transmission with accurate stream coherence has been discussed. Some research issues have been presented that will need more computational hardware for future applications to allow manipulation of more complex video sequences. Finally, accurate performance values and visual results of our approach have been presented.

Performance values given in Table 5.2 show that our approach meets the objective of this work. Individual static objects can be removed in a live video transmission as our approach fulfills two important conditions:

- Our approach is fast enough to process a video frame within a few milliseconds.

- Our algorithm relies only on the current video frame and does not need any information from prospective video frames.

Therefore, our approach significantly differs from all related video inpainting approaches discussed in Subsection 2.2. None of the previously proposed approaches is able to process a video sequence fast enough to allow real-time performance. Most of them need several minutes or hours for the processing of a video sequence composed of only a few video frames. No approach exists that does not rely on the entire video stream as a priori information.

Our real-time tracking approach creates a coherent video stream for unconstrained camera movements. Most related algorithms are applicable for almost stationary cameras or camera movement with strong constraints. Our approach is currently limited to static inpainting objects while most related video manipulation algorithms focus on the removal of moving objects. However, the integration of a more advanced tracking approach, as discussed below in Subsection 6.2.2, will also allow the removal of moving objects in a live video transmission.

6 Conclusion

The following chapter will provide a summary of our work. Our objective was to develop an approach for real-time video manipulation that can also be applied for Diminished Reality. Key findings, challenges, and limitations with the realization of the approach have been discussed. Performance and quality of our approach have been compared with previous approaches in detail. In this Chapter, our work and our approach for real-time manipulation of video streams will be concluded, and an outlook for future refinements and areas of application will be provided.

6.1 Summary

In this work, a novel video manipulation approach has been developed that is fast enough for processing a live video stream in real-time. The approach has been derived using a new real-time capable image inpainting algorithm being several magnitudes faster than state-of-the-art approaches.

The image inpainting approach separates an image into two regions. The target regions covers the undesired image content and the source regions defines the remaining image information. During the inpainting process, image information from the source region is copied into the target region ultimately replacing the undesired image content. Our approach does not apply image patches, but applies individual pixels as the inpainting unit to reach performance values several magnitudes faster than previous approaches. Mapping between inpainting mask pixels and the remaining image content pixels is iteratively improved based on the determined cost measure that has to be minimized for the entire inpainting mask. The cost function is determined by an appearance measure and a novel measure based on the geometric conditions of neighboring mappings. Appearance cost measures the similarity between the image content inside and outside the inpainting mask. The more similar the image content, the lower the appearance cost, and thus the better the mapping.

Our approach allows differential weighting of appearance costs for individual target pixels. The appearance cost for pixels in the center of the inpainting mask is rated with lesser impact than for the pixels close to the boundary of the inpainting mask. Thus, the synthesized image information optimally blends in with the remaining image content and noticeable edges at the inpainting boundary can be avoided.

While the appearance measure is a technique often applied in related works, the geometric cost measure has not previously been used and is, in our approach, applied for the first time. The geometry constraint is comparable to an elastic spring model and guides the optimization algorithm in a way that neighboring pixels inside the inpainting mask preferably map to neighboring pixels outside the inpainting mask. The combination of both cost measures allows fast convergence during the optimization process and the geometric cost can be calculated very efficiently. Both cost constraints are jointly weighted by a simple control parameter adjusting the balance between them.

The application of individual pixels as the inpainting unit in combination with both cost constraints is the basis for the significant performance edge compared to state-of-the-art approaches. The novel geometry cost constraint enables a significantly faster convergence of the iterative optimization algorithm while concurrently ensures high image quality of the final image. Additionally, our approach does not rely on time consuming blending iterations of patches that are necessary in related approaches using image patches as inpainting unit. We found that the performance can be increased further by application of two minor approximations regarding the cost measures. The determination of the appearance cost and the determination of the geometric cost function have slightly been modified. The appearance cost for a single pixel mapping is approximated by the calculation of the direct appearance cost only. The impact of the indirect appearance expense is omitted allowing the matching performance to be improved significantly. Furthermore, the geometric cost measure is approximated to benefit from mappings that are provided by the information propagation during the iterative refinement step.

The image inpainting approach creates high quality images by a heuristic optimization algorithm. Instead of applying a brute-force search optimization for pixel mapping, as the majority of the related inpainting approaches does, mapping is improved by a randomized search operation. Therefore, the complexity of our inpainting algorithm is linear with respect to the number of mask pixels. The combination of the heuristic optimization with the propagation of mapping information from neighboring pixels allows for real-time execution of the mapping optimization. Both low and high frequencies can be synthesized by the application of a multiresolution optimization.

6.1 Summary

Although our pixel-based approach does not need to be explicitly initialized, images with tiny but important structural information may benefit from an explicit initialization. Therefore, explicit initialization strategies have been introduced and compared to each other with respect to performance and resulting image quality. Quality and performance is compared for non-initialized images and for images that have been initialized by the randomized erosion filter, by the contour mapping strategy, and by the patch initialization approach. We found that the randomized erosion filter and the contour mapping are faster than the patch initialization approach. However, patch initialization allows for reconstruction of more complex structural information. The patch initialization strategy that iteratively shrinks the inpainting mask on the lowest pyramid layer is able to reconstruct the essential image structure and is still fast enough for real-time execution of the entire inpainting pipeline. The patch initialization directly provides the initial mapping for the lowest pyramid layer. None of the existing inpainting approaches combined the shrinking and the vanishing inpainting strategy within one algorithm. The novel idea of combining both inpainting strategies is another basis for the creation of high quality images in real-time.

In addition, our introduced inpainting approach supports implicit and explicit constraints guiding the optimization algorithm according to specific visual conditions. The applied image data space implicitly guides the inpainting approach. Our inpainting pipeline is fast enough to handle image information with up to four data channels in real-time. We discussed the differences regarding the application of individual data channels. Inpainting images with almost similar color information but changing visual frequencies significantly benefit from a fourth data channel. This extra data channel covers the visual frequency of the image information ensuring that the inpainting approach maps image content with the corresponding visual frequencies. Explicit constraints guide the inpainting approach due to user-defined constraints that preserve important visual structural information. Straight lines as well as curves or even more complex structural information can reliably be reconstructed. In contrast to other approaches, in our method user-defined constraints can be seamlessly integrated into our optimization process.

Overall, the developed algorithm meets the objective of creation of a real-time capable image inpainting approach that can be used as the basis for video inpainting. It is able to provide visual results comparable to state-of-the-art approaches, while being several magnitudes faster.

The video manipulation approach used to process a live video stream with real-time performance is based on image inpainting. First, an object selection and tracking algorithm has been developed that allows the user to select an arbitrary undesired object in a video frame. In real-time, the approach distinguishes between the desired and undesired image content by the application of fingerprints. Image content that does not match the visual image information of a rough object selection (defined by the user) is identified as undesired in the video sequence. The fingerprints determine the undesired content in real-time within a coarse to fine multiresolution approach. This undesired image content is tracked throughout the video. An accurate object contour is determined for each video frame to prevent an accumulated drift error. Contour tracking in combination with homography calculation is used to determine a rough contour for the current frame before this contour is refined in the second step. Contrarily to all other related video inpainting approaches, the selection and tracking approach avoids the necessity of any a priori information. Neither information about the object to be removed nor information about the background of the object is needed in advance. Thus, the approach is very flexible and can be applied without any preprocessing steps. Tracking works immediately beginning from the first video fame after the user has roughly selected the content.

The final object contour, as provided by the fingerprint segmentation approach, defines an inpainting mask that can be processed by the video manipulation approach. For each video frame, an explicit image inpainting execution is invoked. However, between successive video frames, the previously found pixel mapping is forwarded, transformed by the determined homography, and used as initialization. Further, the homography is used to create a reference model that guides the image inpainting process to create a coherent video stream with high accuracy. The reference model is created by regarding individual key frames in the video sequence. It also compensates for changing lighting conditions within the video stream. Previous approaches either created a video inpainting result by warping the first inpainting video frame to all successive frames in the sequence, or by individual executions of image inpainting iterations. None of these related approaches combines both of these strategies to create a manipulated video stream, no approach is able to compensate changing lighting conditions in the video sequence, or is fast enough to provide a real-time result. In contrast, our video inpainting approach is real-time capable and produces high image quality. Image processing uses only the current video frame for the inpainting process and thus does not rely on subsequent video frames like all previous (non-real-time capable) video inpainting approaches. The approach allows for selection and removal of arbitrary objects in heterogeneous but almost planar backgrounds. Further, any type of camera motion is supported. Thus, a live video stream captured by a static camera or by a

6.1 Summary

hand-held camera applying panning, zooming or rotational motions can be manipulated. Related video inpainting approaches mainly allow the removal of either moving objects captured by a static camera or the manipulation of videos captured by a camera with constrained movements (such as sole panning shots).

Our approach is fast enough to be executed on current standard computer hardware. We implemented the entire video inpainting pipeline in C++ and tested the software on several Windows 7 computers. Our implementation supports multi-core CPUs and distributes the computation to as many CPU cores as available. Thus, the execution performance benefits from the architecture of state-of-the-art CPUs coming soon with at least two or even up to four CPU cores. The more cores available in the device, the faster the execution of our approach. Our implementation avoids the use of the GPU enabling it to be ported to almost any device like tablet PCs or smartphones.

In another contribution, we have conducted a user study with more than 100 participants to measure and to verify the visual quality of the result from our video inpainting approach. The test subjects had to watch several video sequences and afterwards were asked whether they noticed a manipulation of the video. We used 24 short evaluation videos, half of which were manipulated with our video inpainting approach in real-time. We found that most test subjects were not able to correctly identify the manipulated video sequences. We applied several t-tests showing that for half of the evaluation backgrounds no significant difference between the ratings for manipulated and non-manipulated videos could be determined by the test subjects. Further, we found that the majority of test persons not knowing about Diminished Reality and not briefed with an introduction video (showing the difference between a manipulated and an original video sequence) were not able to distinguish between the manipulated and non-manipulated video sequences. The test subjects provided almost the same rating for both types of evaluation videos. Therefore, our live video inpainting approach is not only able to process a video stream in real-time without a priori information but also provides high image quality so that most observers are not able to distinguish the manipulation.

No previous video inpainting approach exists that is comparable to our work. No approach exists that is able to detect and track an arbitrary object without a priori information in real-time. All related approaches are too slow for real-time image processing and need the entire video information in advance not allowing the manipulation of a live video stream.

The major contribution of our work can be briefly summarized by:

- A real-time image inpainting approach creating high image quality
- Introduction of a novel spatial cost constraint
- Development of three individual initialization strategies
- Support for implicit inpainting constraints improving the image quality
- Integration of user-defined constraints into the inpainting pipeline
- Realization of a real-time capable object selection and tracking approach
- Support for homogenous and heterogeneous image content
- A real-time video inpainting approach avoiding any a priori information
- Combination of an image warping and image inpainting strategy providing accurate video coherence
- A detailed performance and quality comparison and analysis of our image and video inpainting approach
- Evaluation of the inpainting quality by a user study with more than 100 test subjects

6.2 Future Work

Although our results are promising, there are some interesting directions for future research that will enhance the visual quality of the video manipulation approach and will allow for an application in more complex environments.

6.2.1 Image Inpainting

As described in Subsection 4.10.1, the pixel-based inpainting approach may fail to reconstruct homogenous image content with a smooth color gradient if the inpainting mask covers too much image content. The pixel-based approach creates a final image result by using several joint pixel blocks copied from the remaining image content. In Figure 4.6, the joint pixel blocks are visualized for three individual weighting parameters. The larger the pixel blocks and the thinner the gap between blocks, the higher the probability that a noticeable border will be visible in an inpainting image with homogeneous content. Accordingly, in the future we could investigate removal of the visual border between large joint pixel blocks by blending or interpolating image content. Fortunately, individual pixel blocks can be determined very efficiently by considering the spatial cost of pixel mappings. Further, the appearance cost of block pixels that are not fully enclosed by the block provide a direct measure of the visible border between two neighboring blocks. An application of the Poisson blending [79] has been used by e.g.,

6.2 Future Work

Sun et al. [93] to remove the visual gaps between image patches. Therefore, in the future, a Poisson blending may be investigated for large joint pixel blocks having high appearance costs at the borders. The blending could be applied in a final image refinement step for the highest image resolution after all mapping refinement iterations have been completed. If a Poisson blending is too slow for real-time execution, an approximated interpolation could be used instead to compensate for the changing lighting conditions of the reference model.

Our inpainting approach creates the final image result mainly by application of an appearance and geometric cost measure. These cost measures have a unique and unchanging orientation and scale values. Image content is copied from the remaining image content into the inpainting mask without any modifications regarding orientation, scale, perspective transformations or reflection. Often, however, image content has symmetric properties that could be used to create a more convincing image result. As discussed in Subsection 4.10.2, the current inpainting approach does not consider perspective issues commonly visible in images or video streams. In the future we could investigate the integration of arbitrary transformations into the mapping cost. Neighboring pixels should apply an almost similar appearance transformation. An additional transformation term, similar to that of the geometry measure, could be integrated into the cost measure addressing transformation costs rather than offsets between neighboring mappings. An inpainting approach integrating complex appearance transformations will evoke significant improvements regarding the visual image quality of the final result.

Neither our approach nor any previous image inpainting approaches analyze the image content in a preprocessing step before the actual image inpainting begins. The algorithms do not automatically apply individual weighting parameters or image patch sizes according to the analyzed image content. However, the size of the applied image patches that are used to measure similarity costs can have an especially significant impact on the final image result. If the patch size is too small, low image frequencies cannot be recovered reliably, but a large image patch reduces the matching performance and, even more importantly, may also result in worse inpainting results. The larger the patch, the smaller the number of image patches located in the remaining image content and not covering pixels of the inpainting mask. An automatic balancing between large image patches reconstructing important image frequencies and small image patches allowing consideration of more visual information may improve the overall image quality. Fore example, a fast Fourier transform (FFT) [94], could be applied in a preprocessing step to determine the most relevant image frequencies. The applied size of the image patches could then be adapted to the lowest relevant image frequency, but although the FFT can be calculated very efficiently, the additional calculation time is very expensive as subsequent tasks in the inpainting pipeline have to compensate the loss of time. This would be relevant during the image inpainting process if real-time performance is required.

As discussed in Subsection 4.6, the inpainting approach allows for integration of user-defined constraints. These constraints guide the inpainting algorithm to reconstruct important visual content that might not be sufficiently recovered by the default algorithm. Future work should automatically detect essential image structures such as straight lines or elliptic elements. Simple structure can be determined in an image by an application of a Hough transform [7]. Structural elements intersecting the inpainting mask should be applied as explicit constraints during the inpainting process. Essential structural information will be recovered automatically, so the overall image quality will be improved. However, like the FFT described above, the Hough transform would also need to be applied in a preprocessing step, therefore reducing the overall performance.

The implementation of our approach is currently only realized for CPUs. Although the implementation supports multi-core CPUs, our current software does not benefit from the high parallelization capabilities of modern GPUs. Therefore, future work should investigate the integration of GPUs into the inpainting pipeline. The pipeline provides a lot of potential for parallelization of the search of best matching image content. Further, the iterative refinement step may be improved by the GPU.

6.2.2 Video Inpainting

Our video inpainting approach applies homography determination partially for object tracking and partially for creating a coherent video stream. The application of the homography can be seen as a generalized tracking of a planar 3D structure between successive video frames. However, the tracking approach has limitations regarding the environment. Determination of a homography does not allow objects to be removed that are surrounded by an absolute non-planar background. A more powerful tracking of camera motion has to be investigated in future works. As the approach has to work without any a priori information, tracking approaches working in arbitrary environments and avoiding any preprocessing steps have to be investigated.

Simultaneous Localization and Mapping (SLAM) approaches may be applied concurrently to track camera motion while also creating a virtual 3D model of the direct environment. Klein et al. [60, 61] proposed an approach using natural feature points to create a 3D model of the environment. The 3D model is iteratively refined and extended by new 3D feature points whenever a new robust feature point becomes visible in the camera frame. In previous years, several feature detectors have been proposed that can be applied for the detection and description of natural feature points. The Harris corner detector [38] detects visible corners. The FAST feature detector [82] also detects corner-like features but is several times faster. Scale invariant feature detectors like the SIFT detector [72] or the SURF feature detector [10] are more robust regarding changing lighting conditions but need significantly more time for detection. Approaches like our previous real-time SURF feature tracker [41, 43], the SIFT feature tracker of Wagner et al. [99], or our recent feature tracking approach avoiding any application of feature descriptors [47] provide the basis for real-time SLAM applications in arbitrary environments. In future work, a tracking approach based on natural feature points has to be developed to allow detection of camera motion under changing lighting conditions and in almost any application environment.

Furthermore, tracking should create and refine a precise 3D model of the environment to synthesize video streams with an artificial 3D structure. Our current approach inpaints an almost planar 3D structure in the video stream. It allows for inpainting of a wide variety of live video sequences while creating a convincing image quality in real-time. However, if a more complex 3D structure could be automatically synthesized by a 3D extension of the current 2D image inpainting approach, video sequences with significantly more complex backgrounds could be inpainted. Realization of the above described enhanced tracking approach is currently restricted by computational performance of current computer devices, because both coexistent applications (enhanced tracking and more complex synthesis) cannot be realized in real-time performance. Application of a more complex tracking algorithm combined with a 3D inpainting approach will need more computation power than available today. Nevertheless, the computational power of computer hardware will increase in the next years so that even smartphones will become fast enough to allow for live video inpainting in highly structured and non planar environments without a priori information.

6.2.3 Fields of Application

In this section, some interesting fields of application will be introduced that may benefit from the approach as developed in this work.

Although the presented approach is designed mainly for manipulation of live video streams, it also can be applied for the task of post processing motion pictures. Today, well known video cutting applications still do not allow automatic removal of undesired objects in video sequences. A minor number of third-party vendors offer plugins that are able to manually warp created image content to successive video frames. Results have to be refined expensively by editors, often requiring several days to create a short video sequence of a few seconds. Thus, our approach could be applied to improve the workflow of post processing tasks. In this case, real-time performance is not the main criteria. Therefore, the video inpainting algorithm could apply a larger number of optimization iterations to provide an image result with higher quality. The motion picture production process may even benefit from a real-time solution, such as for providing for a rough preview directly at the movie set. A direct impression of the final video sequence could be provided and used to modify scenes or camera movements if necessary.

The application of real-time video inpainting in Mediated Reality systems has already been discussed in Section 1. A wide variety of applications could be realized using our real-time inpainting approach. Currently, an Augmented Reality system cannot intuitively hide a real object with a virtual model if the dimensions of the real object are larger than that of the virtual model. Urban planners or architects could use a Mediated Reality application to remove large buildings or fixtures and replace them with virtual objects. Direct visual feedback could be made available for their customers. An additional field of application is in computer gaming. Novel gaming applications allowing the manipulation of the real environment of gamers, e.g. using a tablet computer or smartphone, will provide an entirely new gaming experience. First-person shooter games would be able to integrate destruction of real objects such as cars or buildings without expensive preprocessing steps.

Finally, the video inpainting approach is well suited for live television broadcasting events. Undesired objects such as advertisements or unsightly buildings seen in the background could be removed in real-time without any visual artifacts. One strategy would allow television viewers to be provided with a video stream manipulated directly before being broadcasted to the receiver. The second would manipulate the original video stream at the receiver, just before it is watched. The latter strategy would allow user specific manipulation of the original video information, however, the first strategy would be less error-prone.

In Appendix A.1, three patents are listed that have been filed as part of this thesis.

7 Spatial Cost Convergence

7.1 Spatial Cost for Local Mappings

In the following, the proof is presented that the global spatial cost change between $\hat{f}$ and f, resulting from a modification of $\hat{f}$ at a single position $x \in T$, is twice as high as the local change of the spatial cost directly produced by the mapping.

The proof is based on the condition that the applied spatial neighborhood N_s and the cost weighting $w(\cdot)$ from (4.4) are symmetric. Further, the distance measure $d_s(\cdot)$ needs to provide commutative properties.

Claim 1. $\Delta cost_{spatial}(\alpha, \hat{f}, f) \equiv 2\alpha \cdot \Delta cost_{spatial}(x, \hat{f}, f)$, $\forall x \in T$, if N_s holds for (4.5), $d_s(\cdot)$ holds for (4.7) and $w(\cdot)$ holds for (4.9)

Proof. Let $N_s(p), \forall p \in T$ be a neighborhood filter function filtering elements of N_s according to a given position $p \in T$:

$$N_s(p) = \{\vec{v} \in N_s \mid (p + \vec{v}) \in T\}, \quad p \in T \qquad (7.1)$$

with N_s the set of relative positions defining the neighborhood as specified in Subsection 4.2.1. It holds by definition that

$$N_s(p) \subseteq N_s, \quad \forall p \in T \qquad (7.2)$$

and, as $\mathbf{0} \notin N_s$ (due to (4.6)), it holds that

$$p + \vec{v} \neq p, \quad \forall p \in T, \forall \vec{v} \in N_s(p) \qquad (7.3)$$

In Figure 7.1, the definition of $N_s(p)$ is visualized.

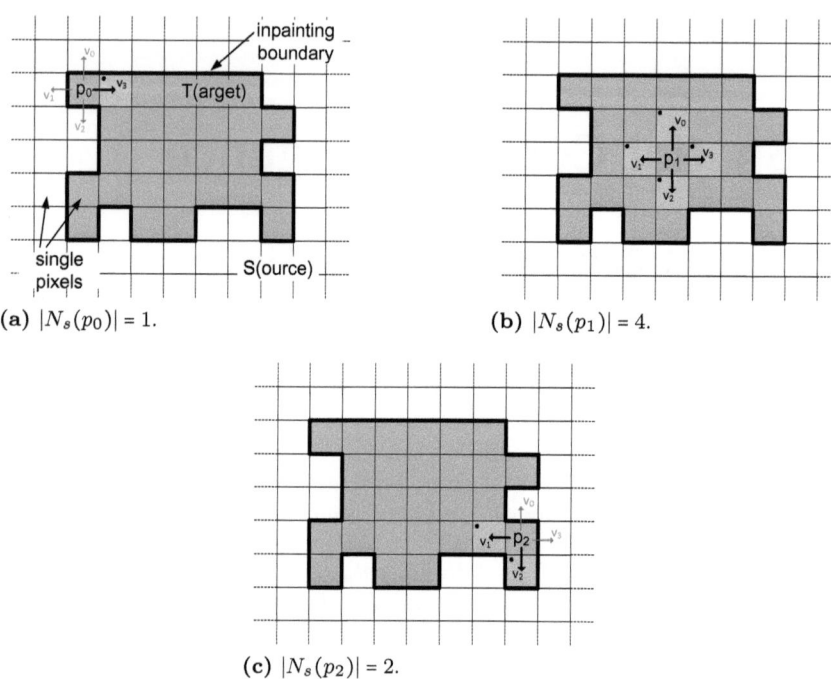

Figure 7.1: Visualization of the neighborhood $N_s(p_i)$ for three individual $p_i \in T$ of the symmetric four-neighborhood $N_s^\delta(\delta_s)$ with $\delta_s = 1$ (see also Figure 4.3a). Elements of $N_s(p_i)$ are depicted by a thick black vector, all elements $q \in \{q \in T \mid p_i + N_s(p_i) = q\}$ are depicted by green pixels (with black dot in the corner).

By application of (4.4) and (7.1), the spatial cost change $\Delta cost_{spatial}(\alpha, \hat{f}, f)$ from (4.50) may be expressed by:

$$\begin{aligned}
&\Delta cost_{spatial}(\alpha, \hat{f}, f) \\
&= \alpha \cdot \sum_{p \in T} \sum_{\substack{\vec{v} \in \{\vec{v} \in N_s \mid \\ (p+\vec{v}) \in T\}}} d_s[f(p) + \vec{v}, f(p+\vec{v})] \cdot \omega_s(\vec{v}) \\
&\quad - \alpha \cdot \sum_{p \in T} \sum_{\substack{\vec{v} \in \{\vec{v} \in N_s \mid \\ (p+\vec{v}) \in T\}}} d_s[\hat{f}(p) + \vec{v}, \hat{f}(p+\vec{v})] \cdot \omega_s(\vec{v}) \\
&= \alpha \cdot \sum_{p \in T} \sum_{\substack{\vec{v} \in \{\vec{v} \in N_s \mid \\ (p+\vec{v}) \in T\}}} \left(d_s[f(p) + \vec{v}, f(p+\vec{v})] - d_s[\hat{f}(p) + \vec{v}, \hat{f}(p+\vec{v})] \right) \cdot \omega_s(\vec{v}) \\
&= \alpha \cdot \sum_{p \in T} \sum_{\vec{v} \in N_s(p)} \Delta d_s(p, \vec{v}, \hat{f}, f) \cdot \omega_s(\vec{v})
\end{aligned}$$

(7.4)

7.1 Spatial Cost for Local Mappings

with single distance difference Δd_s:

$$\Delta d_s(p, \vec{v}, \hat{f}, f)$$
$$= d_s[f(p) + \vec{v}, f(p + \vec{v})] - d_s[\hat{f}(p) + \vec{v}, \hat{f}(p + \vec{v})], \quad p \in T, \vec{v} \in N_s(p) \tag{7.5}$$

Let T_x be a subset of T according to a given $x \in T$. T_x holds x itself and any element of T having x in the neighborhood according to $N_s(\cdot)$:

$$T_x = \{p \in T \mid p = x \ \lor \ \exists \vec{v} \in N_s(p) : (p + \vec{v}) = x\}, \quad x \in T \tag{7.6}$$

By definition, T_x is a subset of T and thus

$$T_x \subseteq T \tag{7.7}$$

holds. As x itself is part of T_x and $x \in T$ it follows that

$$x \in T_x \neq \emptyset \tag{7.8}$$

Further, T may be subdivided into two disjoint subsets T_x and $\overline{T_x}$ so that

$$T = T_x \cup \overline{T_x}, \quad T_x \cap \overline{T_x} = \emptyset \tag{7.9}$$

holds. $\overline{T_x}$ is defined by:

$$\overline{T_x} = T \setminus T_x$$
$$= \{p \in T \mid p \neq x \ \land \ (p + \vec{v}) \neq x, \forall \vec{v} \in N_s(p)\}, \quad x \in T \tag{7.10}$$

In Figure 7.2, the definition of T_x and $\overline{T_x}$ is visualized.

$\Delta cost_{spatial}$ will now be investigated between the initial mapping $\hat{f}$ and the slightly optimized mapping f according to a modification of $\hat{f}$ at one single mapping position $x \in T$ so that

$$f(x) \neq \hat{f}(x) \quad \land \quad f(p) = \hat{f}(p), \forall p \in T \setminus \{x\} \tag{7.11}$$

holds. In the following, f_x denotes the modification of a given mapping $\hat{f}$ at one single position $x \in T$ only:

$$f_x(p) = \begin{cases} f(p), & p = x \\ \hat{f}(p), & \text{else} \end{cases}, \quad \forall p \in T \tag{7.12}$$

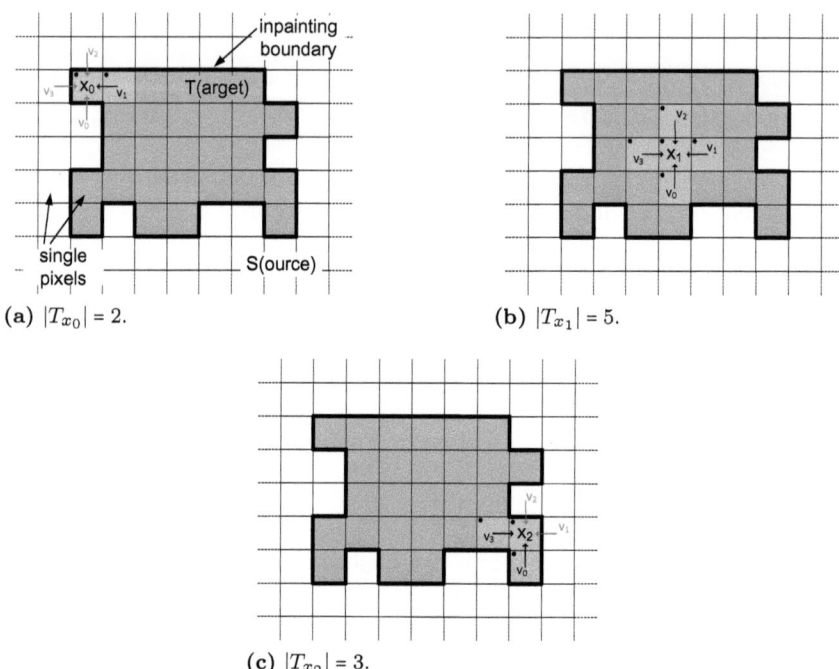

Figure 7.2: Visualization of the subsets T_x and $\overline{T_x}$ for three individual $x_i \in T$ of the symmetric four-neighborhood $N_s^\delta(\delta_s)$ with $\delta_s = 1$. Elements of T_{x_i} are depicted by green pixels (with black dot in the corner), the element of $\overline{T_{x_i}}$ are depicted by blue pixels.

Therefore, with any $x \in T$ and the application of the two disjoint subsets T_x and $\overline{T_x}$, the global spacial cost change from (7.4) can be expressed according to the single mapping modification at x by:

$$\begin{aligned}
&\Delta cost_{spatial}(\alpha, \hat{f}, f_x) \\
&= \alpha \cdot \sum_{p \in T} \sum_{\vec{v} \in N_s(p)} \Delta d_s(p, \vec{v}, \hat{f}, f_x) \cdot \omega_s(\vec{v}) \\
&= \alpha \cdot \Bigg(\sum_{p \in T_x} \sum_{\vec{v} \in N_s(p)} \Delta d_s(p, \vec{v}, \hat{f}, f_x) \cdot \omega_s(\vec{v}) \\
&\quad + \sum_{p \in \overline{T_x}} \sum_{\vec{v} \in N_s(p)} \Delta d_s(p, \vec{v}, \hat{f}, f_x) \cdot \omega_s(\vec{v}) \Bigg) \\
&= \alpha \cdot \left(\Delta_{T_x} + \Delta_{\overline{T_x}} \right)
\end{aligned} \qquad (7.13)$$

with

$$\Delta_{T_x} = \sum_{p \in T_x} \sum_{\vec{v} \in N_s(p)} \Delta d_s(p, \vec{v}, \hat{f}, f_x) \cdot w_s(\vec{v}) \quad (7.14)$$

$$\Delta_{\overline{T_x}} = \sum_{p \in \overline{T_x}} \sum_{\vec{v} \in N_s(p)} \Delta d_s(p, \vec{v}, \hat{f}, f_x) \cdot w_s(\vec{v}) \quad (7.15)$$

In Subsection 7.2, a proof is presented that Δ_{T_x} is twice as high as the single local spatial cost difference for x as defined in (4.51):

$$\Delta_{T_x} = 2 \cdot \Delta cost_{spatial}(x, \hat{f}, f_x)$$

In Subsection 7.3, a proof is given that $\Delta_{\overline{T_x}}$ is equal to zero:

$$\Delta_{\overline{T_x}} = 0$$

Therefore, the global spatial cost change $\Delta cost_{spatial}(\alpha, \hat{f}, f_x)$ from (7.13) for one single mapping modification at $x \in T$ is determined by:

$$\Delta cost_{spatial}(\alpha, \hat{f}, f_x) = 2\alpha \cdot \Delta cost_{spatial}(x, \hat{f}, f_x)$$
$$= 2\alpha \cdot \left(cost_{spatial}(x, f_x) - cost_{spatial}(x, \hat{f}) \right) \quad (7.16)$$

□

7.2 Spatial Cost for Neighbors

In the following, the proof that Δ_{T_x} from (7.14) is equal to $2 \cdot \Delta cost_{spatial}(x, \hat{f}, f_x)$, $\forall x \in T$ is provided.

The proof is based on the condition that the applied spatial neighborhood N_s and the cost weighting $w(\cdot)$ from (4.4) are symmetric. Further, the distance measure $d_s(\cdot)$ needs to provide commutative properties.

Claim 2. $\Delta_{T_x} = \sum_{p \in T_x} \sum_{\vec{v} \in N_s(p)} \Delta d_s(p, \vec{v}, \hat{f}, f_x) \cdot w_s(\vec{v}) \equiv 2 \cdot \Delta cost_{spatial}(x, \hat{f}, f_x)$, $\forall x \in T$
if N_s holds for (4.5), $d_s(\cdot)$ holds for (4.7) and $w(\cdot)$ holds for (4.9)

Proof. Let T_x^1 and T_x^2 be disjoint subsets of T_x from (7.6) so that the following holds:

$$T_x = T_x^1 \cup T_x^2 \quad \wedge \quad T_x^1 \cap T_x^2 = \emptyset \quad (7.17)$$

Due to the definition of T_x in (7.6), T_x^1 and T_x^2 may be defined by:

$$T_x^1 = \{p \in T \mid p = x\}, \quad x \in T \tag{7.18}$$

and

$$T_x^2 = \{p \in T \mid \exists \vec{v} \in N_s(p) : (p + \vec{v}) = x\}, \quad x \in T \tag{7.19}$$

Obviously, the definition of T_x^1 and T_x^2 fulfill condition (7.17).

Therefore, equation (7.14) may be separated according to T_x^1 and T_x^2 by:

$$\begin{aligned}
\Delta_{T_x} &= \sum_{p \in T_x} \sum_{\vec{v} \in N_s(p)} \Delta d_s(p, \vec{v}, \hat{f}, f_x) \cdot \omega_s(\vec{v}) \\
&= \sum_{p \in T_x^1} \sum_{\vec{v} \in N_s(p)} \Delta d_s(p, \vec{v}, \hat{f}, f_x) \cdot \omega_s(\vec{v}) \\
&\quad + \sum_{p \in T_x^2} \sum_{\vec{v} \in N_s(p)} \Delta d_s(p, \vec{v}, \hat{f}, f_x) \cdot \omega_s(\vec{v}) \\
&= \Delta_{T_x^1} + \Delta_{T_x^2}
\end{aligned} \tag{7.20}$$

with terms of the sum:

$$\Delta_{T_x^1} = \sum_{p \in T_x^1} \sum_{\vec{v} \in N_s(p)} \Delta d_s(p, \vec{v}, \hat{f}, f_x) \cdot \omega_s(\vec{v}) \tag{7.21}$$

$$\Delta_{T_x^2} = \sum_{p \in T_x^2} \sum_{\vec{v} \in N_s(p)} \Delta d_s(p, \vec{v}, \hat{f}, f_x) \cdot \omega_s(\vec{v}) \tag{7.22}$$

The cost term $\Delta_{T_x^1}$ represents the direct spatial cost difference while $\Delta_{T_x^2}$ covers the indirect spatial cost difference. From the definition of T_x^1 in (7.18), (7.5) and (4.4) directly follows

$$\begin{aligned}
\Delta_{T_x^1} &= \sum_{p \in T_x^1} \sum_{\vec{v} \in N_s(p)} \Delta d_s(p, \vec{v}, \hat{f}, f_x) \cdot \omega_s(\vec{v}) \\
&= \sum_{\vec{v} \in N_s(x)} \Delta d_s(x, \vec{v}, \hat{f}, f_x) \cdot \omega_s(\vec{v}) \\
&= \sum_{\vec{v} \in N_s(x)} d_s[f_x(x) + \vec{v}, f_x(x + \vec{v})] - d_s[\hat{f}(x) + \vec{v}, \hat{f}(x + \vec{v})] \cdot \omega_s(\vec{v}) \\
&= cost_{spatial}(x, f_x) - cost_{spatial}(x, \hat{f}) \\
&= \Delta cost_{spatial}(x, \hat{f}, f_x)
\end{aligned} \tag{7.23}$$

7.2 Spatial Cost for Neighbors

as by definition $T_x^1 = \{x\}$ holds. Therefore, in the following, $\Delta_{T_x^2}$ has to be investigated to receive the entire cost of Δ_{T_x}.

Let $N_x(p)$ and $N_{\bar{x}}(p)$ be disjoint subsets of $N_s(p)$ from (7.1) so that the following holds:

$$N_s(p) = N_x(p) \cup N_{\bar{x}}(p) \quad \wedge \quad N_x(p) \cap N_{\bar{x}}(p) = \varnothing, \quad \forall x \in T \qquad (7.24)$$

Recalling the definition of $N_s(p)$ from (7.1):

$$N_s(p) = \{\vec{v} \in N_s \mid (p + \vec{v}) \in T\}, \quad p \in T$$

Thus, $N_x(p)$ and $N_{\bar{x}}(p)$ may be defined according to a given $x \in T$ by:

$$N_x(p) = \{\vec{v} \in N_s(p) \mid (p + \vec{v}) = x\}, \quad x \in T \qquad (7.25)$$

and

$$N_{\bar{x}}(p) = \{\vec{v} \in N_s(p) \mid (p + \vec{v}) \neq x\}, \quad x \in T \qquad (7.26)$$

The definition of $N_x(p)$ and $N_{\bar{x}}(p)$ fulfill condition (7.24). Further, as $N_s(p)$ is a subset of N_s it holds that:

$$N_x(p) \subseteq N_s(p) \subseteq N_s \quad \wedge \quad N_{\bar{x}}(p) \subseteq N_s(p) \subseteq N_s, \quad \forall x \in T \qquad (7.27)$$

Therefore, equation (7.22) may be separated according to $N_x(p)$ and $N_{\bar{x}}(p)$ by:

$$\begin{aligned}
\Delta_{T_x^2} &= \sum_{p \in T_x^2} \sum_{\vec{v} \in N_s(p)} \Delta d_s(p, \vec{v}, \hat{f}, f_x) \cdot \omega_s(\vec{v}) \\
&= \sum_{p \in T_x^2} \sum_{\vec{v} \in N_x(p)} \Delta d_s(p, \vec{v}, \hat{f}, f_x) \cdot \omega_s(\vec{v}) \\
&\quad + \sum_{p \in T_x^2} \sum_{\vec{v} \in N_{\bar{x}}(p)} \Delta d_s(p, \vec{v}, \hat{f}, f_x) \cdot \omega_s(\vec{v}) \\
&= \Delta_{T_x^2}^a + \Delta_{T_x^2}^b
\end{aligned} \qquad (7.28)$$

with terms of the sum:

$$\Delta_{T_x^2}^a = \sum_{p \in T_x^2} \sum_{\vec{v} \in N_x(p)} \Delta d_s(p, \vec{v}, \hat{f}, f_x) \cdot \omega_s(\vec{v}) \qquad (7.29)$$

$$\Delta_{T_x^2}^b = \sum_{p \in T_x^2} \sum_{\vec{v} \in N_{\bar{x}}(p)} \Delta d_s(p, \vec{v}, \hat{f}, f_x) \cdot \omega_s(\vec{v}) \qquad (7.30)$$

First, $\Delta^a_{T^2_x}$ will be determined, the determination of $\Delta^b_{T^2_x}$ follows. By inserting the definition of T^2_x and $N_x(p)$, equation (7.29) may be expressed by:

$$\Delta^a_{T^2_x} = \sum_{\substack{p \in T^2_x = \{p \in T \mid \\ \exists \vec{u} \in N_s(p) : (p+\vec{u})=x\}}} \sum_{\substack{\vec{v} \in N_x(p) = \{\vec{v} \in N_s(p) \mid \\ (p+\vec{v})=x\}}} \Delta d_s(p, \vec{v}, \hat{f}, f_x) \cdot \omega_s(\vec{v}) \quad (7.31)$$

Obviously, for (7.31) regarding T^2_x, it holds that $|N_x(p)| = 1$ because $N_x(p)$ cannot hold any value except from $\vec{u}$. Thus, (7.31) can significantly be simplified by the application of $N_x(p) = \{\vec{u}\}$:

$$\begin{aligned}\Delta^a_{T^2_x} &= \sum_{\substack{p \in \{p \in T \mid \exists \vec{u} \in N_s(p): \\ (p+\vec{u})=x\}}} \sum_{\vec{v} \in N_x(p) = \{\vec{u}\}} \Delta d_s(p, \vec{v}, \hat{f}, f_x) \cdot \omega_s(\vec{v}) \\ &= \sum_{\substack{p \in \{p \in T \mid \exists \vec{u} \in N_s(p): \\ (p+\vec{u})=x\}}} \Delta d_s(p, \vec{u}, \hat{f}, f_x) \cdot \omega_s(\vec{u})\end{aligned} \quad (7.32)$$

Further, as T^2_x forces that $p + \vec{u} = x$ holds, p may be replaced:

$$\Delta^a_{T^2_x} = \sum_{\substack{p \in \{p \in T \mid \exists \vec{u} \in N_s(p): \\ (p+\vec{u})=x\}}} \Delta d_s(x - \vec{u}, \vec{u}, \hat{f}, f_x) \cdot \omega_s(\vec{u}) \quad (7.33)$$

Now, by back-substitution of (7.5), $\Delta^a_{T^2_x}$ is expressed by:

$$\Delta^a_{T^2_x} = \sum_{\substack{p \in \{p \in T \mid \exists \vec{u} \in N_s(p): \\ (p+\vec{u})=x\}}} \begin{pmatrix} d_s[f_x(x - \vec{u}) + \vec{u}, f_x(x)] \\ -d_s[\hat{f}(x - \vec{u}) + \vec{u}, \hat{f}(x)] \end{pmatrix} \cdot \omega_s(\vec{u}) \quad (7.34)$$

By (4.5), a symmetric neighborhood $N_s : \vec{v} \in N_s \iff -\vec{v} \in N_s$ is forced. Thus, u may be replaced by $-v$:

$$\Delta^a_{T^2_x} = \sum_{\substack{p \in \{p \in T \mid \exists \vec{v} \in N_s(p): \\ (p-\vec{v})=x\}}} \begin{pmatrix} d_s[f_x(x + \vec{v}) - \vec{v}, f_x(x)] \\ -d_s[\hat{f}(x + \vec{v}) - \vec{v}, \hat{f}(x)] \end{pmatrix} \cdot \omega_s(-\vec{v}) \quad (7.35)$$

7.2 Spatial Cost for Neighbors

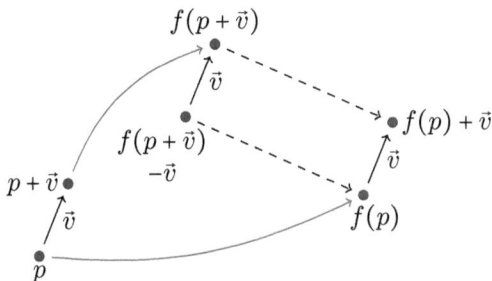

Figure 7.3: Visualization of the rearrangement of the distance measure $d_s(\cdot)$ for any point $p \in T$: $d_s[f(p), f(p+\vec{v}) - \vec{v})] = d_s[f(p) + \vec{v}, f(p+\vec{v})]$

Further, by (4.9) a symmetric $w_s(\cdot)$ with $w_s(\vec{v}) = w_s(-\vec{v})$, $\forall \vec{v} \in N_s$ is requested and thus:

$$\Delta^a_{T^2_x} = \sum_{\substack{p \in \{p \in T \,|\, \exists \vec{v} \in N_s(p):\\(p-\vec{v})=x\}}} \begin{pmatrix} d_s[f_x(x+\vec{v}) - \vec{v}, f_x(x)] \\ -d_s[\hat{f}(x+\vec{v}) - \vec{v}, \hat{f}(x)] \end{pmatrix} \cdot w_s(\vec{v}) \qquad (7.36)$$

The distance measure $d_s(\cdot)$ has commutative properties due to (4.7). With $d_s(a,b) = d_s(b,a)$, $\forall a,b \in I$ it follows:

$$\Delta^a_{T^2_x} = \sum_{\substack{p \in \{p \in T \,|\, \exists \vec{v} \in N_s(p):\\(p-\vec{v})=x\}}} \begin{pmatrix} d_s[f_x(x), f_x(x+\vec{v}) - \vec{v}] \\ -d_s[\hat{f}(x), \hat{f}(x+\vec{v}) - \vec{v}] \end{pmatrix} \cdot w_s(\vec{v}) \qquad (7.37)$$

Now, as visualized in Figure 7.3 the following rearrangement of $d_s(\cdot)$ holds:

$$d_s[f(p), f(p+\vec{v}) - \vec{v})] = d_s[f(p) + \vec{v}, f(p+\vec{v})], \forall p \in T, \forall \vec{v} \in N_s \qquad (7.38)$$

Thus, $\Delta^a_{T^2_x}$ may be expressed by:

$$\Delta^a_{T^2_x} = \sum_{\substack{p \in \{p \in T \,|\, \exists \vec{v} \in N_s(p):\\(p-\vec{v})=x\}}} d_s[f_x(x) + \vec{v}, f_x(x+\vec{v})] - d_s[\hat{f}(x) + \vec{v}, \hat{f}(x+\vec{v})]$$

$$= \sum_{\substack{p \in \{p \in T \,|\, \exists \vec{v} \in N_s(p):\\(p-\vec{v})=x\}}} \Delta d_s(x, \vec{v}, \hat{f}, f_x) \cdot w_s(\vec{v})$$

$$(7.39)$$

Finally, we have to investigate the set of elements applied by the sum operator in (7.39). This set is a variation of T_x^2 which is called $\hat{T}_x^2$ in the following:

$$\begin{aligned}\hat{T}_x^2 &= \{p \in T \mid \exists \vec{v} \in N_s(p) : (p - \vec{v}) = x\} \\ &= \{p \in T \mid \exists \vec{v} \in N_s(p) : (x + \vec{v}) = p\}\end{aligned} \quad (7.40)$$

As in $\hat{T}_x^2$ the position p is forced to be defined in T and the terms of the sum of (7.39) do not depend on p, the equation can expressed by:

$$\Delta_{T_x^2}^a = \sum_{\vec{v} \in \{\vec{v} \in N_s \mid (x+\vec{v}) \in T\}} \Delta d_s(x, \vec{v}, \hat{f}, f_x) \cdot \omega_s(\vec{v}) \quad (7.41)$$

And thus we receive by definition of $N_s(p), p \in T$ from (7.1):

$$\begin{aligned}\Delta_{T_x^2}^a &= \sum_{v \in N_s(x)} \Delta d_s(x, \vec{v}, \hat{f}, f_x) \cdot \omega_s(\vec{v}) \\ &= \Delta cost_{spatial}(x, \hat{f}, f_x) \\ &= \Delta_{T_x^1}\end{aligned} \quad (7.42)$$

Determination of $\Delta_{T_x^2}^b$ has to be investigated in the following. From the definition of T_x^2, $N_{\bar{x}}(p)$, and f_x directly follows that

$$\begin{aligned}\Delta_{T_x^2}^b &= \sum_{p \in T_x^2} \sum_{\vec{v} \in N_{\bar{x}}(p)} \Delta d_s(p, \vec{v}, \hat{f}, f_x) \cdot \omega_s(\vec{v}) \\ &= \sum_{p \in T_x^2} \sum_{\vec{v} \in N_{\bar{x}}(p)} \left(d_s[f_x(p) + \vec{v}, f_x(p+\vec{v})] - d_s[\hat{f}(p) + \vec{v}, \hat{f}(p+\vec{v})]\right) \cdot \omega_s(\vec{v}) \\ &= 0\end{aligned} \quad (7.43)$$

as $p \neq x$ (7.19) and $(p + \vec{v}) \neq x$ (7.26).

By application of (7.42) and (7.43), the cost difference $\Delta_{T_x^2}$ from (7.22) is fully determined by:

$$\begin{aligned}\Delta_{T_x^2} &= \Delta_{T_x^2}^a + \Delta_{T_x^2}^b \\ &= \Delta_{T_x^1}\end{aligned} \quad (7.44)$$

7.2 Spatial Cost for Neighbors

Finally, (7.23) and (7.44) allows Δ_{T_x} to be expressed by:

$$\begin{aligned} \Delta_{T_x} &= \Delta_{T_x^1} + \Delta_{T_x^2} \\ &= 2 \cdot \Delta_{T_x^1} \\ &= 2 \cdot \Delta cost_{spatial}(x, \hat{f}, f_x) \end{aligned} \qquad (7.45)$$

$\square$

In Figure 7.4, a scheme of the two individual spatial costs $\Delta_{T_x^1}$ and $\Delta_{T_x^2}$ for a neighborhood with four elements is depicted.

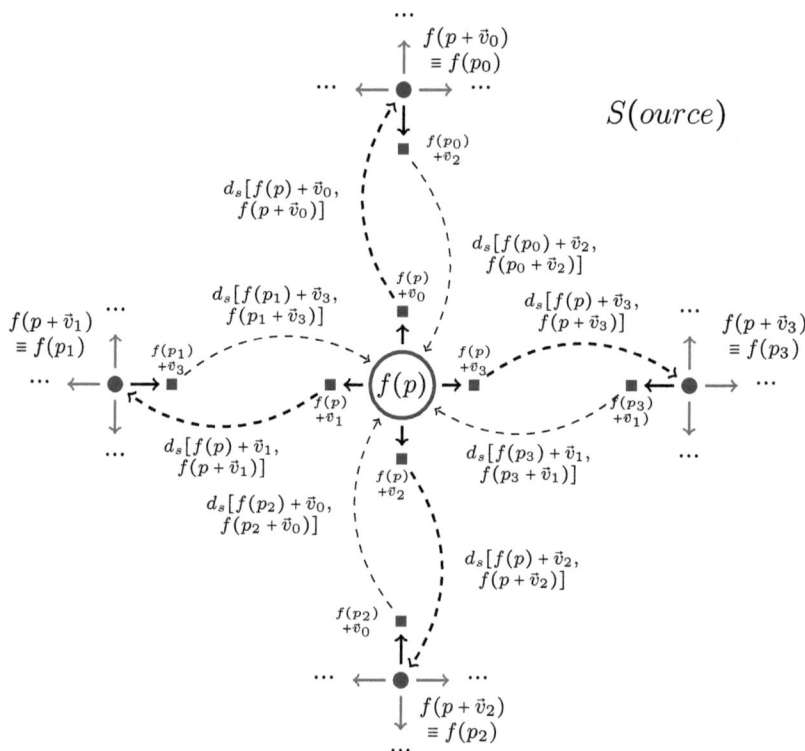

Figure 7.4: Scheme of the direct and indirect spatial cost of a mapping $f(p) \in S$ at position $p \in T$. Due to visibility reasons, the scheme is depicted for a symmetric neighborhood N_s^δ with four elements as defined in equation (4.11). Obviously, the general case of a symmetric neighborhood with arbitrary size gets more complex with increasing number of neighbors defined in N_s. The direct spatial cost $\Delta_{T_x^1}$ from (7.21) corresponds to outgoing distance measures $d_s(\cdot)$ starting at $f(p)$, while the indirect costs $\Delta_{T_x^2}$ from (7.22) are depicted by incoming distance measures. The direct neighbors of $p \in T$ according to $\vec{v}_i \in N_s$ are depicted as p_0, p_1, p_3 and p_3.

7.3 Spatial Cost for Non-Neighbors

In the following, the proof that $\Delta_{\overline{T_x}}$ of (7.15) is equal to 0 is provided:

Claim 3. $\Delta_{\overline{T_x}} = \sum_{p \in \overline{T_x}} \sum_{\vec{v} \in N_s(p)} \Delta d_s(p, \vec{v}, \hat{f}, f_x) \cdot \omega_s(\vec{v}) \equiv 0, \quad \forall x \in T$

Proof. Back substitution of (7.5) results in:

$$\Delta_{\overline{T_x}} = \sum_{p \in \overline{T_x}} \sum_{\vec{v} \in N_s(p)} \left(d_s[f_x(p) + \vec{v}, f_x(p + \vec{v})] - d_s[\hat{f}(p) + \vec{v}, \hat{f}(p + \vec{v})] \right) \quad (7.46)$$

Recalling the definition $\overline{T_x}$ from (7.10)

$$\overline{T_x} = \{p \in T \mid p \neq x \wedge (p + \vec{v}) \neq x, \forall \vec{v} \in N_s(p)\}, \quad x \in T$$

and f_x from (7.12)

$$f_x(p) = \begin{cases} f(p), & p = x \\ \hat{f}(p), & \text{else} \end{cases}, \quad \forall p \in T$$

it follows that

$$f_x(p) \equiv \hat{f}(p), \quad \forall p \in \overline{T_x} \quad (7.47)$$

as $x \notin \overline{T_x}$ by definition of $\overline{T_x}$.

Further, by definition of $\overline{T_x}$ it holds that $\forall p \in \overline{T_x}, \forall \vec{v} \in N_s(p) : (p + \vec{v}) \neq x$ and thus it follows that

$$f_x(p + \vec{v}) = \hat{f}(p + \vec{v}), \quad \forall p \in \overline{T_x}, \forall \vec{v} \in N_s(p) \quad (7.48)$$

Therefore, no direct cost differences exist between the two mappings $\hat{f}$ and f_x for any position $p \in \overline{T_x}$:

$$d_s[f_x(p) + \vec{v}, f_x(p + \vec{v})] = d_s[\hat{f}(p) + \vec{v}, \hat{f}(p + \vec{v})], \quad \forall p \in \overline{T_x}, \forall \vec{v} \in N_s(p) \quad (7.49)$$

and by application of (7.5)

$$\Delta d_s(p, \vec{v}, \hat{f}, f_x) = 0, \quad \forall p \in \overline{T_x}, \forall \vec{v} \in N_s(p) \quad (7.50)$$

follows.

Finally (7.50) directly provides

$$\Delta_{\overline{T_x}} = \sum_{p \in \overline{T_x}} \sum_{\vec{v} \in N_s(p)} \Delta d_s(p, \vec{v}, \hat{f}, f_x) \cdot \omega_s(\vec{v}) = 0, \quad \forall x \in T \qquad (7.51)$$

□

8 Appearance Cost Convergence

8.1 Appearance Cost for Local Mappings

In the following, the proof is given that the global appearance cost change between $\hat{f}$ and f, resulting from a modification of $\hat{f}$ at a single position $y \in T$, may be expressed by the sum of two individual parts (apart from the control variable α). The first part represents the direct cost change produced at the position y itself by $\Delta cost_{appear}(y, \hat{f}, f_y)$, while the second part $\Delta cost_{appear}^{N_a}(y, \hat{f}, f_y)$ represents indirect cost changes gathered by neighboring positions at their relative positions corresponding to y.

Claim 4.
$$\Delta cost_{appear}(\alpha, \hat{f}, f)$$
$$\equiv (1-\alpha) \cdot \left(\Delta cost_{appear}(y, \hat{f}, f_y) + \Delta cost_{appear}^{N_a}(y, \hat{f}, f_y) \right)$$

Proof. Let $N_a(p, f), \forall p \in T$ be a neighborhood filter function filtering elements of N_a according to a given position $p \in T$ and mapping f:

$$N_a(p, f) = \{\vec{v} \in N_a \mid (f(p) + \vec{v}) \in S\}, \quad p \in T \qquad (8.1)$$

with N_a the set of relative positions defining the neighborhood as specified in Subsection 4.2.2. Obviously, it holds by definition that

$$N_a(p, f) \subseteq N_a, \quad \forall p \in T \qquad (8.2)$$

and due to (4.14) $\mathbf{0} \notin N_a$, it holds that

$$p + \vec{v} \neq p, \quad \forall p \in T, \forall \vec{v} \in N_a(p, f) \qquad (8.3)$$

In Figure 8.1 the definition of $N_a(p, f)$ is visualized.

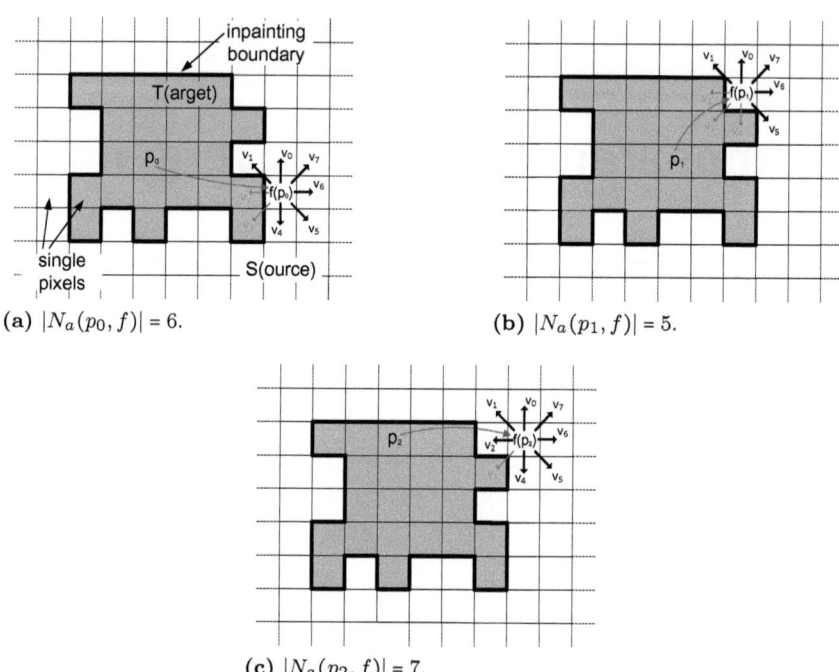

Figure 8.1: Visualization of the neighborhood $N_a(p_i, f)$ for three individual $p_i \in T$ of a square patch neighborhood $N_a^{\delta}(\delta_a)$ from (4.16) with $\delta_a = 3$ (edge length).

By applying (4.13) and (8.1), the appearance cost change $\Delta cost_{appear}(\alpha, \hat{f}, f)$ from (4.52) may be expressed by:

$$\begin{aligned}
&\Delta cost_{appear}(\alpha, \hat{f}, f) \\
&= (1-\alpha) \sum_{p \in T} \rho_{N_a}(p, f) \sum_{\substack{\vec{v} \in \{\vec{v} \in N_a | \\ (f(p)+\vec{v}) \in S\}}} d_a[i(p+\vec{v}), i(f(p)+\vec{v})] \omega_a^1(\vec{v}) \omega_a^2(p+\vec{v}) \\
&- (1-\alpha) \sum_{p \in T} \rho_{N_a}(p, \hat{f}) \sum_{\substack{\vec{v} \in \{\vec{v} \in N_a | \\ (\hat{f}(p)+\vec{v}) \in S\}}} d_a[i(p+\vec{v}), i(\hat{f}(p)+\vec{v})] \omega_a^1(\vec{v}) \omega_a^2(p+\vec{v})
\end{aligned}$$

(8.4)

As the mapping function f assigns pixel values from the source region S to positions in the target region T, the following holds:

$$i(p) = i(f(p)), \quad \forall p \in \quad (8.5)$$

8.1 Appearance Cost for Local Mappings

The mapping f for all points lying outside the inpainting mask $p \in S$ is expected to be the identity:

$$f(p) = p, \quad \forall p \in S \tag{8.6}$$

Thus, (8.4) may be expressed by:

$$\begin{aligned}
&\Delta cost_{appear}(\alpha, \hat{f}, f) \\
&= (1-\alpha) \sum_{p \in T} \rho_{N_a}(p, f) \sum_{\substack{\vec{v} \in \{\vec{v} \in N_a | \\ (f(p)+\vec{v}) \in S\}}} d_a[i(f(p+\vec{v})), i(f(p)+\vec{v})] \omega_a^1(\vec{v}) \omega_a^2(p+\vec{v}) \\
&\quad -(1-\alpha) \sum_{p \in T} \rho_{N_a}(p, \hat{f}) \sum_{\substack{\vec{v} \in \{\vec{v} \in N_a | \\ (\hat{f}(p)+\vec{v}) \in S\}}} d_a[i(\hat{f}(p+\vec{v})), i(\hat{f}(p)+\vec{v})] \omega_a^1(\vec{v}) \omega_a^2(p+\vec{v}) \\
&= (1-\alpha) \sum_{p \in T} \Bigg(\rho_{N_a}(p, f) \sum_{\vec{v} \in N_a(p,f)} d_a[i(f(p+\vec{v})), i(f(p)+\vec{v})] \omega_a^1(\vec{v}) \omega_a^2(p+\vec{v}) \\
&\quad - \rho_{N_a}(p, \hat{f}) \sum_{\vec{v} \in N_a(p,\hat{f})} d_a[i(\hat{f}(p+\vec{v})), i(\hat{f}(p)+\vec{v})] \omega_a^1(\vec{v}) \omega_a^2(p+\vec{v}) \Bigg) \\
&= (1-\alpha) \sum_{p \in T} \Bigg(\rho_{N_a}(p, f) \sum_{\vec{v} \in N_a(p,f)} d_a^{\omega}(p, \vec{v}, f) - \rho_{N_a}(p, \hat{f}) \sum_{\vec{v} \in N_a(p,\hat{f})} d_a^{\omega}(p, \vec{v}, \hat{f}) \Bigg) \\
&= (1-\alpha) \sum_{p \in T} \Delta cost_{appear}(p, \hat{f}, f)
\end{aligned} \tag{8.7}$$

with the weighted distance measure $d_a^{\omega} : T \times N_a \times (T \to S)$:

$$d_a^{\omega}(p, \vec{v}, f) = d_a[i(f(p+\vec{v})), i(f(p)+\vec{v})] \cdot \omega_a^1(\vec{v}) \cdot \omega_a^2(p+\vec{v}), \quad p \in T, \vec{v} \in N_a \tag{8.8}$$

and the appearance cost difference for a single position $p \in T$:

$$\begin{aligned}
&\Delta cost_{appear}(p, \hat{f}, f) \\
&= \rho_{N_a}(p, f) \sum_{\vec{v} \in N_a(p,f)} d_a^{\omega}(p, \vec{v}, f) - \rho_{N_a}(p, \hat{f}) \sum_{\vec{v} \in N_a(p,\hat{f})} d_a^{\omega}(p, \vec{v}, \hat{f})
\end{aligned} \tag{8.9}$$

Let T_y be a subset of T according to a given $y \in T$. T_y holds y itself and any element of T having y in the neighborhood according to $N_a(\cdot)$:

$$T_y = \{p \in T \mid p = y \lor \exists \vec{v} \in N_a(p, f) : (p + \vec{v}) = y\}, \quad y \in T \tag{8.10}$$

Obviously, by definition T_y is a subset of T and thus

$$T_y \subseteq T \tag{8.11}$$

holds. As y itself is part of T_y and $y \in T$ it follows that

$$y \in T_y \neq \varnothing \tag{8.12}$$

Further, T may be subdivided into two disjoint subsets T_y and $\overline{T_y}$ so that

$$T = T_y \cup \overline{T_y}, \quad T_y \cap \overline{T_y} = \emptyset \qquad (8.13)$$

holds. Obviously, $\overline{T_y}$ is defined by:

$$\begin{aligned}\overline{T_y} &= T \setminus T_y \\ &= \{p \in T \mid p \neq y \wedge (p + \vec{v}) \neq y, \vec{v} \in N_a(p, f)\}, \quad y \in T\end{aligned} \qquad (8.14)$$

Now, $\Delta cost_{appear}$ will be investigated between the initial mapping $\hat{f}$ and a slightly optimized mapping f_y according to a modification of $\hat{f}$ at one single mapping position $y \in T$ equivalent defined as for f_x in (7.12):

$$f_y(p) = \begin{cases} f(p), & p = y \\ \hat{f}(p), & \text{else} \end{cases}, \quad \forall p \in T \qquad (8.15)$$

With any $y \in T$ and the application of the two disjoint subsets T_y and $\overline{T_y}$, the global appearance cost change from (8.7) can be expressed according to the single mapping modification at y by:

$$\begin{aligned}&\Delta cost_{appear}(\alpha, \hat{f}, f_y) \\ &= (1 - \alpha) \cdot \sum_{p \in T} \Delta cost_{appear}(p, \hat{f}, f_y) \\ &= (1 - \alpha) \cdot \left(\sum_{p \in T_y} \Delta cost_{appear}(p, \hat{f}, f_y) + \sum_{p \in \overline{T_y}} \Delta cost_{appear}(p, \hat{f}, f_y) \right) \\ &= (1 - \alpha) \cdot \left(\Delta_{T_y} + \Delta_{\overline{T_y}} \right)\end{aligned} \qquad (8.16)$$

with

$$\Delta_{T_y} = \sum_{p \in T_y} \Delta cost_{appear}(p, \hat{f}, f_y) \qquad (8.17)$$

$$\Delta_{\overline{T_y}} = \sum_{p \in \overline{T_y}} \Delta cost_{appear}(p, \hat{f}, f_y) \qquad (8.18)$$

In Subsection 8.2, a proof is presented that Δ_{T_y} may be expressed by:

$$\begin{aligned}\Delta_{T_y} &= \Delta cost_{appear}(y, \hat{f}, f_y) + \Delta cost_{appear}^{N_a}(y, \hat{f}, f_y) \\ &= \Delta cost_{appear}(y, \hat{f}, f_y) \\ &\quad + \sum_{\substack{(p, \vec{v}) \in \{(p, \vec{v}) \mid p \in T, \\ \vec{v} \in N_a(p, f) : (p + \vec{v}) = y\}}} \rho_{N_a}(p, f_y) \cdot \left[d_a^{\omega}(p, \vec{v}, f_y) - d_a^{\omega}(p, \vec{v}, \hat{f}) \right]\end{aligned}$$

Further, in Subsection 8.3, a proof is given that $\Delta_{\overline{T_y}}$ is equal to zero:

$$\Delta_{\overline{T_y}} = 0$$

Therefore, the global appearance cost change $\Delta cost_{appear}(\alpha, \hat{f}, f_y)$ from (8.16) for one single mapping modification of $\hat{f}$ at $y \in T$ is determined by:

$$\begin{aligned}
&\Delta cost_{appear}(\alpha, \hat{f}, f_y) \\
&= (1-\alpha) \cdot \Delta_{T_y} \\
&= (1-\alpha) \cdot \left(\Delta cost_{appear}(y, \hat{f}, f_y) + \Delta cost_{appear}^{N_a}(y, \hat{f}, f_y) \right) \\
&= (1-\alpha) \cdot \left(\Delta cost_{appear}(y, \hat{f}, f_y) \right. \\
&\quad + \left. \sum_{\substack{(p,\vec{v}) \in \{(p,\vec{v}) \mid p \in T, \\ \vec{v} \in N_a(p,f) : (p+\vec{v})=y\}}} \rho_{N_a}(p, f_y) \cdot \left[d_a^\omega(p, \vec{v}, f_y) - d_a^\omega(p, \vec{v}, \hat{f}) \right] \right)
\end{aligned} \quad (8.19)$$

□

8.2 Appearance Cost for Neighbors

In the following, the proof is given that Δ_{T_y} from (8.17) may be expressed by the sum of two parts:

$$\Delta_{T_y} = \Delta cost_{appear}(y, \hat{f}, f_y) + \Delta cost_{appear}^{N_a}(y, \hat{f}, f_y)$$

with

$$\Delta cost_{appear}^{N_a}(y, \hat{f}, f_y) = \sum_{\substack{(p,\vec{v}) \in \{(p,\vec{v}) \mid p \in T, \\ \vec{v} \in N_a(p,f) : (p+\vec{v})=y\}}} \rho_{N_a}(p, f_y) \cdot \left[d_a^\omega(p, \vec{v}, f_y) - d_a^\omega(p, \vec{v}, \hat{f}) \right]$$

Claim 5. $\Delta_{T_y} \equiv \Delta cost_{appear}(y, \hat{f}, f_y) + \Delta cost_{appear}^{N_a}(y, \hat{f}, f_y)$

Proof. Let T_y^1 and T_y^2 be disjoint subsets of T_y from (8.10) so that the following holds:

$$T_y = T_y^1 \cup T_y^2 \quad \wedge \quad T_y^1 \cap T_y^2 = \varnothing \quad (8.20)$$

Due to the definition of T_y in (8.10), T_y^1 and T_y^2 may be defined by:

$$T_y^1 = \{ p \in T \mid p = y \}, \quad y \in T \quad (8.21)$$

and

$$T_y^2 = \{ p \in T \mid \exists \vec{v} \in N_a(p, f) : (p + \vec{v}) = y \}, \quad y \in T \quad (8.22)$$

Obviously, the definition of T_y^1 and T_y^2 fulfill condition (8.20).

Therefore, equation (8.17) may be separated according to T_y^1 and T_y^2 by:

$$\Delta_{T_y} = \sum_{p \in T_y} \Delta cost_{appear}(p, \hat{f}, f_y)$$
$$= \sum_{p \in T_y^1} \Delta cost_{appear}(p, \hat{f}, f_y) + \sum_{p \in T_y^2} \Delta cost_{appear}(p, \hat{f}, f_y) \qquad (8.23)$$
$$= \Delta_{T_y^1} + \Delta_{T_y^2}$$

with terms of the sum:

$$\Delta_{T_y^1} = \sum_{p \in T_y^1} \Delta cost_{appear}(p, \hat{f}, f_y) \qquad (8.24)$$

$$\Delta_{T_y^2} = \sum_{p \in T_y^2} \Delta cost_{appear}(p, \hat{f}, f_y) \qquad (8.25)$$

The cost term $\Delta_{T_y^1}$ represents the direct appearance cost difference, while $\Delta_{T_y^2}$ covers the direct appearance cost difference. From the definition of T_y^1 in (8.21) directly follows that

$$\Delta_{T_y^1} = \sum_{p \in T_y^1} \Delta cost_{appear}(p, \hat{f}, f_y)$$
$$= \Delta cost_{appear}(y, \hat{f}, f_y) \qquad (8.26)$$

as by definition $T_y^1 = \{y\}$ holds. Therefore, in the following, $\Delta_{T_y^2}$ has to be investigated to receive the entire cost of Δ_{T_y}.

Let $N_y(p, f)$ and $N_{\bar{y}}(p, f)$ be disjoint subsets of $N_a(p, f)$ from (8.1) so that the following holds:

$$N_a(p, f) = N_y(p, f) \cup N_{\bar{y}}(p, f) \quad \wedge \quad N_y(p, f) \cap N_{\bar{y}}(p, f) = \emptyset, \quad \forall y \in T \quad (8.27)$$

Respecting the definition of $N_a(p, f)$ from (8.1), $N_y(p, f)$ and $N_{\bar{y}}(p, f)$ may be defined according to a given $y \in T$ by:

$$N_y(p, f) = \{\vec{v} \in N_a(p, f) \mid (p + \vec{v}) = y\}, \quad \forall p \in T, y \in T \qquad (8.28)$$

and

$$N_{\bar{y}}(p, f) = \{\vec{v} \in N_a(p, f) \mid (p + \vec{v}) \neq y\}, \quad \forall p \in T, y \in T \qquad (8.29)$$

Obviously, the definition of $N_y(p, f)$ and $N_{\bar{y}}(p, f)$ fulfill condition (8.27). Further, as $N_a(p, f)$ is a subset of N_a it holds that:

$$N_y(p, f) \subseteq N_a(p, f) \subseteq N_a \quad \wedge \quad N_{\bar{y}}(p, f) \subseteq N_a(p, f) \subseteq N_a, \quad \forall y \in T \qquad (8.30)$$

8.2 Appearance Cost for Neighbors

Therefore, $\Delta_{T_y^2}$ from equation (8.25) may be separated according to the subsets $N_y(p, f)$ and $\bar{N}_{\bar{y}}(p, f)$ by:

$$\Delta_{T_y^2} = \sum_{p \in T_y^2} \Delta cost_{appear}(p, \hat{f}, f_y)$$

$$= \sum_{p \in T_y^2} \left(\rho_{N_a}(p, f_y) \cdot \sum_{\vec{v} \in N_a(p, f_y)} d_a^\omega(p, \vec{v}, f_y) - \rho_{N_a}(p, \hat{f}) \cdot \sum_{\vec{v} \in N_a(p, \hat{f})} d_a^\omega(p, \vec{v}, \hat{f}) \right)$$

$$= \sum_{p \in T_y^2} \left(\rho_{N_a}(p, f_y) \cdot \left[\sum_{\vec{v} \in N_y(p, f_y)} d_a^\omega(p, \vec{v}, f_y) + \sum_{\vec{v} \in N_{\bar{y}}(p, f_y)} d_a^\omega(p, \vec{v}, f_y) \right] \right.$$

$$\left. - \rho_{N_a}(p, \hat{f}) \cdot \left[\sum_{\vec{v} \in N_y(p, \hat{f})} d_a^\omega(p, \vec{v}, \hat{f}) + \sum_{\vec{v} \in N_{\bar{y}}(p, \hat{f})} d_a^\omega(p, \vec{v}, \hat{f}) \right] \right)$$

$$= \sum_{p \in T_y^2} \left[\rho_{N_a}(p, f_y) \cdot \sum_{\vec{v} \in N_y(p, f_y)} d_a^\omega(p, \vec{v}, f_y) - \rho_{N_a}(p, \hat{f}) \cdot \sum_{\vec{v} \in N_y(p, \hat{f})} d_a^\omega(p, \vec{v}, \hat{f}) \right]$$

$$+ \sum_{p \in T_y^2} \left[\rho_{N_a}(p, f_y) \cdot \sum_{\vec{v} \in N_{\bar{y}}(p, f_y)} d_a^\omega(p, \vec{v}, f_y) - \rho_{N_a}(p, \hat{f}) \cdot \sum_{\vec{v} \in N_{\bar{y}}(p, \hat{f})} d_a^\omega(p, \vec{v}, \hat{f}) \right]$$

(8.31)

Due to the definition of T_y^2 in (8.22), f_y in (8.15) and $\rho_{N_a}(\cdot)$ in (4.15), it holds that

$$\rho_{N_a}(p, f_y) = \frac{1}{\sum_{\substack{\vec{v} \in \{\vec{v} \in N_a \mid \\ (f_y(p) + \vec{v}) \in S\}}} 1} = \frac{1}{\sum_{\substack{\vec{v} \in \{\vec{v} \in N_a \mid \\ (\hat{f}(p) + \vec{v}) \in S\}}} 1} = \rho_{N_a}(p, \hat{f}), \quad y \in T, \forall p \in T_y^2 \quad (8.32)$$

as $y \notin T_y^2$.

Thus, $\Delta_{T_y^2}$ may be expressed by:

$$\Delta_{T_y^2} = \sum_{p \in T_y^2} \left(\rho_{N_a}(p, f_y) \cdot \left[\sum_{\vec{v} \in N_y(p, f_y)} d_a^\omega(p, \vec{v}, f_y) - \sum_{\vec{v} \in N_y(p, \hat{f})} d_a^\omega(p, \vec{v}, \hat{f}) \right] \right)$$

$$+ \sum_{p \in T_y^2} \left(\rho_{N_a}(p, f_y) \cdot \left[\sum_{\vec{v} \in N_{\bar{y}}(p, f_y)} d_a^\omega(p, \vec{v}, f_y) - \sum_{\vec{v} \in N_{\bar{y}}(p, \hat{f})} d_a^\omega(p, \vec{v}, \hat{f}) \right] \right) \quad (8.33)$$

$$= \Delta_{T_y^2}^a + \Delta_{T_y^2}^b$$

with terms of the sum:

$$\Delta_{T_y^2}^a = \sum_{p \in T_y^2} \left(\rho_{N_a}(p, f_y) \cdot \left[\sum_{\vec{v} \in N_y(p, f_y)} d_a^\omega(p, \vec{v}, f_y) - \sum_{\vec{v} \in N_y(p, \hat{f})} d_a^\omega(p, \vec{v}, \hat{f}) \right] \right) \quad (8.34)$$

$$\Delta_{T_y^2}^b = \sum_{p \in T_y^2} \left(\rho_{N_a}(p, f_y) \cdot \left[\sum_{\vec{v} \in N_{\bar{y}}(p, f_y)} d_a^\omega(p, \vec{v}, f_y) - \sum_{\vec{v} \in N_{\bar{y}}(p, \hat{f})} d_a^\omega(p, \vec{v}, \hat{f}) \right] \right) \quad (8.35)$$

By back substitution of (8.8), $\Delta_{T_y^2}^b$ is expressed by:

$$\begin{aligned}\Delta_{T_y^2}^b = \sum_{p \in T_y^2} \rho_{N_a}(p, f_y) \cdot \Bigg[& \sum_{\vec{v} \in N_{\bar{y}}(p, f_y)} d_a[i(f_y(p+\vec{v})), i(f_y(p)+\vec{v})] \cdot \omega_a^1(\vec{v}) \cdot \omega_a^2(p+\vec{v}) \\ & - \sum_{\vec{v} \in N_{\bar{y}}(p, \hat{f})} d_a[i(\hat{f}(p+\vec{v})), i(\hat{f}(p)+\vec{v})] \cdot \omega_a^1(\vec{v}) \cdot \omega_a^2(p+\vec{v}) \Bigg]\end{aligned}$$
(8.36)

Due to the definition of T_y^2 in (8.22) and f_y in (8.15) it follows that

$$f_y(p) = \hat{f}(p), \quad \forall p \in T_y^2 \quad (8.37)$$

as $p \neq y$.

Further it follows, that

$$N_{\bar{y}}(p, f_y) = N_{\bar{y}}(p, \hat{f}), \quad \forall p \in T_y^2 \quad (8.38)$$

Thus, due to the definition of $N_{\bar{y}}$ in (8.29), it follows that

$$f_y(p+\vec{v}) = \hat{f}(p+\vec{v}), \quad \forall p \in T_y^2, \forall \vec{v} \in N_{\bar{y}}(p, f_y) \equiv N_{\bar{y}}(p, \hat{f}) \quad (8.39)$$

Therefore, it directly follows that:

$$i(f_y(p+\vec{v})) = i(\hat{f}(p+\vec{v})) \quad \wedge \quad i(f_y(p)+\vec{v}) = i(\hat{f}(p)+\vec{v}) \quad (8.40)$$

and thus

$$\Delta_{T_y^2}^b = 0 \quad (8.41)$$

8.2 Appearance Cost for Neighbors

Therefore, $\Delta_{T_y^2}$ is determined by $\Delta_{T_y^2}^a$ only:

$$\Delta_{T_y^2} = \Delta_{T_y^2}^a$$

$$= \sum_{p \in T_y^2} \rho_{N_a}(p, f_y) \cdot \left[\sum_{\vec{v} \in N_y(p, f_y)} d_a^\omega(p, \vec{v}, f_y) - \sum_{\vec{v} \in N_y(p, \hat{f})} d_a^\omega(p, \vec{v}, \hat{f}) \right]$$

$$= \sum_{p \in T_y^2} \rho_{N_a}(p, f_y) \cdot \left[\sum_{\vec{v} \in N_y(p, f_y)} d_a[i(f_y(p+\vec{v})), i(f_y(p)+\vec{v})] \cdot \omega_a^1(\vec{v}) \cdot \omega_a^2(p+\vec{v}) \right.$$

$$\left. - \sum_{\vec{v} \in N_y(p, \hat{f})} d_a[i(\hat{f}(p+\vec{v})), i(\hat{f}(p)+\vec{v})] \cdot \omega_a^1(\vec{v}) \cdot \omega_a^2(p+\vec{v}) \right] \tag{8.42}$$

Further, due to the definition of T_y^2 and $N_y(\cdot)$, the following holds:

$$|N_y(p, f_y)| = \begin{cases} 1, & \exists \vec{v} \in N_a(p, f_y) : f_y(p) + \vec{v} \in S \\ 0, & \text{else} \end{cases}, \quad \forall p \in T_y^2 \tag{8.43}$$

Thus, $\Delta_{T_y^2}$ may be simplified to

$$\Delta_{T_y^2} = \sum_{(p,\vec{v}) \in \hat{T}_y^2} \rho_{N_a}(p, f_y) \cdot \Big(d_a[i(f_y(p+\vec{v})), i(f_y(p)+\vec{v})]$$

$$- d_a[i(\hat{f}(p+\vec{v})), i(\hat{f}(p)+\vec{v})] \Big) \cdot \omega_a^1(\vec{v}) \cdot \omega_a^2(p+\vec{v}) \tag{8.44}$$

$$= \sum_{(p,\vec{v}) \in \hat{T}_y^2} \rho_{N_a}(p, f_y) \cdot \big(d_a^\omega(p, \vec{v}, f_y) - d_a^\omega(p, \vec{v}, \hat{f}) \big)$$

with

$$\hat{T}_y^2 = \{(p, \vec{v}) \mid p \in T, \vec{v} \in N_a(p, f_y) : (p+\vec{v}) = y\}, \quad y \in T \tag{8.45}$$

Therefore, $\Delta_{T_y^2}$ is determined by summing single appearance differences from all direct neighbors p of y at their relative positions corresponding to y. Thus, we receive the indirect appearance cost $\Delta cost_{appear}^{N_a}(\cdot)$ by:

$$\Delta cost_{appear}^{N_a}(y, \hat{f}, f_y) = \Delta_{T_y^2}$$

$$= \sum_{(p,\vec{v}) \in \hat{T}_y^2} \rho_{N_a}(p, f_y) \cdot \big[d_a^\omega(p, \vec{v}, f) - d_a^\omega(p, \vec{v}, \hat{f}) \big] \tag{8.46}$$

Finally, by application of (8.26), (8.44) and (8.46) the following holds:

$$\Delta_{T_y} = \Delta_{T_y^1} + \Delta_{T_y^2}$$
$$= \Delta cost_{appear}(y, \hat{f}, f_y) + \Delta cost_{appear}^{N_a}(y, \hat{f}, f_y) \tag{8.47}$$

□

8.3 Appearance Cost for Non-Neighbors

In the following, the proof that $\Delta_{\overline{T_y}}$ of (8.18) is equal to 0 is provided:

Claim 6. $\Delta_{\overline{T_y}} = \sum_{p \in \overline{T_y}} \Delta cost_{appear}(p, \hat{f}, f_y) \equiv 0, \quad \forall y \in T$

Proof. Back substitution of (8.9) results in:

$$\Delta_{\overline{T_y}} = \sum_{p \in \overline{T_y}} \Delta cost_{appear}(p, \hat{f}, f_y)$$

$$= \sum_{p \in \overline{T_y}} \left(\rho_{N_a}(p, f_y) \cdot \sum_{\vec{v} \in N_a(p, f_y)} d_a^\omega(p, \vec{v}, f_y) - \rho_{N_a}(p, \hat{f}) \cdot \sum_{\vec{v} \in N_a(p, \hat{f})} d_a^\omega(p, \vec{v}, \hat{f}) \right) \tag{8.48}$$

Due to the definition of $\overline{T_y}$ in (8.14), $\rho_{N_a}(\cdot)$ in (4.15) and $N_a(\cdot)$ in (8.1), it holds that

$$\rho_{N_a}(p, f_y) = \frac{1}{\sum_{\substack{\vec{v} \in \{\vec{v} \in N_a \mid \\ (f_y(p) + \vec{v}) \in S\}}} 1} = \frac{1}{\sum_{\substack{\vec{v} \in \{\vec{v} \in N_a \mid \\ (\hat{f}(p) + \vec{v}) \in S\}}} 1} = \rho_{N_a}(p, \hat{f}), \quad \forall p \in \overline{T_y} \tag{8.49}$$

and

$$N_a(p, f_y) = N_a(p, \hat{f}), \quad \forall p \in \overline{T_y} \tag{8.50}$$

as

$$f_y(p) = \hat{f}(p), \quad \forall p \in \overline{T_y} \tag{8.51}$$

holds.

Therefore, $\Delta_{\overline{T_y}}$ can be expressed by application of (8.8):

$$\Delta_{\overline{T_y}} = \sum_{p \in \overline{T_y}} \left(\rho_{N_a}(p, f_y) \cdot \sum_{\vec{v} \in N_a(p, f_y)} [d_a^\omega(p, \vec{v}, f_y) - d_a^\omega(p, \vec{v}, \hat{f})] \right)$$

$$= \sum_{p \in \overline{T_y}} \rho_{N_a}(p, f_y) \cdot \sum_{\vec{v} \in N_a(p, f_y)} \left(d_a[i(f_y(p+\vec{v})), i(f_y(p)+\vec{v})] \right. \tag{8.52}$$

$$\left. - d_a[i(\hat{f}(p+\vec{v})), i(\hat{f}(p)+\vec{v})] \right) \cdot \omega_a^1(\vec{v}) \cdot \omega_a^2(p+\vec{v})$$

8.3 Appearance Cost for Non-Neighbors

Further, also due to the definition of $\overline{T_y}$, the following holds:

$$f_y(p + \vec{v}) = \hat{f}(p + \vec{v}), \quad \forall p \in \overline{T_y}, \forall \vec{v} \in N_a(p, f_y) \tag{8.53}$$

Finally, by application of (8.51) and (8.53) equation (8.52) can be thus expressed by:

$$\Delta_{\overline{T_y}} = \sum_{p \in \overline{T_y}} \rho_{N_a}(p, f_y) \cdot \sum_{\vec{v} \in N_a(p, f_y)} \Big(d_a[i(f_y(p + \vec{v})), i(f_y(p) + \vec{v})]$$
$$- d_a[i(f_y(p + \vec{v})), i(f_y(p) + \vec{v})] \Big) \cdot \omega_a^1(\vec{v}) \cdot \omega_a^2(p + \vec{v}) \tag{8.54}$$
$$= 0$$

□

A Appendix

A.1 Patents

As part of this work, three individual patents have been filed. The first patent [49] covers our previous work [40] realizing a real-time Diminished Reality approach. The previous work is the first real-time capable approach allowing removal of previously unknown objects in a video stream. A second patent [45] has been recently filed that covers the pixel-based video inpainting approach as developed in this work and partially discussed in [46]. This patent protects the mapping improvement with the spatial and appearance cost measure as well as the creation of coherent video streams. Finally, a patent has also been filed for the feature tracking approach [47] avoiding any application of feature describing structures as discussed in the previous section. This patent [44] covers the creation and tracking of a virtual feature map in real-time performance, even on smartphones. At this present moment, due diligence of the patents is pending.

A.2 Additional Patch Initialization Comparisons

In the following subsection, the patch initialization approach as described in Subsection 4.4.3 is depicted for several further benchmark images. Patch initialization is applied on a pyramid layer with low image resolution iteratively shrinking the inpainting mask. First, the important structural image content is recovered. Afterwards, homogenous image regions are inpainted. The combination of the patch initialization with the pixel mapping approach allows for real-time image inpainting. High image quality can be reached for images with heterogeneous content.

For the *Elephant* image (see Figure A.1), the algorithm first inpaints the visual content of the river as the straight structure intersects orthogonal to the inpainting mask. The foreground and the blurred trees in the background are recovered with a lower priority afterwards.

In Figure A.2, patch initialization first reconstructs the thin sash bar of the window and synthesizes the remaining homogenous image content afterwards.

The algorithm behaves similarly for the *Bungee* image (see Figure A.3). The structure of the building in the background is inpainted first, followed by the less structured green forest content. Finally, the homogenous water region is reconstructed.

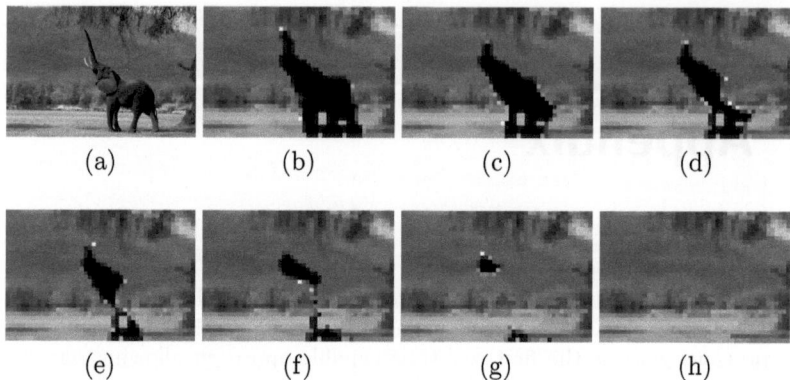

Figure A.1: Patch initialization for the *Elephant* image with original image (a), six intermediate results (b-g), and the final initial mapping result (h) with 271 mask pixels. White contour pixels have a high inpainting priority. The original image has been taken from Xu et al. [106], kindly authorized by the author, ©2010 IEEE.

Figure A.2: Patch initialization for the *Window* image. The original image a) has been taken from Pritch et al. [81] ©2009 IEEE, kindly authorized by the author, six intermediate results b)-g), and the final initial mapping result h) with 477 inpainting mask pixels.

Figure A.4 depicts one of the most complex benchmark images of related approaches. None of the related approaches is able to create a convincing inpainting result without explicit user constraints. Our patch initialization approach is able

A.2 Additional Patch Initialization Comparisons

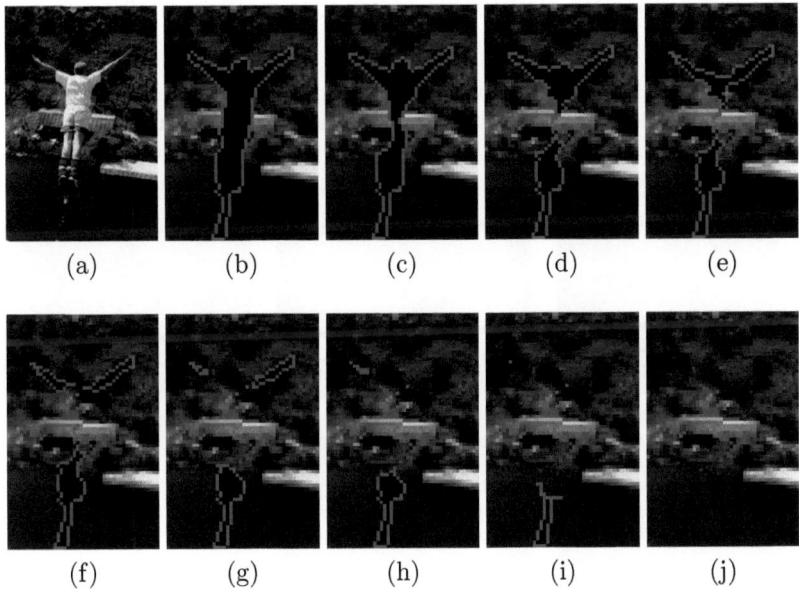

Figure A.3: Patch initialization for the *Bungee* image with original image a); the original image has been taken from Criminisi et al. [25], kindly authorized by the author, ©2004 IEEE; three intermediate results b)-i); and the final initial mapping result j) with 501 inpainting mask pixels.

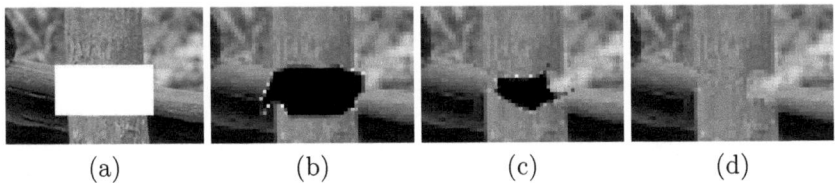

Figure A.4: Patch initialization for the *Wood* image with original image a); the original image has been taken from Shen et al. [85], kindly authorized by the author, ©2007 IEEE; two intermediate results b)-c); and the final initial mapping result d) with 450 inpainting mask pixels. The patch initialization algorithm fails to reliably reconstruct the corners of the crossing wood sticks.

to recover the major structure of the image. However, the corners of the crossing wood pieces cannot be synthesized sufficiently as the remaining image information does not provide any similar visual content.

A.3 Additional Initialization Comparisons

In the following, several additional inpainting results are provided that result from individual initialization strategies as developed in Subsection 4.4. Subsection 4.4.4 already compared the strategies for images with individual image content. Now, further examples are provided showing the individual characteristics of the inpainting strategies.

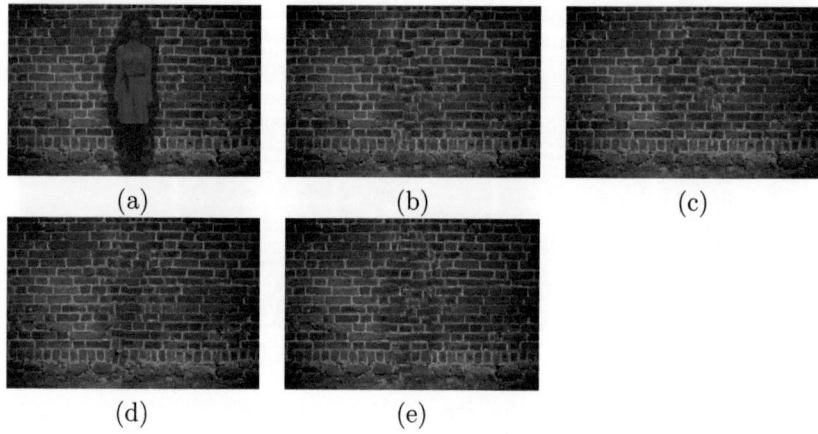

Figure A.5: Initialization comparison for the *Wall* image. a) original image combined with inpainting mask; ©2012 Paul Träger kindly authorized by the author, b) final inpainting result without explicit initialization, c) result with randomized erosion initialization, d) contour mapping initialization, e) final result with patch initialization.

In the *Wall* image as depicted in Figure A.5, a similar effect as for the *Elephant* image can be observed (compare Figure 4.17). Although the wall is comprised of a highly structured texture, the texture is almost regular. Therefore, visual differences between the four individual initialization techniques result mainly from the random optimization iterations of the core inpainting approach. However, patch initialization seems to provide slightly worse result compared to contour mapping or erosion initialization. An analysis of this issue showed that patch initialization mapping fails to reconstruct the individual stones of the wall more sufficiently as the pyramid layer on which the initialization is applied is too coarse and does not cover the significant image frequencies. Therefore, patch initialization should be applied on a pyramid layer with more image information applying a larger patch for the appearance similarity measure. The better image quality would then be compensated by a longer processing time. In Subsection 6.2.1, a

A.3 Additional Initialization Comparisons

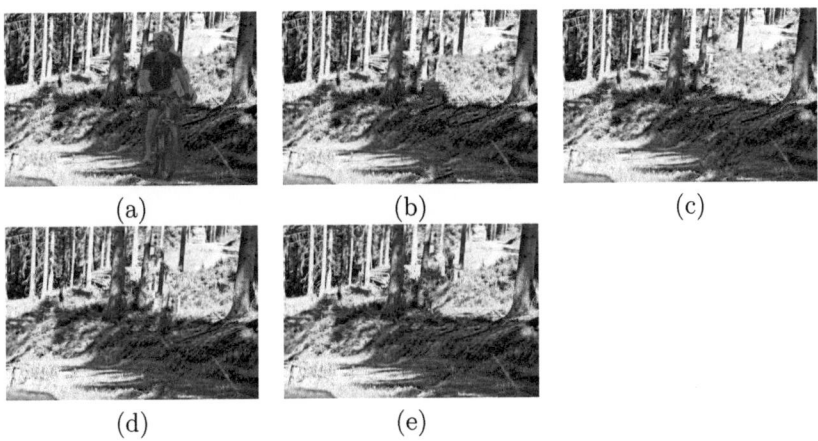

Figure A.6: Initialization comparison for the *Biker* image. a) original combined with inpainting mask ©2012 Manuel Neunkirchen, NEMIN.de, viewed 20 August 2012, kindly authorized by the author; b) no explicit initialization; c) randomized erosion initialization; d) contour mapping initialization; e) patch initialization.

draft of an algorithmic solution handling the automatic adjustment of patch size is discussed.

The *Biker* image (see Figure A.6) shows minor differences between the individual initialization techniques. The most significant differences appear in the reconstruction of the trees in the background of the biker. As the trees have straight contours, an irregular reconstruction of the tree structures is very sensitively distinguished by the human eye. Less important visual differences can be observed in the foreground for the reconstruction of the cycle track. Overall, patch initialization seems to provide the best visual result. The comparison between our previous inpainting result and the current proposed approach shows significant differences in the image quality.

A geometrically regular structure for inpainting is shown in Figure A.7. Human eyes are very sensitive to even tiny reconstruction errors due to the regular shape of the *Blobs* image. An almost perfect result is provided by application of the patch initialization strategy. All in all, the remaining initialization strategies result in the same visual image quality after the core inpainting approach has finished.

The Figures A.8 and A.9 depict the final inpainting results for images with more than one visual structure intersecting the inpainting mask. For the image in Figure A.8, all initialization techniques allow creation of a final image with the reconstructed window frame. The window frame is visible even on the coarsest pyramid layer and thus can be reconstructed even if no initialization is applied

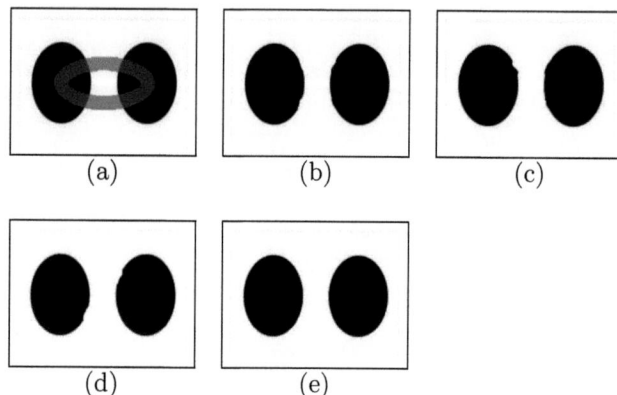

Figure A.7: Initialization comparison for the *Blobs* image. a) original combined with inpainting mask, taken from [65], kindly authorized by the author, ©2010 IEEE; b) no explicit initialization; c) randomized erosion initialization; d) contour mapping initialization; e) patch initialization.

as depicted in A.8c. However, the thin sash bar is preserved only by patch initialization, as this structure is almost invisible on the coarse pyramid layer.

The inpainting result of the *Wood* image as depicted in Figure A.9 can still be improved. None of the initialization techniques allow final result to be provided that would be able to spoof an observer not knowing that these images have been manipulated. As the remaining image information in the *Wood* image do not provide any visual elements similar to crossing wood pieces, iterative refinement repetitions cannot find perfect matching image content and thus have to create the final result by piecing up the remaining image content.

The *Wood* image is one of the most challenging benchmark images and none of the related inpainting algorithms as introduced in Subsection 2.1.2 are able to provide a more convincing result without using user-defined guiding information.

Also, the result of the *Biker* image (Figure A.6) shows contradictions in the background region intersected by the trees. The inpainting pipeline is not able to recover the individual elements of the environment sufficiently. Thus, the approach needs further improvements to allow the manipulation of such complex scenes.

A.3 Additional Initialization Comparisons

Figure A.8: Initialization comparison for the *Window* image. a) original image, b) original combined with inpainting mask, c) no explicit initialization, d) randomized erosion initialization, e) contour mapping initialization, f) patch initialization. The original image has been taken from Pritch et al. [81] ©2009 IEEE, kindly authorized by the author.

Figure A.9: Initialization comparison for the *Wood* image. a) original image combined with inpainting mask taken from Shen et al. [85], kindly authorized by the author, ©2007 IEEE; b) final result without explicit initialization; c) randomized erosion initialization; d) contour mapping initialization; e) final result image started with a patch initialization.

A.4 Additional Image Inpainting Results

In Subsection 4.9, several image inpainting results have already been provided for individual benchmark images. In the following, further image inpainting results will be presented.

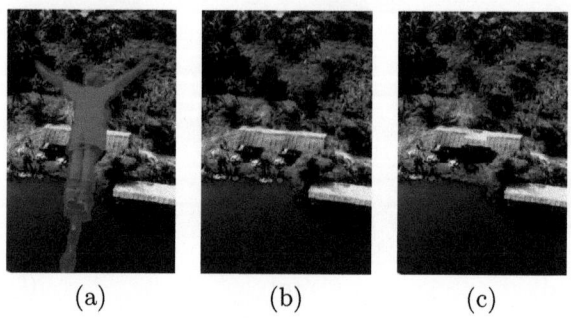

(a)   (b)   (c)

Figure A.10: Result comparison for the *Bungee* image with the algorithm of Pritch et al. a) Original image with inpainting mask (notice that this time the mask covers the small gray area behind the man's chest), b) result by Pritch et al. [81], c) our result. The reference images have been taken from [81], kindly authorized by the author. ©2009 IEEE

Pritch et al. [81] used a *Bungee* image with better image contrast and a more optimized inpainting mask covering image content more difficult to integrate into the final image. As the approach of Pritch et al. also applies pixel mapping during their inpainting process (as we do), a comparison of our approach with image data of Pritch et al. is given in Figure A.10. Our algorithm shows the same performance as for the original bungee image (see Figure 4.43). Unfortunately, Pritch et al. do not give accurate performance values but a performance range for all their results in their work (between 0.5 and 30 seconds).

Similar to other benchmark images, the *Window* image in Figure A.11 has important structural information that has to be recovered during the inpainting process. Our approach is able to provide a similar result as Sun et al. [93] or Pritch et al. [81]. Our final inpainting result is determined within 19 ms. Neither Sun nor Pritch provide unique performance values for this benchmark image. However, Sun and Pritch give performance ranges for other test images. These values allow us to conclude that their approach is at least one or two magnitudes slower than the approach as developed in this work. In Table 4.8, the detailed performance values for the *Window* image are provided.

Figure A.12 compares our result for the *Wood* image with the approach of Drori et al. and Shen et al. The inpainting mask covers four straight lines crossing each other. None of the approaches not applying any user-defined constraints provide a

A.4 Additional Image Inpainting Results

Figure A.11: Result comparison for the *Window* image. a) Original image, b) original with inpainting mask, c) result by Pritch et al. [81], d) our result. The reference images are taken from [81] ©2009 IEEE, kindly authorized by the author.

perfect result. However, our recent approach does not provide worse results than all other approaches but also has proven to be several times faster. In Table 4.8, the performance of our approach is depicted showing that the overall inpainting pipeline needs 16.4 ms for the *Wood* picture.

Figure A.13 compares our result with an another inpainting result from Drori et al. [30]. Our algorithm needs less than 18 ms for the entire inpainting process while the approach of Drori would need more than 15 minutes on our test hardware (with an estimated performance increase of $\Theta = 10$). Thus, our approach is more then 50,000 times faster than the algorithm of Drori. Further, the result by Drori has blurred areas especially around the reconstructed trees.

In Figure A.14, an inpainting comparison for the *Still Life* with four related image manipulation approaches is depicted. Although this image does not match with the objective of this work (the apple is only partially removed), the image quality of our approach is almost identical to that of all other algorithms.

Often, related inpainting approaches use the *Microphone* picture for benchmarking. In Figure A.15, the image quality of our algorithm is compared with that of Bertalmio et al. [13], Shen et al. [85] and that of Kwok et al. [65]. The approach

Figure A.12: Result comparison for the *Wood* image. a) Original image with inpainting mask; b) result by Drori et al. [30] ©2003 ACM, c) result by Shen et al. [85], d) our result. The reference images are kindly authorized by the authors.

of Bertalmio creates undesired blurring effects while our approach and that of Shen and Kwok provide similarly convincing image qualities.

In Figure A.16, an inpainting image of Criminisi et al. [24] is depicted. On the one hand, the image shows important structural image information that has to be recovered in the final image. On the other hand, the surrounding image content is covered by simple textures. The combination of the patch initialization strategy with the iterative mapping refinement approach allows both tasks to be handled concurrently with high performance results.

As already discussed in the introduction in Chapter 1, the objective of this work is not to support the inpainting of a partial region or element of a visible object. Instead, this work is designed to removed one undesired object in one piece while recovering the unknown background. However, it should be mentioned that all related image inpainting approaches cannot reliably remove parts of undesired object, either. In Figure A.17, a part of a train is removed and the final image is compared to the approach of Drori et al. [30]. None of the resulting inpainting images is able to spoof an observer not knowing the original image.

In Figure A.18, a direct comparison between our previous and our new inpainting approach is presented. Although, the inpainting of the undesired objects lying on

A.4 Additional Image Inpainting Results

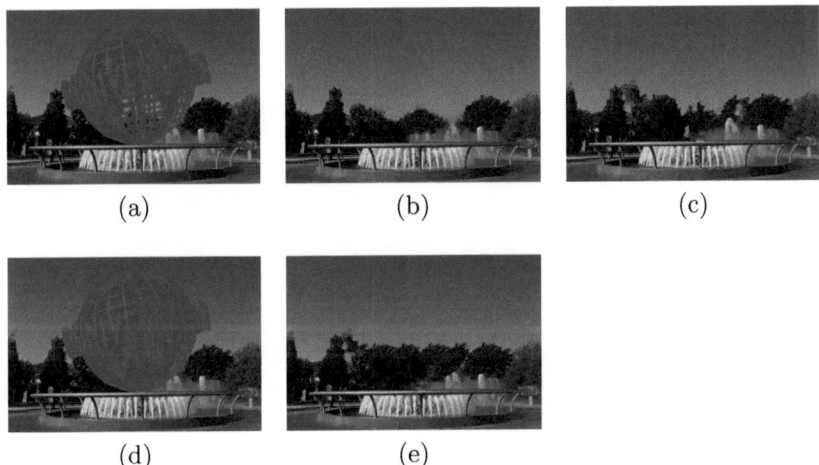

Figure A.13: *Universal Studios* image from Drori [30] ©2003 ACM, kindly authorized by the author. a) Original with inpainting mask; b) result by Drori; c) our result with the original mask; d) dense mask without tiny holes in the middle (as these holes have an intermediate alpha value in the original work), e) our result for the dense mask.

the chair seems to be trivial, our previous approach provided a final image with smooth image content. In contrast, the image manipulation approach as developed in this work creates a final image with sharp image content.

Figure A.19 depicts that our inpainting approach is able to handle individual background content still provides a convincing image result. The individually structured green grass as well as the dry leaves are reconstructed reliably. Our approach creates the final inpainting image with resolution 1842×1266 and 182,860 inpainting pixels in less than 200 ms.

The previous inpainting images did not apply explicit used-defined constraints as introduced in Subsection 4.6. Therefore, in Figure A.20, a comparison for inpainting constraints is provided. The inpainting result without user-defined line constraints show minor undesired jumps at the yellow bar on the street. In contrast, the inpainting result created with the application of four finite line constraints provide absolute strait borders at the yellow bar.

Figure A.14: Result comparison for the *Still Life with Apples* image with four individual approaches. a) Original picture, b) original image with inpainting mask, c) result by Drori et al. [30] ©2003 ACM, d) result by Shen et al. [85], e) result by Xu et al. [106] ©2010 IEEE, f) our result. The reference images are kindly authorized by the authors.

A.4 Additional Image Inpainting Results

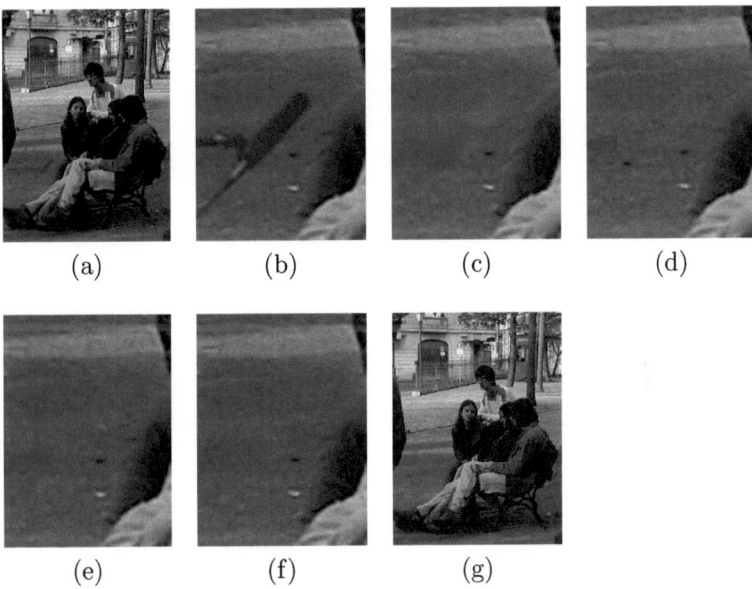

Figure A.15: Result comparison for an image introduced by Bertalmio et al. a) Original image with inpainting mask, b) zoomed original with inpainting mask, c) zoomed result by Bertalmio et al. [13] ©2000 ACM, d) zoomed result by Shen et al. [85], e) zoomed result by Kwok et al. [65] ©2010 IEEE; f) our zoomed result, g) our result. The reference images are kindly authorized by the authors.

(a) Original image with inpainting mask.   (b) Our result (similar to that of Criminisi et al. [25].

Figure A.16: Result comparison for the *Dog* image. The original image is taken from Criminisi et al. [25], ©2004 IEEE, kindly authorized by the author.

(a) (b) (c)

Figure A.17: Result comparison for the *Train* image. a) Original image with inpainting mask, b) result by Drori et al. [30], c) our result. The reference images are taken from [30] ©2003 IEEE, kindly authorized by the author.

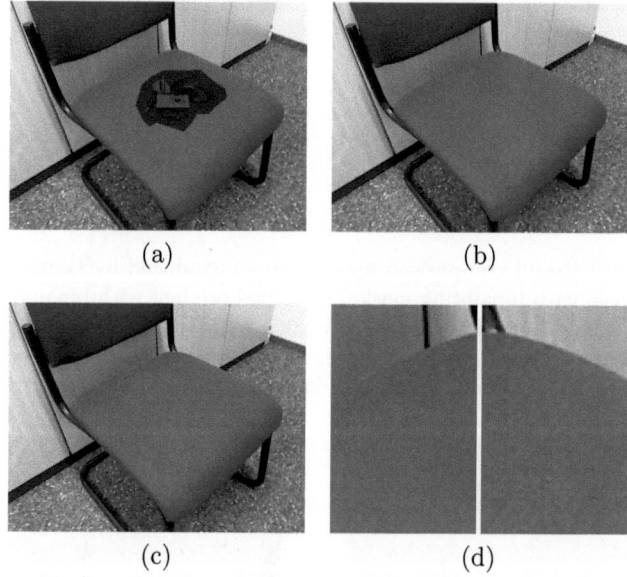

Figure A.18: Result comparison for the *Chair* image. a) Original image with inpainting mask, b) result by our previous approach [40], c) our result not blurring the structure of the sitting area, d) zoom-in of our previous result (left) and the new result (right).

A.4 Additional Image Inpainting Results

Figure A.19: Inpainting result example with leaves in the background. a) Original image with inpainting mask, b) inpainting result. Image source: bbroianigo / pixelio.de (creative commons image database), viewed 19 September 2012

Figure A.20: Constraint image inpainting example. a) original image, b) original image with inpainting mask and four finite line constraints, c) inpainting result without constraints, d) inpainting result with constraints. Image source: Peter Smola / pixelio.de (creative commons image database), viewed 19 September 2012

A.5 Additional Video Inpainting Results

In the following, additional results of the video inpainting approach that has been developed in this work will be provided. In Subsection 5.7.3, some visual results have already been presented. In the following, additional video sequences with individually selected visual environments and inpainting objects are presented.

In A.21, the video inpainting result for a house facade is given. An undesired window is removed in the video sequence while a coherent video stream is provided. By precisely synthesizing the texture of the remaining house facade, the inpainting mask is filled with image content

Another video with frame resolution 640 × 480 has been inpainted in Figure A.22. The video sequence is composed of more than 500 frames and shows an undesired object in front of a regular textured background. The background is almost planar and the hand-held camera moves around the object. The screenshots in Figure A.22 show that resulting video quality is comparable to the remaining image content in each video frame. Further, the video shows a stream coherency with high accuracy.

In Figure A.23 an inpainting video stream is depicted with an absolute planar background. A nut is removed on a homogenous and regular textured sidewalk. The resulting video stream has high accuracy although the camera captures the scene with extreme zooming, rotation and panning movements.

In Figure A.24, a backpack is removed in a video sequence. On the one hand, motion detection of the inpainting contour is a nontrivial task as the background does not provide unique feature points. On the other hand, the contour refinement step can reliably distinguish between desired and undesired video pixels due to the unique contour. The camera moves around the object with a circular sector of about 180°.

The real-time tracking algorithm as developed in this work is also able to reliably identify and track the undesired drain in the street as depicted in Figure A.25. Undesired image content is removed by a synthesized flagstone perfectly fitting into the inpainting mask. The hand-held camera captures the drain and rotates around the object.

In Figure A.26, a snowball is removed covering important structural information. The strong edge between the grass and the side walk is reconstructed reliably as patch initialization is able to reconstruct the straight line.

However, the patch initialization approach fails to reconstruct circular geometry as depicted in Figure A.27. Although the individual video frames provide a high image quality with an accurate stream coherence, an observer cannot be spoofed by the real-time result as the reconstructed drain shows minor geometric errors. An automatic detection of an elliptical constraints as described in Subsection 6.2.1 might be applied to create a more convincing result.

The homogenous background in Figure A.28 is a complex tracking environment. However, due to the individual tracking sub-algorithms as developed in Subsection

A.5 Additional Video Inpainting Results

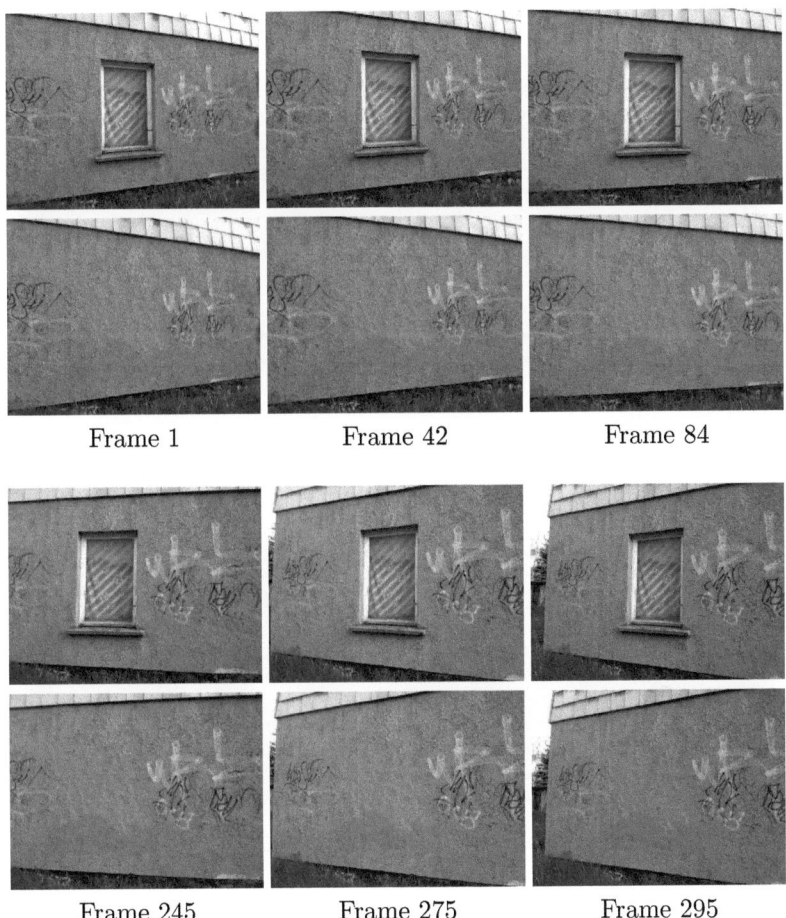

Figure A.21: Real-time video inpainting removing a window in a textured house facade. A reliable stream coherence is provided. The video has been captured by a hand-held camera with an image resolution of 640 × 480 pixels and is composed of almost 300 frames.

5.2, a convincing video stream is provided showing a wall without the undesired light switch. Further, the shadow near the undesired object does not influence the final video result.

In Figure A.29, a volumetric object has been removed in a video sequence captured with an almost stationary (but hand-held) camera. Although the video inpainting approach generally is not able to handle volumetric objects as discussed in Subsection 5.8, a convincing video result is provided due to the restricted camera motion. Thus, comparable to all related video inpainting approaches as presented in Subsection 2.2, our algorithm allows for manipulation of video sequences with arbitrary static objects as long as the camera is almost stationary. The video sequence shows two moving persons behind the objects that do not reduce the image quality.

A.5 Additional Video Inpainting Results

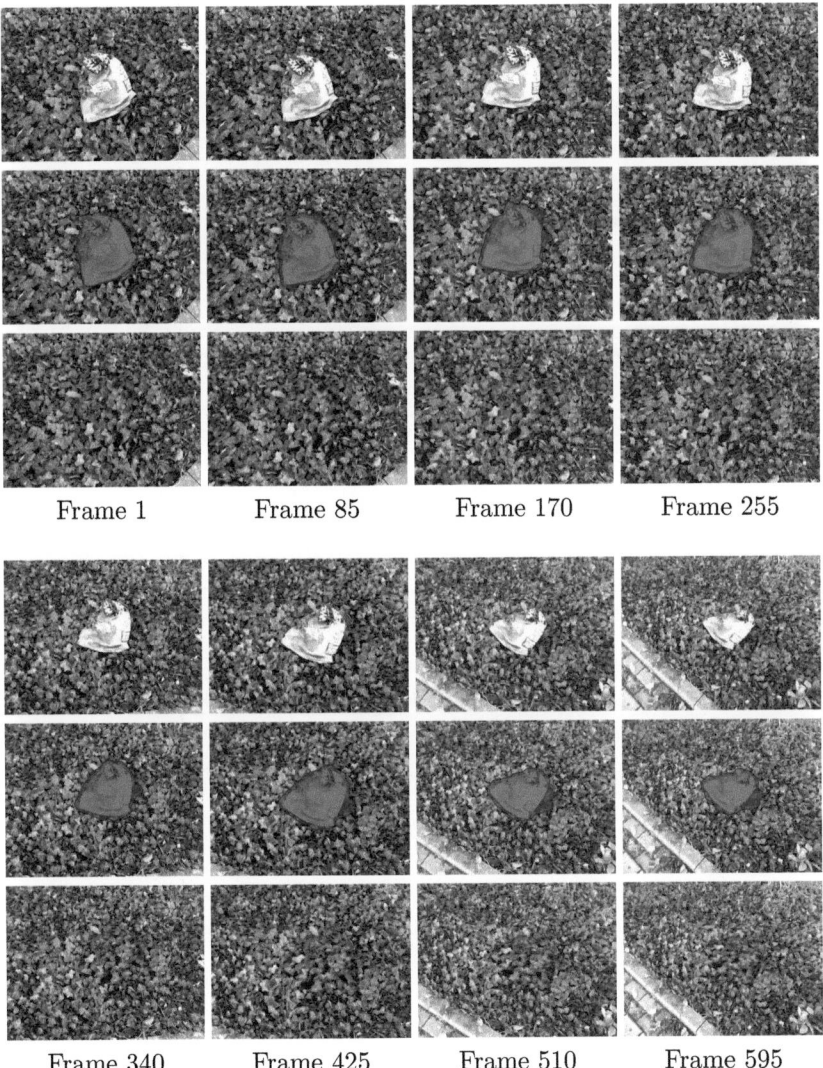

| Frame 1 | Frame 85 | Frame 170 | Frame 255 |

| Frame 340 | Frame 425 | Frame 510 | Frame 595 |

Figure A.22: Real-time video inpainting with a background composed of ivy plants. The video has been captured by a hand-held camera with an image resolution of 640 × 480 pixels and is composed of almost 600 frames. The corresponding performance values are discussed in Table 5.1 and 5.2.

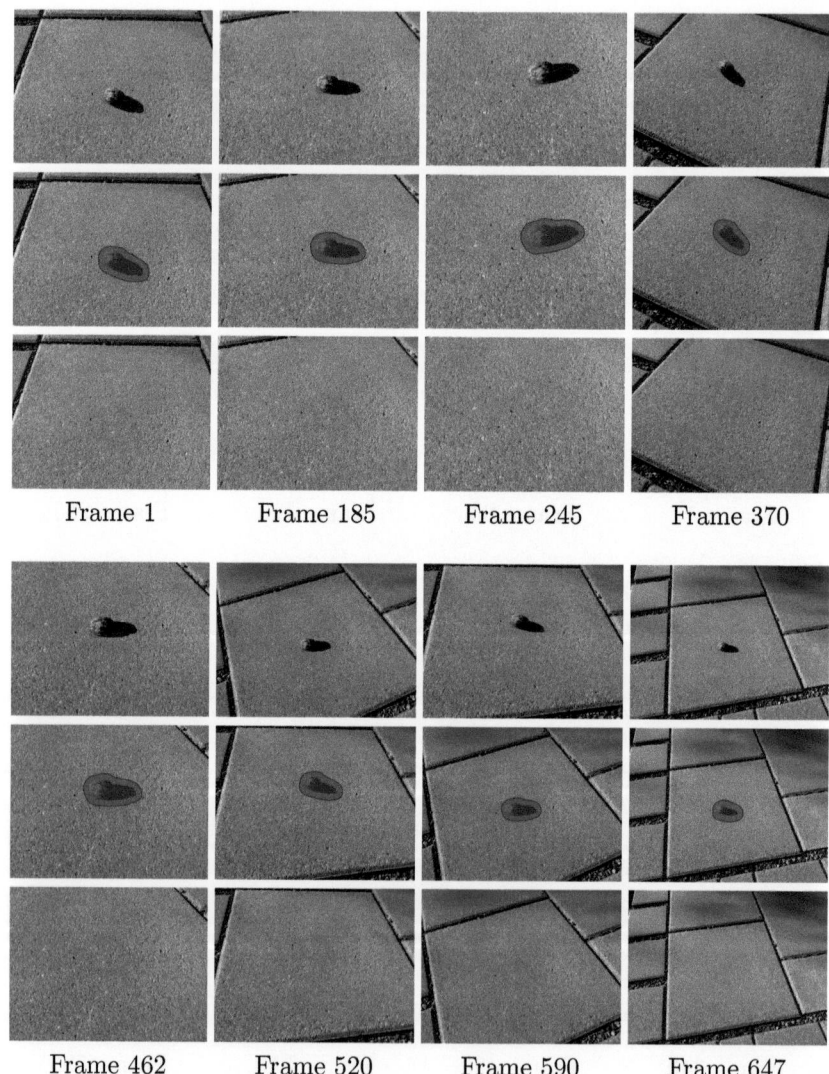

Figure A.23: Real-time video inpainting with an almost homogenous but structured texture background. The video has been captured by a hand-held camera with an image resolution of 640 × 480 pixels and is composed of almost 700 frames. The corresponding performance values are discussed in Table 5.1 and 5.2.

A.5 Additional Video Inpainting Results

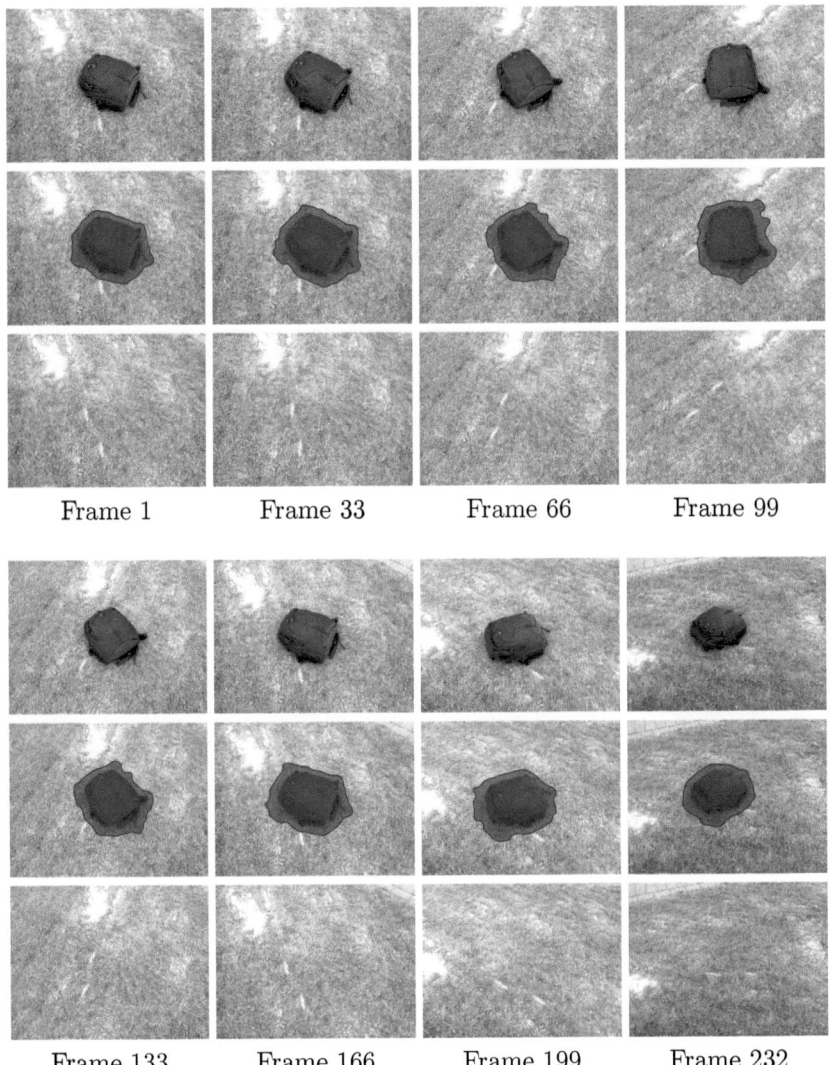

Frame 1 Frame 33 Frame 66 Frame 99

Frame 133 Frame 166 Frame 199 Frame 232

Figure A.24: Real-time video inpainting with a grass background. The video has been captured by a hand-held camera with an image resolution of 640 × 480 pixels and is composed of about 230 frames.

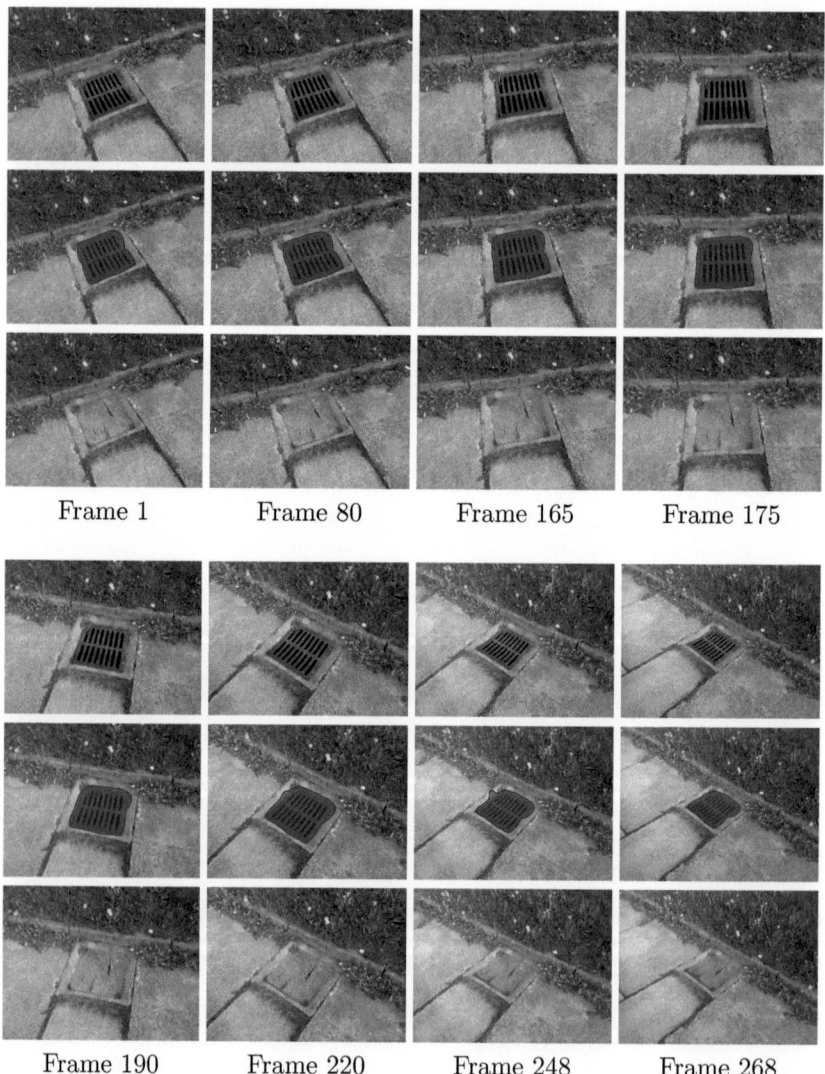

Figure A.25: Real-time video inpainting removing a drain in the street. The video has been captured by a hand-held camera with an image resolution of 640 × 480 pixels and is composed of almost 270 frames.

A.5 Additional Video Inpainting Results

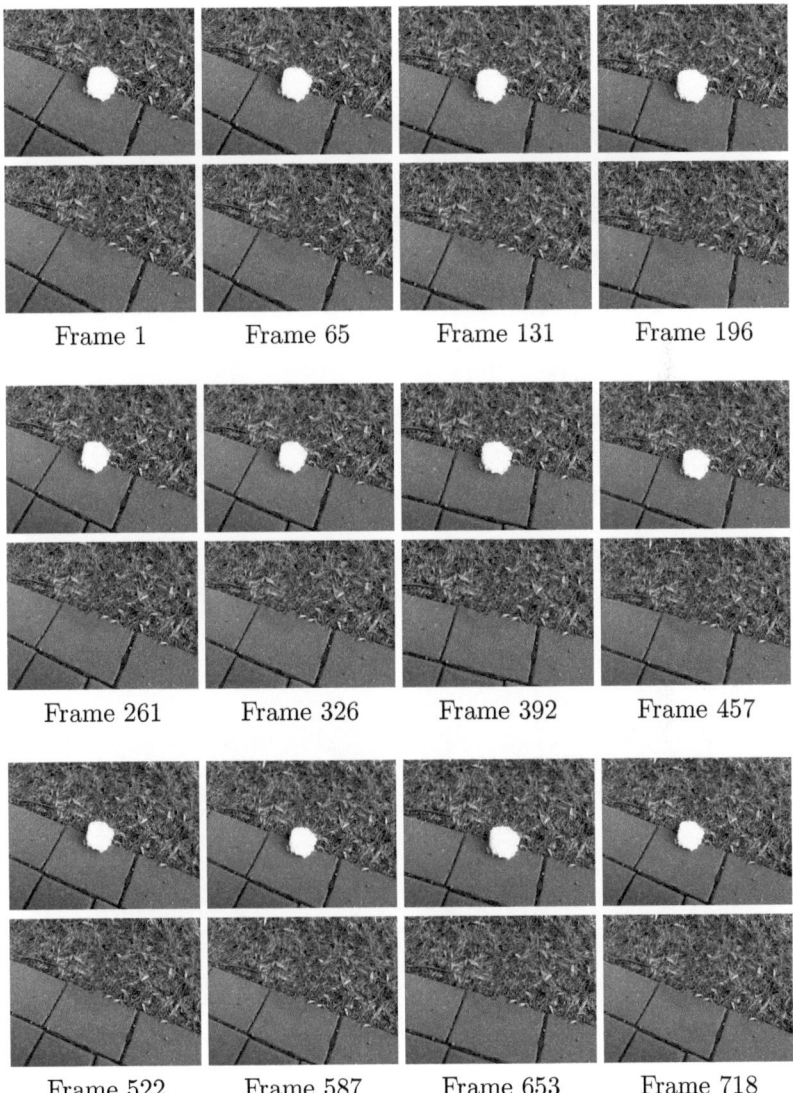

Figure A.26: Real-time video inpainting removing a snow ball lying at the border of a sidewalk. The straight line is reliably reconstructed while a coherent video stream is provided. The video has been captured by a hand-held camera with an image resolution of 640×480 pixels and is composed of about 700 frames.

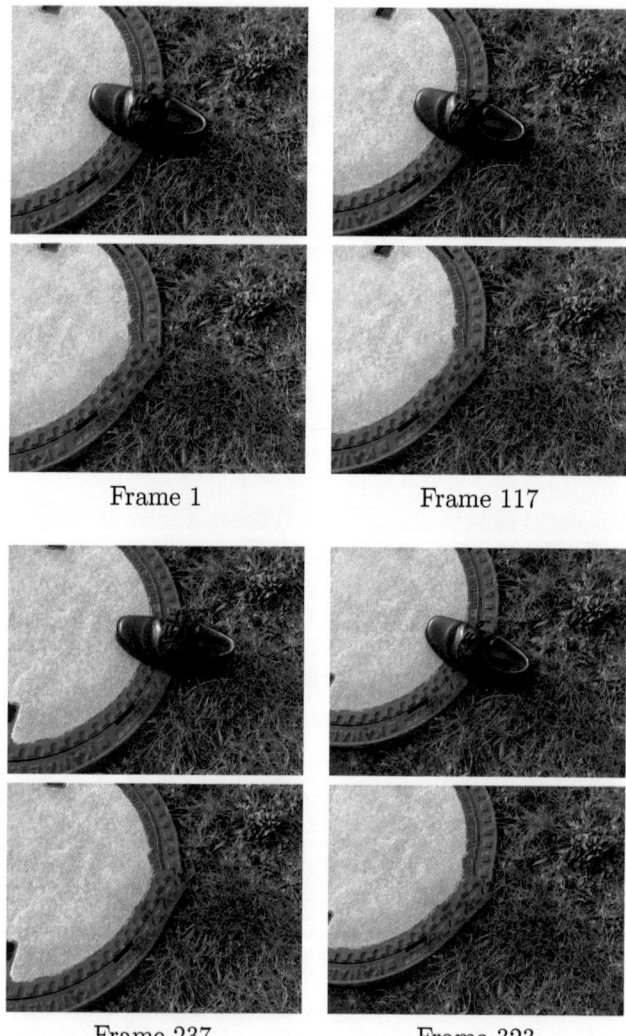

Frame 1 Frame 117

Frame 237 Frame 323

Figure A.27: Real-time video inpainting removing a shoe lying on a circular drain. The circular structure of the drain is partially recovered. The video has been captured by a hand-held camera with an image resolution of 640 × 480 pixels and is composed of about 320 frames.

A.5 Additional Video Inpainting Results

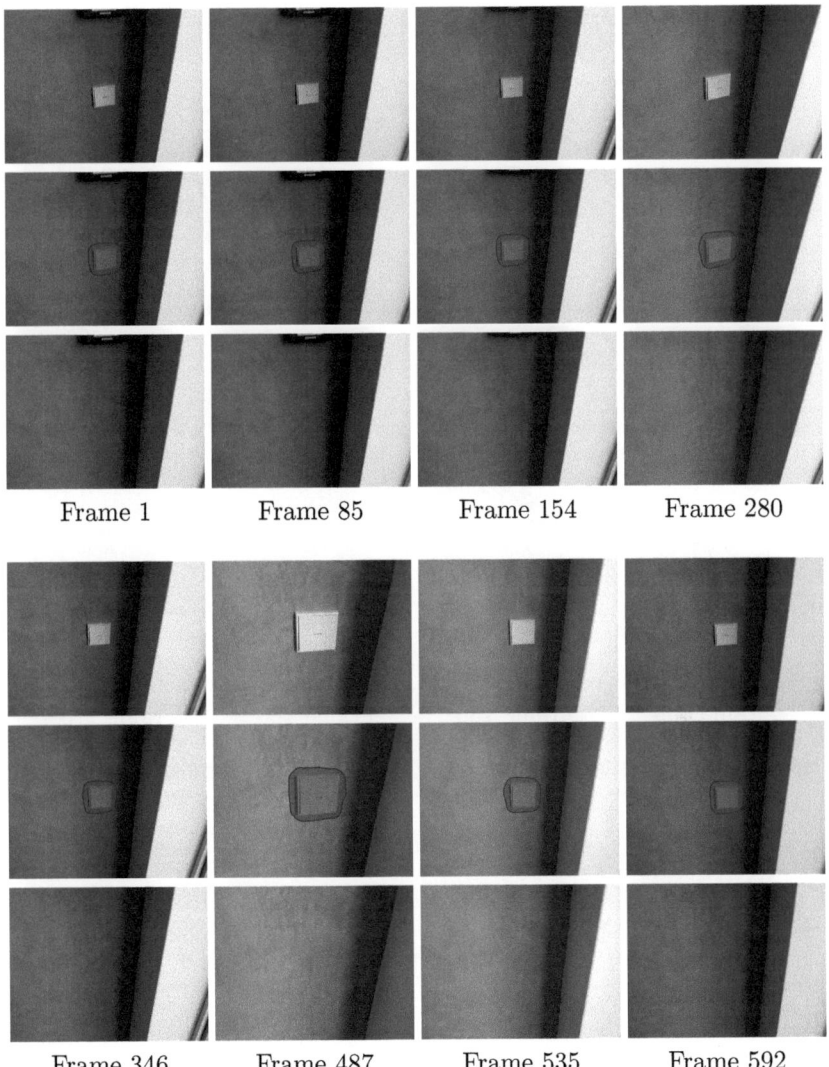

Frame 1   Frame 85   Frame 154   Frame 280

Frame 346   Frame 487   Frame 535   Frame 592

Figure A.28: Real-time video inpainting removing a light switch in a homogenous background. A reliable real-time tracking of the undesired object is provided. The video has been captured by a hand-held camera with an image resolution of 640 × 480 pixels and is composed of almost 600 frames.

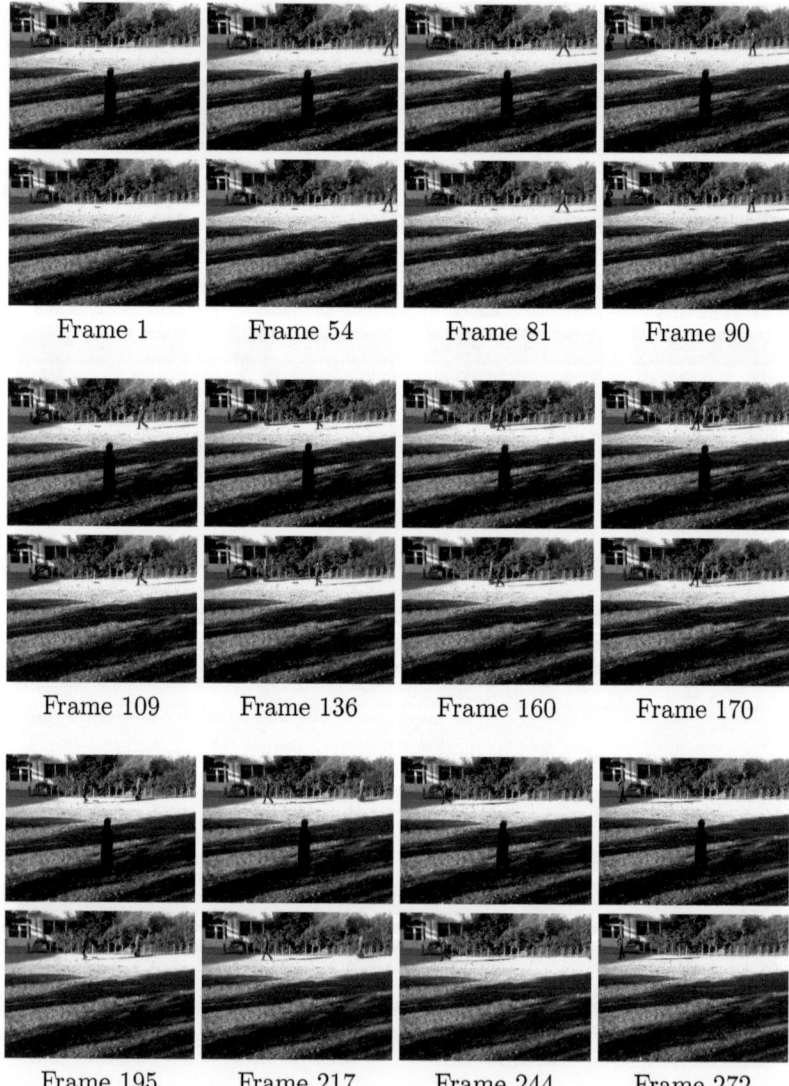

Figure A.29: Real-time video inpainting removing a statue captured by an almost stationary camera. The moving persons in the background do not disturb the inpainting algorithm. The video has been captured by a hand-held camera with an image resolution of 640 × 480 pixels and is composed of almost 300 frames.

A.6 Additional Study Results

In the following, additional user ratings and measurements determined by our user study as presented in Subsection 5.7.2 are presented.

A.6.1 User Ratings

In Subsection 5.7.2, the test subjects ratings for the two first evaluation backgrounds B_0 and B_1 have been presented. In the following, the ratings for the remaining 10 backgrounds are presented. The Figures A.30 - A.34 show the individual background characteristics and the corresponding ratings of all participants.

The manipulated videos for the backgrounds B_2, B_6 and B_7 received almost the same ratings as the original test sequences. Although the visual information of the backgrounds is regularly structured and is composed of complex visual elements, our video inpainting algorithm is able to create a final video sequence able to convincingly spoof the test subjects.

The manipulated test video of background B_5 (Figure A.31b) is exposed by a majority of the test subjects as manipulated video information. The test persons did not decide a unique rating for background B_{10}. The participants rated the manipulated video sequence as well as the original video sequence as original or as manipulated to the same extent.

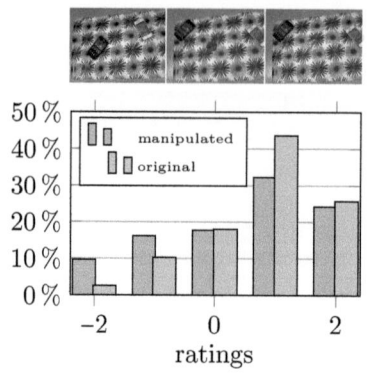
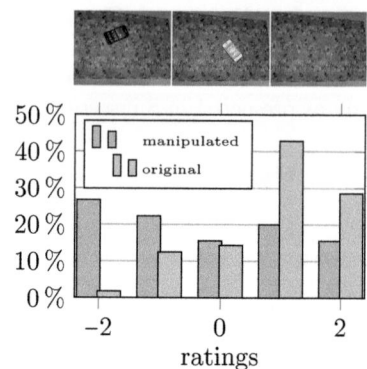

(a) Rates for the original and manipulated video of background B_2 (see Figure A.35).

(b) Rates for the original and manipulated video of background B_3.

Figure A.30: Test subject rates for evaluation background B_2 and B_3. Top (from left to right): screen shot of original video test sequence, original video sequence that will be manipulated, manipulated video sequence, bottom: corresponding ratings of test persons. The meaning of the ratings is provides in Table 5.3.

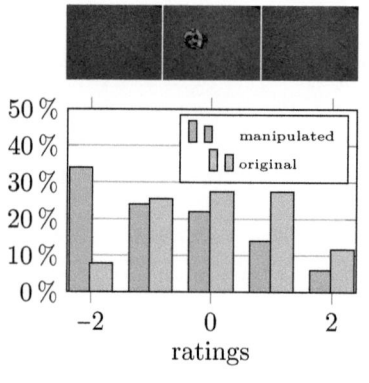
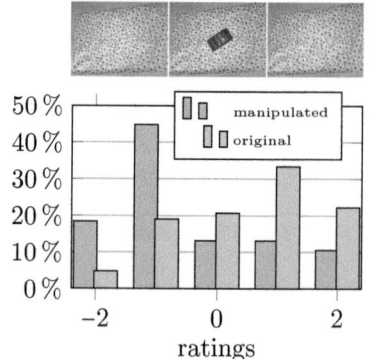

(a) Rates for the original and manipulated video of background B_4.

(b) Rates for the original and manipulated video of background B_5.

Figure A.31: Test subject rates for evaluation background B_4 and B_5. Top (from left to right): screen shot of original video test sequence, original video sequence that will be manipulated, manipulated video sequence, bottom: corresponding ratings of test persons.

A.6 Additional Study Results

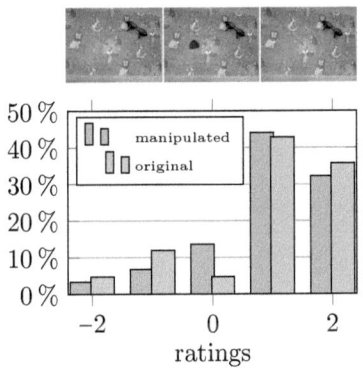

(a) Rates for the original and manipulated video of background B_6.

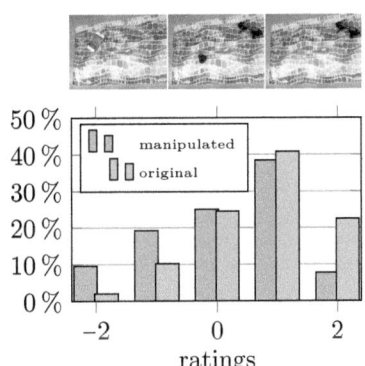

(b) Rates for the original and manipulated video of background B_7.

Figure A.32: Test subject rates for evaluation background B_6 and B_7. Top (from left to right): screen shot of original video test sequence, original video sequence that will be manipulated, manipulated video sequence, bottom: corresponding ratings of test persons.

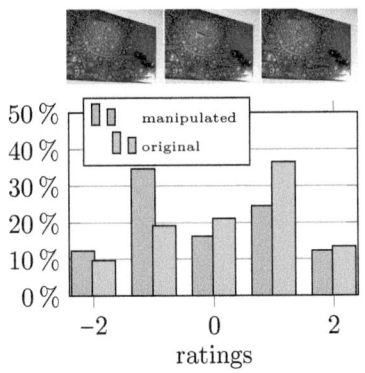

(a) Rates for the original and manipulated video of background B_8.

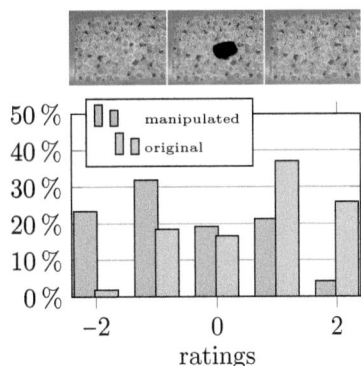

(b) Rates for the original and manipulated video of background B_9.

Figure A.33: Test subject rates for evaluation background B_8 and B_9. Top (from left to right): screen shot of original video test sequence, original video sequence that will be manipulated, manipulated video sequence, bottom: corresponding ratings of test persons.

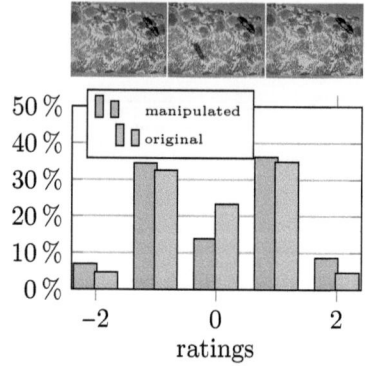
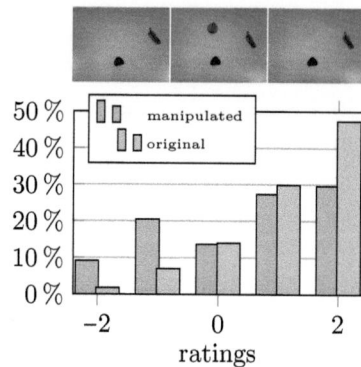

(a) Rates for the original and manipulated video of background B_{10}.

(b) Rates for the original and manipulated video of background B_{11}.

Figure A.34: Test subject rates for evaluation background B_{10} and B_{11}. Top (from left to right): screen shot of original video test sequence, original video sequence that will be manipulated, manipulated video sequence, bottom: corresponding ratings of test persons.

In Table A.1, the detailed ratings for individual groups of test subjects are given. The table provides the absolute number of participants in the individual groups. Further, the average rating μ is provided and the deviation σ of the entire data set in the individual groups is calculated. The individual groups of test subjects have been introduced in Subsection 5.7.2.3. A visualization of the data given in the table is depicted in Figure 5.16.

A.6 Additional Study Results

Table A.1: Accumulated ratings of the test subjects in individual groups. $\bar{x}$ determines the average rating, s the deviation of all ratings in the correspondig group.

Group of subjects	Subjects	Evaluation videos	Ratings (absolute)						sum	$\bar{x}$	s
			-2	-1	0	1	2				
all	101	manipulated	82	142	105	178	99		606	0.116	1.307
		original	27	105	108	225	141		606	0.574	1.151
males	48	manipulated	42	62	54	83	47		288	0.108	1.315
		original	14	56	47	103	68		288	0.538	1.184
females	53	manipulated	40	80	51	95	52		318	0.123	1.301
		original	13	49	61	122	73		318	0.607	1.118
briefed	50	manipulated	54	72	48	68	58		300	0.013	1.400
		original	7	41	58	105	89		300	0.760	1.090
nonbriefed	51	manipulated	28	70	57	110	41		306	0.216	1.202
		original	20	64	50	120	52		306	0.392	1.179
knowledge	27	manipulated	34	39	19	46	24		162	-0.080	1.396
		original	4	19	31	65	43		162	0.765	1.045
no knowledge	74	manipulated	48	103	86	132	75		444	0.187	1.266
		original	23	86	77	160	98		444	0.505	1.179
briefed & knowledge	13	manipulated	23	16	10	16	13		78	-0.256	1.480
		original	0	9	17	29	23		78	0.846	0.975
nonbriefed & no knowledge	37	manipulated	17	47	48	80	30		222	0.266	1.161
		original	16	54	36	84	32		222	0.279	1.187

A.6.2 Evaluation Video

In Figure A.35, the manipulated evaluation video of the test background B_2 is depicted. The forward as well as the background panning shot is depicted.

A.7 Performance Measurements

In the previous subsections, a wide variety of related approaches have been introduced. Most of them are prototypes implemented with high-level programming languages such as Matlab [3].

A reliable comparison regarding performance and image quality would need highly optimized implementations of the individual approaches applying the same programming language and using the same computer hardware for evaluation. Nevertheless, most authors of the related approaches do not provide any source code realizing their algorithms. We decided to not re-implement the related approaches, as code and algorithmic validation could never be guaranteed. Instead, the claimed performance results and presented visual qualities, provided in the related works, are used for comparison. However, as the performance of computers increases with each new hardware generation, an exact comparison is almost impossible.

Thus, the performance values of related approaches have to be transformed to our evaluation hardware. Figure A.36 depicts the well known SPEC 2006 benchmark for the most recent years and shows the average computational performance. Between 2005 and 2010, average hardware performance has been increased by a factor of at most 2.58, as evaluated in the Stanford CPU database [27] (see the trendline in Figure A.36). However, we double the increase factor for a generous upper bound estimate and further assume an exponential performance growth. Thus, we take an exponential performance increase factor of $\sqrt[5]{5.12} \approx 1.39$ per year as a basis to allow a convenient performance comparison. In Figure A.37, the exponential performance factor is depicted. The upper bound growth rate is visualized in Figure A.36, allowing comparison of the real performance increase measured by the SEPC 2006 benchmark with the upper bound estimation.

The platform independent implementation of our approach is realized with C++ and extends our previous work [42]. If not mentioned otherwise, all performance tests in this work are applied using a laptop Intel i7 Nehalem Core with 2.13 GHz released in 2010 and running Windows 7.

A.7 Performance Measurements

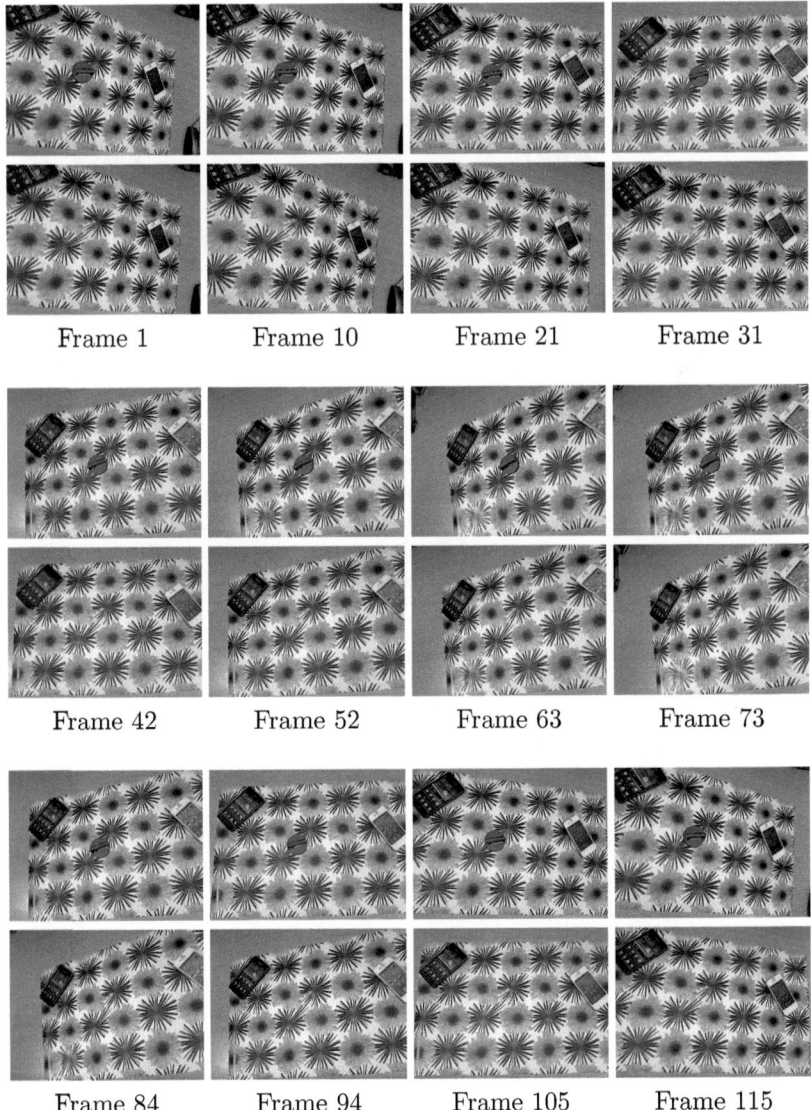

Figure A.35: The manipulated evaluation video of test background B_2. Top row: live video information, bottom row: live manipulated video information that was provided as (manipulated) evaluation video (see Figure A.30a for the corresponding user ratings).

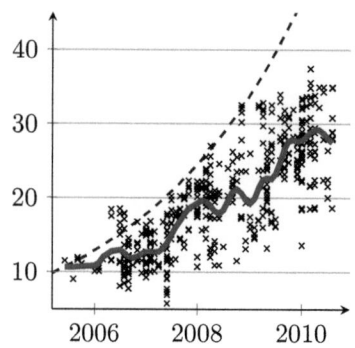
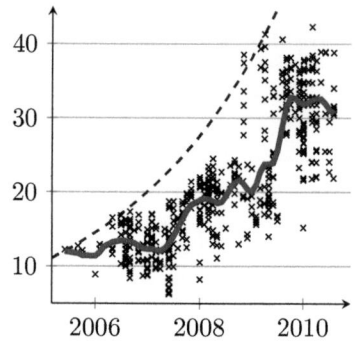

(a) SPEC 2006 integer base mean, with trendline endpoints (2005-06-01, 10.6) and (2010-08-01, 27.5).

(b) SPEC 2006 floating point base mean, with trend line endpoints (2005-06-01, 12.0) and (2010-08-01, 30.6).

Figure A.36: SPEC 2006 benchmarks for more than 550 standard and workstation CPUs between 2005 and 2010 separated for integer and floating point calculations. A trend line (thick red), and the upper bound estimation line (dashed blue) has been added. Data source: *Stanford CPU Database* (http://cpudb.stanford.edu/, viewed 20 August 2012), kindly authorized by the author of [27].

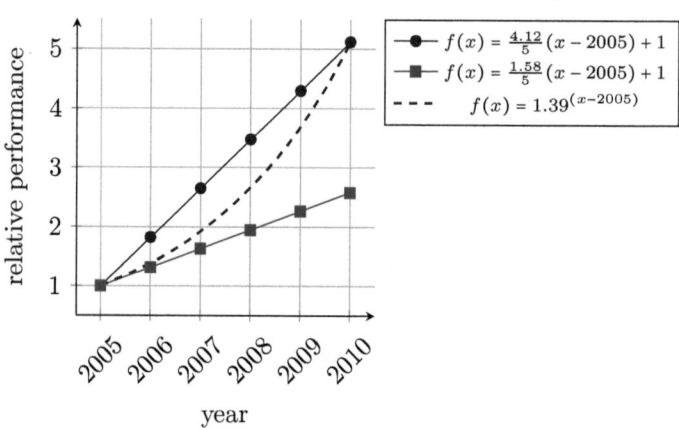

Figure A.37: Visualization of the estimated performance increase of computational hardware between 2005 and 2010 oriented on the SPEC 2006 benchmark database (see Figure A.36). Linear performance increase of factor 2.58 (red), doubled linear factor of 5.12 (blue) and exponential increase with base 1.39 (blue dotted).

Bibliography

[1] Pablo Arbelaez, Michael Maire, Charless Fowlkes, and Jitendra Malik. Contour detection and hierarchical image segmentation. *IEEE Transactions on Pattern Analysis and Machine Intelligence*, 33:898–916, 2011.

[2] Michael Ashikhmin. Synthesizing natural textures. In *Proceedings of the 2001 symposium on Interactive 3D graphics*, I3D '01, pages 217–226, New York, NY, USA, 2001. ACM.

[3] Stormy Attaway. *Matlab, Second Edition: A Practical Introduction to Programming and Problem Solving*. Butterworth-Heinemann, Newton, MA, USA, 2nd edition, 2011.

[4] Shai Avidan and Ariel Shamir. Seam carving for content-aware image resizing. In *ACM SIGGRAPH 2007 papers*, SIGGRAPH '07, New York, NY, USA, 2007. ACM.

[5] Ronald T. Azuma. A survey of augmented reality. *Presence*, 6:355–385, 1997.

[6] Xue Bai, Jue Wang, David Simons, and Guillermo Sapiro. Video snapcut: robust video object cutout using localized classifiers. In *ACM SIGGRAPH 2009 papers*, SIGGRAPH '09, pages 1–11, New York, NY, USA, 2009. ACM.

[7] D. H. Ballard. Generalizing the hough transform to detect arbitrary shapes. In Martin A. Fischler and Oscar Firschein, editors, *Readings in computer vision: issues, problems, principles, and paradigms*, pages 714–725. Morgan Kaufmann Publishers Inc., San Francisco, CA, USA, 1987.

[8] Connelly Barnes, Eli Shechtman, Adam Finkelstein, and Dan B Goldman. Patchmatch: a randomized correspondence algorithm for structural image editing. In *ACM SIGGRAPH 2009 papers*, SIGGRAPH '09, pages 1–11, New York, NY, USA, 2009. ACM.

[9] Connelly Barnes, Eli Shechtman, Dan B. Goldman, and Adam Finkelstein. The generalized patchmatch correspondence algorithm. In *Proceedings of the 11th European conference on computer vision conference on Computer vision: Part III*, ECCV'10, pages 29–43, Berlin, Heidelberg, 2010. Springer-Verlag.

[10] Herbert Bay, Andreas Ess, Tinne Tuytelaars, and Luc Van Gool. Speeded-up robust features (surf). *Computer Vision and Image Understanding*, 110(3):346–359, June 2008.

[11] James R. Bergen, P. Anandan, Keith J. Hanna, and Rajesh Hingorani. Hierarchical model-based motion estimation. In *Proceedings of the Second European Conference on Computer Vision*, ECCV '92, pages 237–252, London, UK, UK, 1992. Springer-Verlag.

[12] Marcelo Bertalmio, Andrea L. Bertozzi, and Guillermo Sapiro. Navier-stokes, fluid dynamics, and image and video inpainting. In *Proceedings of the 2001 IEEE Computer Society Conference on Computer Vision and Pattern Recognition*, volume 1 of *CVPR '01*, pages 355–362, 2001.

[13] Marcelo Bertalmio, Guillermo Sapiro, Vincent Caselles, and Coloma Ballester. Image inpainting. In *Proceedings of the 27th annual conference on Computer graphics and interactive techniques*, SIGGRAPH '00, pages 417–424, New York, NY, USA, 2000. ACM Press/Addison-Wesley Publishing Co.

[14] Marcelo Bertalmio, Luminita A. Vese, Guillermo Sapiro, and Stanley J. Osher. Simultaneous structure and texture image inpainting. In *Proceedings of 2003 IEEE Computer Society Conference on Computer Vision and Pattern Recognition*, volume 2 of *CVPR '03*, pages 1–6, June 2003.

[15] Mark Billinghurst, Hirokazu Kato, and Ivan Poupyrev. The magicbook: a transitional ar interface. *Computers & Graphics*, 25:745–753, 2001.

[16] Raphaël Bornard, Emmanuelle Lecan, Louis Laborelli, and Jean-Hugues Chenot. Missing data correction in still images and image sequences. In *Proceedings of the tenth ACM international conference on Multimedia*, MULTIMEDIA '02, pages 355–361, New York, NY, USA, 2002. ACM.

[17] Jack Bresenham. Algorithm for computer control of a digital plotter. *IBM Systems Journal*, 4(1):25–30, 1965.

[18] Wolfgang Broll. Interacting in distributed collaborative virtual environments. In *Proceedings of the Virtual Reality Annual International Symposium (VRAIS'95)*, VRAIS '95, pages 148–155, Washington, DC, USA, 1995. IEEE Computer Society.

[19] Wolfgang Broll and Jan Herling. Supporting reusability of vr and ar interface elements and interaction techniques. In *Proceedings of the 3rd International Conference on Virtual and Mixed Reality: Held as Part of HCI International 2009*, VMR '09, pages 145–153, Berlin, Heidelberg, 2009. Springer-Verlag.

[20] Wolfgang Broll, Jan Herling, and Lisa Blum. Interactive bits: Prototyping of mixed reality applications and interaction techniques through visual programming. In *IEEE Symposium on 3D User Interfaces*, 3DUI '08, pages 109–115, March 2008.

[21] Aurélie Bugeau, Marcelo Bertalmío, Vicent Caselles, and Guillermo Sapiro. A comprehensive framework for image inpainting. *IEEE Transactions on Image Processing - Special section on distributed camera networks: sensing,*

processing, communication, and implementation, 19(10):2634–2645, October 2010.

[22] Sen-Ching S. Cheung, Jian Zhao, and M. Vijay Venkatesh. Efficient object-based video inpainting. In *Proceedings of IEEE International Conference on Image Processing, 2006*, pages 705 –708, October 2006.

[23] Dorin Comaniciu, Visvanathan Ramesh, and Peter Meer. Real-time tracking of non-rigid objects using mean shift. In *Proceedings of the IEEE Conference on Computer Vision and Pattern Recognition*, volume 2 of *CVPR '00*, pages 142 –149, 2000.

[24] Antonio Criminisi, Patrick Pérez, and Kentaro Toyama. Object removal by exemplar-based inpainting. In *IEEE Computer Vision and Pattern Recognition (CVPR)*, pages 721–728, June 2003.

[25] Antonio Criminisi, Patrick Perez, and Kentaro Toyama. Region filling and object removal by exemplar-based image inpainting. *IEEE Transactions on Image Processing*, 13(9):1200 –1212, September 2004.

[26] Boguslaw Cyganek and Jan Borgosz. Maximum disparity threshold estimation for stereo imaging systems via variogram analysis. In *Proceedings of the 1st international conference on Computational science: Part I*, ICCS '03, pages 591–600, Berlin, Heidelberg, 2003. Springer-Verlag.

[27] Andrew Danowitz, Kyle Kelley, James Mao, John P. Stevenson, and Mark Horowitz. Cpu db: recording microprocessor history. *Communications of the ACM*, 55(4):55–63, April 2012.

[28] Soheil Darabi, Eli Shechtman, Connelly Barnes, Dan B Goldman, and Pradeep Sen. Image Melding: Combining Inconsistent Images using Patch-based Synthesis. *ACM Transactions on Graphics (TOG) (Proceedings of SIGGRAPH 2012)*, 31(4), 2012.

[29] Laurent Demanet, Bing Song, and Tony Chan. Image inpainting by correspondence maps: a deterministic approach. *Computer*, 1100(03-40):21750, 2003.

[30] Iddo Drori, Daniel Cohen-Or, and Hezy Yeshurun. Fragment-based image completion. In *ACM SIGGRAPH 2003 Papers*, SIGGRAPH '03, pages 303–312, New York, NY, USA, 2003. ACM.

[31] Alexei A. Efros and William T. Freeman. Image quilting for texture synthesis and transfer. In *Proceedings of the 28th annual conference on Computer graphics and interactive techniques*, SIGGRAPH '01, pages 341–346, New York, NY, USA, 2001. ACM.

[32] Alexei A. Efros and Thomas K. Leung. Texture synthesis by non-parametric sampling. In *Proceedings of the International Conference on Computer Vision*, volume 2 of *ICCV '99*, pages 1033–1038, Washington, DC, USA, 1999. IEEE Computer Society.

[33] Akihito Enomoto and Hideo Saito. Diminished reality using multiple hand-held cameras. In *ACCV'07 Workshop on Multidimensional and Multi-view Image Processing*, 2007.

[34] Chih-Wei Fang and Jenn-Jier James Lien. Rapid image completion system using multiresolution patch-based directional and nondirectional approaches. *IEEE Transactions on Image Processing*, 18(12):2769–2779, December 2009.

[35] Raanan Fattal, Dani Lischinski, and Michael Werman. Gradient domain high dynamic range compression. In *Proceedings of the 29th annual conference on Computer graphics and interactive techniques*, SIGGRAPH '02, pages 249–256, New York, NY, USA, 2002. ACM.

[36] Martin A. Fischler and Robert C. Bolles. Random sample consensus: a paradigm for model fitting with applications to image analysis and automated cartography. *Communications of the ACM*, 24(6):381–395, June 1981.

[37] Allen Gersho and Robert M. Gray. *Vector quantization and signal compression*. Kluwer Academic Publishers, Norwell, MA, USA, 1991.

[38] Chris Harris and Mike Stephens. A combined corner and edge detector. In *In Proceedings of Fourth Alvey Vision Conference*, pages 147–151, 1988.

[39] James Hays and Alexei A. Efros. Scene completion using millions of photographs. In *ACM SIGGRAPH 2007 papers*, SIGGRAPH '07, New York, NY, USA, 2007. ACM.

[40] Jan Herling and Wolfgang Broll. Advanced Self-contained Object Removal for Realizing Real-time Diminished Reality in Unconstrained Environments. In *Proceedings of the 9th IEEE International Symposium on Mixed and Augmented Reality*, ISMAR '00, pages 207–212, October 2010.

[41] Jan Herling and Wolfgang Broll. An Adaptive Training-free Feature Tracker for Mobile Phones. In *Proceedings of the 17th ACM Symposium on Virtual Reality Software and Technology*, VRST '10, pages 35–42, New York, NY, USA, 2010. ACM.

[42] Jan Herling and Wolfgang Broll. The Ocean Framework: Providing the Basis for Next-gen MR Applications. In *Proceedings of the IEEE Virtual Reality 2010 Workshop, 3rd Workshop on Software Engineering and Architectures for Realtime Interactive Systems*, SEARIS' 10, 2010.

[43] Jan Herling and Wolfgang Broll. Markerless tracking for augmented reality. In Borko Furht, editor, *Handbook of Augmented Reality*, pages 255–272. Springer New York, 2011.

[44] Jan Herling and Wolfgang Broll. International patent: Verfahren und Bildverarbeitungsanlage zum Bestimmen von Parametern einer Kamera. Patent (pending), PCT/EP2012/069161, Den Haag, September 2012.

[45] Jan Herling and Wolfgang Broll. International patent: Verfahren und Bildverarbeitungsanlage zum Entfernen eines visuellen Objektes aus einem Bild. Patent (pending), PCT/EP2012/067352, Den Haag, September 2012.

[46] Jan Herling and Wolfgang Broll. PixMix: A Real-Time Approach to High-Quality Diminished Reality. In *11th IEEE International Symposium on Mixed and Augmented Reality*, ISMAR' 12, pages 141–150, USA, November 2012. IEEE.

[47] Jan Herling and Wolfgang Broll. Random model variation for universal feature tracking. In *Proceedings of the 18th ACM symposium on Virtual reality software and technology*, VRST '12, pages 169–176, New York, NY, USA, 2012. ACM.

[48] Jan Herling and Wolfgang Broll. High-quality Real-time Video Inpainting with PixMix. *IEEE Transactions on Visualization and Computer Graphics*, PP(99):1, 2014.

[49] Jan Herling and Wolfgang Broll. Method and Apparatus for Removing a Visual Object from a Visual Data Stream. Patent No.: US 8,660,305 B2, Date of Patent: February 25, 2014; Filed: October 11, 2011.

[50] Somayeh Hesabi, Mansour Jamzad, and Nezam Mahdavi-Amiri. Structure and texture image inpainting. In *2010 International Conference on Signal and Image Processing (ICSIP)*, pages 119 –124, December 2010.

[51] Bernd Jähne. *Digital image processing (3rd ed.): concepts, algorithms, and scientific applications*. Springer-Verlag, London, UK, UK, 1995.

[52] Songkran Jarusirisawad, Takahide Hosokawa, and Hideo Saito. Diminished reality using plane-sweep algorithm with weakly-calibrated cameras. *Progress in Informatics*, 7:11–20, 2010.

[53] Jiaya Jia, Tai pang Wu, Yu wing Tai, and Chi keung Tang. Video repairing: Inference of foreground and background under severe occlusion. In *Proceedings of Computer Vision and Pattern Recognition*, pages 364–371, 2004.

[54] Jiaya Jia, Yu-Wing Tai, Tai-Pang Wu, and Chi-Keung Tang. Video repairing under variable illumination using cyclic motions. *IEEE Transactions on Pattern Analysis and Machine Intelligence*, 28(5):832–839, May 2006.

[55] Jiaya Jia and Chi-Keung Tang. Image repairing: robust image synthesis by adaptive nd tensor voting. In *Proceedings of the 2003 IEEE computer society conference on Computer vision and pattern recognition*, CVPR'03, pages 643–650, Washington, DC, USA, 2003. IEEE Computer Society.

[56] Michael Kass, Andrew Witkin, and Demetri Terzopoulos. Snakes: Active contour models. *International Journal of Computer Vision*, 1(4):321–331, 1988.

[57] Hirokazu Kato and Mark Billinghurst. Marker tracking and hmd calibration for a video-based augmented reality conferencing system. In *Proceedings of the 2nd IEEE and ACM International Workshop on Augmented Reality*, IWAR '99, pages 85–94, Washington, DC, USA, 1999. IEEE Computer Society.

[58] Norihiko Kawai, Tomokazu Sato, and Naokazu Yokoya. Image inpainting considering brightness change and spatial locality of textures and its evaluation. In *Proceedings of the 3rd Pacific Rim Symposium on Advances in Image and Video Technology*, PSIVT '09, pages 271–282, Berlin, Heidelberg, 2008. Springer-Verlag.

[59] Ross Kindermann and J. Laurie Snell. *Markov random fields and their applications.* Contemporary mathematics. American Mathematical Society, 1980.

[60] Georg Klein and David Murray. Parallel tracking and mapping for small ar workspaces. In *Proceedings of the 2007 6th IEEE and ACM International Symposium on Mixed and Augmented Reality*, ISMAR '07, pages 1–10, Washington, DC, USA, 2007. IEEE Computer Society.

[61] Georg Klein and David Murray. Parallel tracking and mapping on a camera phone. In *Proceedings of the 2009 8th IEEE International Symposium on Mixed and Augmented Reality*, ISMAR '09, pages 83–86, Washington, DC, USA, 2009. IEEE Computer Society.

[62] Nikos Komodakis. Image completion using global optimization. In *Proceedings of the 2006 IEEE Computer Society Conference on Computer Vision and Pattern Recognition*, volume 1 of *CVPR '06*, pages 442–452, Washington, DC, USA, 2006. IEEE Computer Society.

[63] Nikos Komodakis and Georgios Tziritas. Image completion using efficient belief propagation via priority scheduling and dynamic pruning. *IEEE Transactions on Image Processing*, 16(11):2649–2661, November 2007.

[64] Otto Korkalo, Miika Aittala, and Sanni Siltanen. Light-weight marker hiding for augmented reality. In *9th IEEE International Symposium on Mixed and Augmented Reality, ISMAR 2010, Seoul, Korea, 13-16 October 2010*, pages 247–248. IEEE, 2010.

[65] Tsz-Ho Kwok, Hoi Sheung, and Charlie C. L. Wang. Fast query for exemplar-based image completion. *IEEE Transactions on Image Processing*, 19(12):3106–3115, December 2010.

[66] Vincent Lepetit and Marie-Odile Berger. An intuitive tool for outlining objects in video sequences: Applications to augmented and diminished reality. In *International Symposium of Mixed Reality*, March 2001.

[67] Kenneth Levenberg. A method for the solution of certain problems in least squares. *Quarterly of Applied Mathematics*, 2:164–168, 1944.

[68] Anat Levin, Dani Lischinski, and Yair Weiss. A closed-form solution to natural image matting. *IEEE Transactions on Pattern Analysis and Machine Intelligence*, 30(2):228–242, February 2008.

[69] Anat Levin, Assaf Zomet, and Yair Weiss. Learning how to inpaint from global image statistics. In *Proceedings of the Ninth IEEE International*

Conference on Computer Vision, volume 1 of *ICCV '03*, pages 305–312, Washington, DC, USA, 2003. IEEE Computer Society.

[70] Yin Li, Jian Sun, and Heung-Yeung Shum. Video object cut and paste. In *ACM SIGGRAPH 2005 Papers*, SIGGRAPH '05, pages 595–600, New York, NY, USA, 2005. ACM.

[71] Ming Liu, Shifeng Chen, Jianzhuang Liu, and Xiaoou Tang. Video completion via motion guided spatial-temporal global optimization. In *Proceedings of the 17th ACM international conference on Multimedia*, MM '09, pages 537–540, New York, NY, USA, 2009. ACM.

[72] David G. Lowe. Distinctive image features from scale-invariant keypoints. *International Journal of Computer Vision*, 60(2):91–110, November 2004.

[73] Steve Mann. Mediated reality. Tr 260, M.I.T. Media Lab Perceptual Computing Section, Cambridge, Massachusetts, 1994.

[74] Paul Milgram, Haruo Takemura, Akira Utsumi, and Fumio Kishino. Augmented reality: A class of displays on the reality-virtuality continuum. In *Proceedings of the SPIE Conference on Telemanipulator and Telepresence Technologies*, volume 2351 of *Proceedings of SPIE*, pages 42–48, Boston, Massachusetts, USA, November 1994.

[75] Patrick Ndjiki-Nya, Martin Köppel, Dimitar Doshkov, and Thomas Wiegand. Automatic structure-aware inpainting for complex image content. In *Proceedings of the 4th International Symposium on Advances in Visual Computing*, ISVC '08, pages 1144–1156, Berlin, Heidelberg, 2008. Springer-Verlag.

[76] Jifeng Ning, Lei Zhang, David Zhang, and Chengke Wu. Interactive image segmentation by maximal similarity based region merging. *Pattern Recognition*, 43(2):445–456, February 2010.

[77] Kedar A. Patwardhan, Guillermo Sapiro, and Marcelo Bertalmio. Video inpainting of occluding and occluded objects. In *Proceedings of the IEEE International Conference on Image Processing*, volume 2 of *ICIP '05*, pages 69–72, September 2005.

[78] Kedar A. Patwardhan, Guillermo Sapiro, and Marcelo Bertalmio. Video inpainting under constrained camera motion. *IEEE Transactions on Image Processing*, 16(2):545–553, Februar 2007.

[79] Patrick Pérez, Michel Gangnet, and Andrew Blake. Poisson image editing. In *ACM SIGGRAPH 2003 Papers*, SIGGRAPH '03, pages 313–318, New York, NY, USA, 2003. ACM.

[80] William H. Press, Saul A. Teukolsky, William T. Vetterling, and Brian P. Flannery. *Numerical Recipes 3rd Edition: The Art of Scientific Computing*. Cambridge University Press, New York, NY, USA, 3 edition, 2007.

[81] Yael Pritch, Eitam Kav-Venaki, and Shmuel Peleg. Shift-map image editing. In *Proceedings of the IEEE 12th International Conference on Computer Vision*, pages 151–158, October 2009.

[82] Edward Rosten and Tom Drummond. Fusing points and lines for high performance tracking. In *Proceedings of the Tenth IEEE International Conference on Computer Vision - Volume 2*, ICCV '05, pages 1508–1515, Washington, DC, USA, 2005. IEEE Computer Society.

[83] Carsten Rother, Vladimir Kolmogorov, and Andrew Blake. "grabcut": interactive foreground extraction using iterated graph cuts. In *ACM SIGGRAPH 2004 Papers*, SIGGRAPH '04, pages 309–314, New York, NY, USA, 2004. ACM.

[84] Hanno Scharr. *Optimal operators in digital image processing*. PhD thesis, Interdisziplinaeres Zentrum fuer Wissenschaftliches Rechnen, 2000.

[85] Jianbing Shen, Xiaogang Jin, Chuan Zhou, and Charlie C. L. Wang. Technical section: Gradient based image completion by solving the poisson equation. *Computers and Graphics*, 31(1):119–126, January 2007.

[86] Yuping Shen, Fei Lu, Xiaochun Cao, and Hassan Foroosh. Video completion for perspective camera under constrained motion. In *Proceedings of the 18th International Conference on Pattern Recognition - Volume 03*, ICPR '06, pages 63–66, Washington, DC, USA, 2006. IEEE Computer Society.

[87] Takashi Shibata, Akihiko Iketani, and Shuji Senda. Image inpainting based on probabilistic structure estimation. In *Proceedings of the 10th Asian conference on Computer vision - Volume Part III*, ACCV'10, pages 109–120, Berlin, Heidelberg, 2011. Springer-Verlag.

[88] Timothy K. Shih, Nick C. Tang, and Jenq-Neng Hwang. Exemplar-based video inpainting without ghost shadow artifacts by maintaining temporal continuity. *IEEE Transactions on Circuits and Systems for Video Technology*, 19(3):347–360, March 2009.

[89] Timothy K. Shih, Nick C. Tang, Wei-Sung Yeh, Ta-Jen Chen, and Wonjun Lee. Video inpainting and implant via diversified temporal continuations. In *Proceedings of the 14th annual ACM international conference on Multimedia*, MULTIMEDIA '06, pages 133–136, New York, NY, USA, 2006. ACM.

[90] Takaaki Shiratori, Yasuyuki Matsushita, Xiaoou Tang, and Sing Bing Kang. Video completion by motion field transfer. In *Proceedings of the 2006 IEEE Computer Society Conference on Computer Vision and Pattern Recognition*, volume 1 of *CVPR '06*, pages 411–418, Washington, DC, USA, 2006. IEEE Computer Society.

[91] Sanni Siltanen. Texture generation over the marker area. In *Proceedings of the 5th IEEE and ACM International Symposium on Mixed and Augmented Reality*, ISMAR '06, pages 253–254, Washington, DC, USA, 2006. IEEE Computer Society.

[92] Denis Simakov, Yaron Caspi, Eli Shechtman, and Michal Irani. Summarizing visual data using bidirectional similarity. In *IEEE Conference on Computer*

Bibliography

Vision and Pattern Recognition (CVPR), pages 1–8. IEEE Computer Society, June 2008.

[93] Jian Sun, Lu Yuan, Jiaya Jia, and Heung-Yeung Shum. Image completion with structure propagation. In *ACM SIGGRAPH 2005 Papers*, SIGGRAPH '05, pages 861–868, New York, NY, USA, 2005. ACM.

[94] Richard Szeliski. *Computer Vision: Algorithms and Applications*. Springer, 2010.

[95] Kosuke Takeda and Ryuuki Sakamoto. Diminished reality for landscape video sequences with homographies. In *Proceedings of the 14th international conference on Knowledge-based and intelligent information and engineering systems: Part III*, KES'10, pages 501–508, Berlin, Heidelberg, 2010. Springer-Verlag.

[96] Ruo-Feng Tong, Yun Zhang, and Meng Ding. Video brush: A novel interface for efficient video cutout. *Computer Graphics Forum*, 30(7):2049–2057, September 2011.

[97] John W. Tukey. *Exploratory Data Analysis*. Addison-Wesley, 1977.

[98] M. Vijay Venkatesh, Sen-Ching Samson Cheung, and Jian Zhao. Efficient object-based video inpainting. *Pattern Recognition Letters*, 30(2):168–179, January 2009.

[99] Daniel Wagner, Gerhard Reitmayr, Alessandro Mulloni, Tom Drummond, and Dieter Schmalstieg. Pose tracking from natural features on mobile phones. In *Proceedings of the 7th IEEE/ACM International Symposium on Mixed and Augmented Reality*, ISMAR '08, pages 125–134, Washington, DC, USA, 2008. IEEE Computer Society.

[100] Li-Yi Wei. Deterministic texture analysis and synthesis using tree structure vector quantization. In *Proceedings of the XII Brazilian Symposium on Computer Graphics and Image Processing*, SIBGRAPI '99, pages 207–214, Washington, DC, USA, 1999. IEEE Computer Society.

[101] Li-Yi Wei and Marc Levoy. Fast texture synthesis using tree-structured vector quantization. In *Proceedings of the 27th annual conference on Computer graphics and interactive techniques*, SIGGRAPH '00, pages 479–488, New York, NY, USA, 2000. ACM Press/Addison-Wesley Publishing Co.

[102] Yonatan Wexler, Eli Shechtman, and Michal Irani. Space-time completion of video. *IEEE Conference Computer Vision and Pattern Recognition*, 1:120–127, 2004.

[103] Yonatan Wexler, Eli Shechtman, and Michal Irani. Space-time completion of video. *IEEE Transactions on Pattern Analysis and Machine Intelligence*, 29(3):463–476, March 2007.

[104] Alexander Wong and Jeff Orchard. A nonlocal-means approach to exemplar-based inpainting. In *Proceedings of the 15th IEEE International Conference on Image Processing*, ICIP '08, pages 2600–2603, October 2008.

[105] Ying-Qing Xu, Baining Guo, and Harry Shum. Chaos mosaic: Fast and memory efficient texture synthesis. TechReport MSR-TR-2000-32, Microsoft Research, April 2000.

[106] Zongben Xu and Jian Sun. Image inpainting by patch propagation using patch sparsity. *IEEE Transactions on Image Processing*, 19(5):1153–1165, May 2010.

[107] Yimin Yu, Duanqing Xu, Chun Chen, and Lei Zhao Zhao. Video completion based on improved belief propagation. In *Proceedings of the 6th WSEAS International Conference on Multimedia, Internet & Video Technologies*, MIV'06, pages 53–58, Stevens Point, Wisconsin, USA, 2006. World Scientific and Engineering Academy and Society (WSEAS).

[108] Yunjun Zhang, Jiangjian Xiao, and Mubarak Shah. Region completion in a single image. In *Proceedings of Eurographics 2004*, 2004.

[109] Yunjun Zhang, Jiangjian Xiao, and Mubarak Shah. Motion layer based object removal in videos. In *Proceedings of the Seventh IEEE Workshops on Application of Computer Vision*, volume 1 of *WACV-MOTION '05*, pages 516–521, Washington, DC, USA, 2005. IEEE Computer Society.

[110] Feng Zhou, Henry Been-Lirn Duh, and Mark Billinghurst. Trends in augmented reality tracking, interaction and display: A review of ten years of ismar. In *Proceedings of the 7th IEEE/ACM International Symposium on Mixed and Augmented Reality*, ISMAR '08, pages 193–202, Washington, DC, USA, 2008. IEEE Computer Society.

[111] Siavash Zokai, Julien Esteve, Yakup Genc, and Nassir Navab. Multiview paraperspective projection model for diminished reality. In *Proceedings of the 2nd IEEE/ACM International Symposium on Mixed and Augmented Reality*, ISMAR '03, pages 217–226, Washington, DC, USA, 2003. IEEE Computer Society.

MIX
Papier aus verantwortungsvollen Quellen
Paper from responsible sources
FSC® C105338

If you have any concerns about our products,
you can contact us on
ProductSafety@springernature.com

In case Publisher is established outside the EU,
the EU authorized representative is:
**Springer Nature Customer Service Center GmbH
Europaplatz 3, 69115 Heidelberg, Germany**

Printed by Libri Plureos GmbH
in Hamburg, Germany